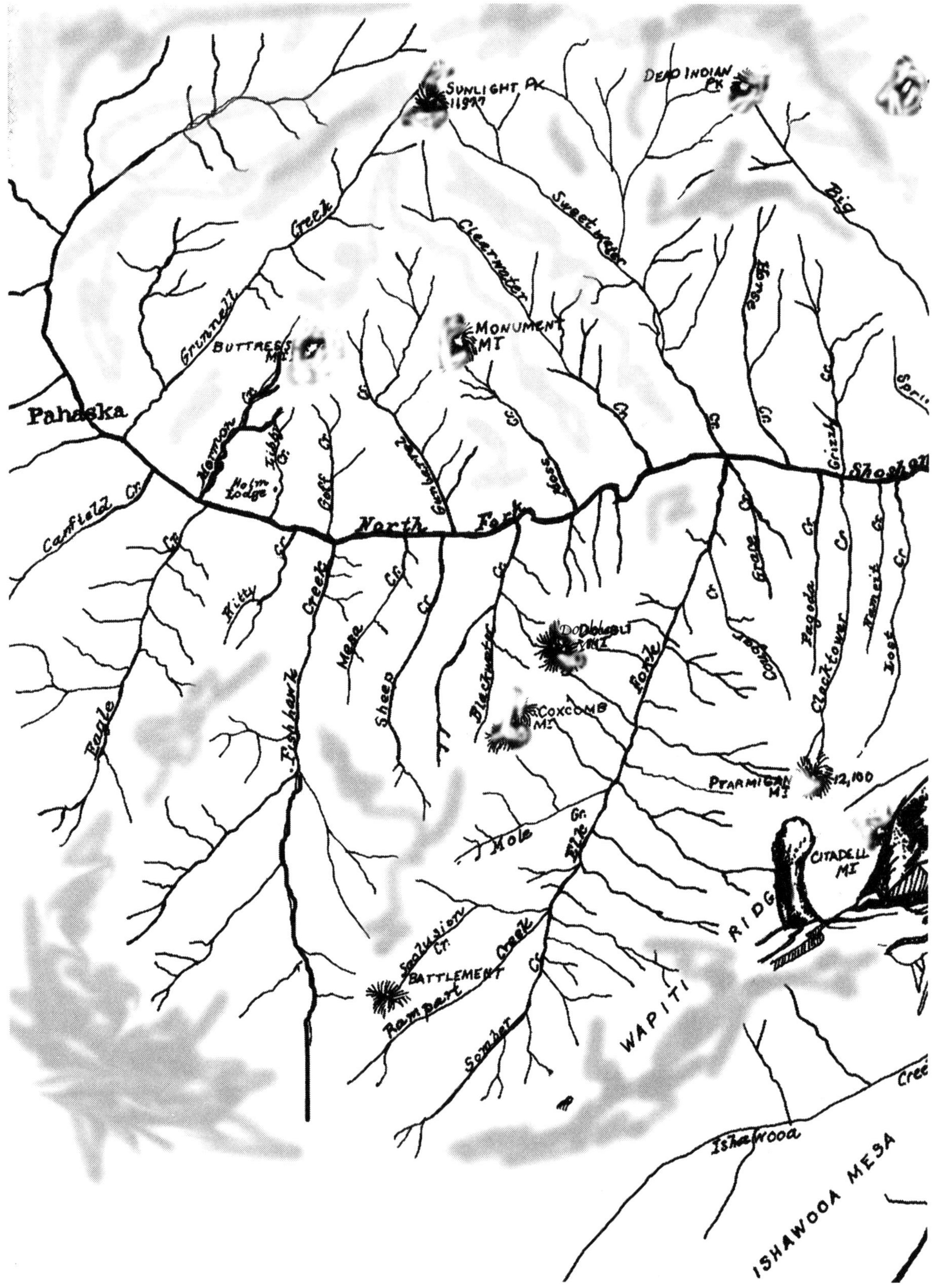

Sunlight Pk
11977
Dead Indian Pk
Pahaska
Buttress Mt
Monument Mt
Grinnell Creek
Clearwater
Sweetwater
Big
Mormon Cr
Holm Lodge
Canfield Cr
North Fork
Shoshone
Kitty Cr
Fishhawk Creek
Eagle
Sheep Cr
Blackwater Cr
Doubleli Mt
Coxcomb Mt
Elk Fork
Ptarmigan Mt
12,100
Citadell Mt
Mole Cr
Battlement
Rampart Creek
Somber Cr
Wapiti Ridge
Ishawooa
Ishawooa Mesa
Clocktower Cr
Pagoda Cr
Grizzly Cr
Lost Cr

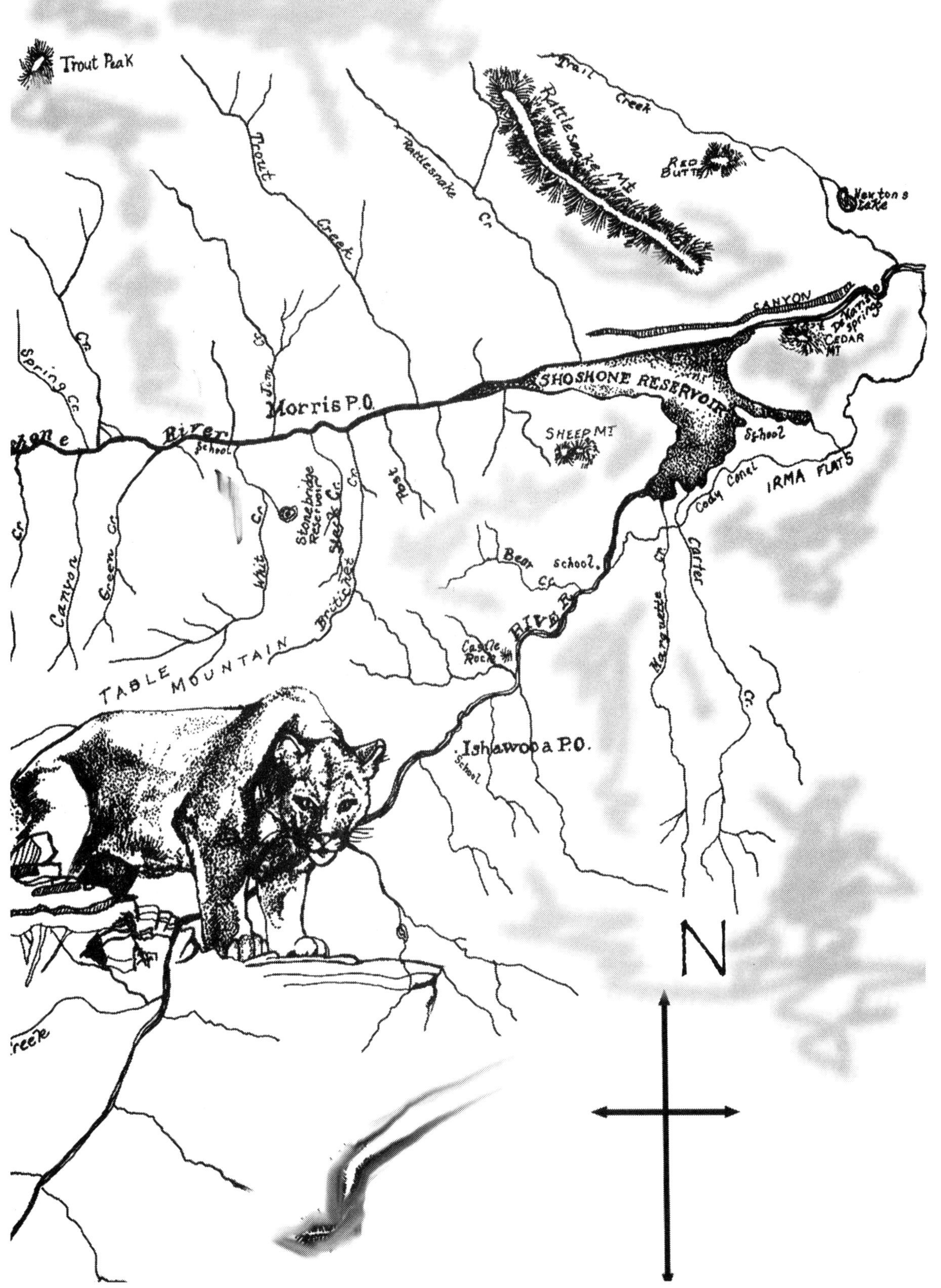
Trout Peak
Trail Creek
Rattlesnake Mt
Red Butte
Trout Creek
Rattlesnake Cr
Canyon
Cedar Mt
Shoshone Reservoir
Morris P.O.
River
School
Spring Cr
Jim Cr
Sheep Mt
School
Cody Canal
Irma Flats
Stonebridge Reservoir
Green Cr
Canyon
White Cr
Post
Bear Cr
School
Marquette Cr
Carter
River
Castle Rock
Table Mountain
Ishawooa P.O.
School
Cr
N

By Ester Johansson Murray

To Diane Walsh
Best Wishes
Ester Johansson Murray

First Edition

Cody, Wyoming
November 16, 1996

Lone Eagle MultiMedia

Cody Wyoming, USA

Lone Eagle MultiMedia, Cody Wyoming 82414

Printed in the United States of America

Cover Design: Marik Turbes
Book Design/Illustrations: Marik Turbes
The body text in this book is set in Times; headlines are set in Letraset Papyrus and map notations are set in Fontec and ITC FineHand.

ISBN 0- 9651378- 0- 5 Linen cover
ISBN 0- 9651378- 1- 3 Soft cover

. . . to all those
who have lifted up their eyes
unto Jim Mountain. . .

TABLE OF CONTENTS

PREFACE

A region that never has been definitively researched is ripe for exhaustive study. Because I enjoy historical research I tackled the history of the North Fork of the Shoshone River. To make it manageable, I chose to research the era from 1800 to the end of the 1930's. My affection for the North Fork comes from personal experience. My father homesteaded there and my family worked during summers on area ranches.

I wanted to present as accurate a history as possible with anecdotal material to complement the story. By the time I began researching, all the oldtimers were gone. I talked to many later residents who had lived in the Wapiti Valley for many years and am grateful for their interviews.

The Montana Room of the Parmly Billings Library furnished useful background material. The Wyoming State Historical Archives filled requests for material from early brands to school records. The Park County Historical Archives staff were most helpful, pulling files and furnishing photographs. The librarians at the Park County Library, gave me access to Cody newspapers on microfilm. The collection of Western Americana at the Harold McCracken Research Library of the Buffalo Bill Historical Center was a source of local items.

The lines from " If you would love Wyoming" by Ginny Odenbach,* reflected my feelings about this project:

" You must let
The long arms
Of the past
Wrap themselves
Around your heart"

John A. Yeates offered personal memories of his early life on Jim Creek and eight years of attending Wapiti School. His contributions rounded out the story, unfortunately lack of space precluded my using much of his research material, but all of it is available at the Park County Archives.

** used by permission of the author.*

INTRODUCTION

How does a regional history of a small river valley fifty miles long and twenty miles wide fit into the history of the western United States? In a very small way. And yet there is a uniqueness to this valley of the North Fork of the Shoshone River in northwestern Wyoming, due to its location, late settlement, and scenery. The time frame for the research covers roughly 1800-1940, so if we use the classic date of 1890 for the closing of the western frontier, this study area was just beginning to be opened up in the last decade of the nineteenth century. More applicable would be the date given by Michael P. Malone and Richard W. Etulain in *The American West,* (1989) "Postwar (1918) collapse of agriculture signaled the close of the frontier." In 1909, the North Fork was part of the undivided Big Horn County. Friction between cattlemen and sheepmen was bitter on the west slope of the Big Horn mountains, erupting in the brutal murder of three sheepmen by seven cattlemen because the sheepmen had crossed the cattlemen's deadline. The trial of the Spring Creek raiders resulted in the conviction of Herbert Brink and four of the other raiders. John W. Davis in his book, *A Vast Amount of Trouble*, states, "The case of State v. Brink signified the end of the frontier in Wyoming." Thus, the closing of the frontier is subject to various interpretations and dates according to various authors.

This river valley felt the influence of the federal government in many ways, the first was the free land enticing homesteaders. However, it was not prime Homestead Act land and was good mostly for grazing and small irrigated fields. What today is prime property for a summer home or scenic cabin was only viewed in the early 1900s as land to provide a livelihood. A number of early dude ranches did capitalize on western scenery, including the Morris ranch, Frost and Richard, and P-P.

Settlers came by wagons and horseback until 1901, when a spur of the Chicago, Burlington, and Quincy Railroad reached Cody. The railroads, subsidized by the federal government, advertised for settlers, some of whom were lured by railroad brochures. Here, again, the area was touched by the federal government. The newcomers did not displace any previous inhabitants as in many western states. No Indians were driven out, although in historic times it had been the hunting grounds of Arapahoes, Crows, and Shoshone "Sheep Eaters." The people did displace the grizzlies and mountain sheep, driving them to higher elevations.

The Reclamation Act of 1894, or then called Carey Act, authored by Wyoming's Senator Joseph M. Carey, to provide federal aid to irrigation projects, had the greatest impact on the earliest settlers, whose farms lay in the lower valley around the converging forks of the river. The federal government bought the farms and ranches and the residents moved out. For those times, the people were well compensated for their displacement. Important too, the Shoshone reservoir, at first called Shoshone Lake, caused the geographical separation of the two river valleys, severing the oneness of early times.

Very important is the fact the upper two thirds of the river valley lies in federally owned forest reserve, and much of the lower valley's private land abuts forest reserve or wilderness areas. Only three small parcels of state lands remain in the valley.

The aid given by the federal government to expand roads had a tremendous affect on the North Fork, connecting it with Yellowstone Park road system and coaxing east-west federal highways 14, 16, and 20 travel through the river valley for at least five months of the year. Tourism had great impact on the North Fork. By 1926 cheap cars and roads had revolutionized the lifestyle of Westerners where places were separated by great distances. Cars and roads brought ever increasing numbers of tourists from all parts of the United States to the area.

Some residents of the North Fork were affected by the federal government during Prohibition when federal agents were chasing bootleggers.

In 1934 the Taylor Grazing Act brought a degree of order and regulation to grazing livestock on federal land. The Federal Bureau of Land Management (BLM) began to improve western rangelands for livestock and wildlife.

Finally, the New Deal with its Civilian Conservation Corp (CCC) camp at Clearwater had quite an impact on the area. It helped the local economy during the Great Depression, employing a few local men, and buying the supplies locally. The CCCs upgraded campgrounds, built trails and bridges, and fought forest fires.

The extractive industry did not affect the valley to any extent. Prospectors, searched for minerals, mostly in vain, and left no toxic waste sites. The minerals in Silver Tip Basin between Sunlight and North Fork were remote and unprofitable.

Lumbering proved marginal to unprofitable, producing lumber for only local use and there were no tie camps or plants like near Dubois, Sheridan, Medicine Bow, or Green River. And if oil lies deep under the Overthrust Belt where it crosses the Wapiti Valley, it has not been tapped.

The North Forkers felt the post World War I Depression, since most ranchers were involved in agriculture. Then a decade after the closing of the frontier, according to Malone and Etulain, the Great Depression hit the North Fork, somewhat later than the East. By 1931 it was painful. Luckily, no major drought, devastating dust storm or grasshopper plague accompanied the hard times."The Great Depression brought about the crises of that old, exploitative economic order that was based on unrestricted taking of the West's bounty; and the New Deal and World War II signaled the beginning of the new order in which we still live today," according to Malone and Etulain.

The North Fork would fall into what Patricia Nelson Limerick in *A Legacy of Conquest,* (1987) calls "White-American-mainstream-centered history." The North Fork lacked ethnic diversity and provided no occasion for racism in early days. The KKK burned no crosses in the river valley. However, Italian immigrants imported to work on building the Shoshone dam 1905-1910, were labeled "A bunch of Dagoes" in a Cody newspaper. The Italians did not stay. A few Japanese internees from the Heart Mountain Relocation Camp during WWII worked outside the camp, some at the Whit Creek sawmill. At first there was considerable bias, but eventually they were accepted. They did not stay after the war.

In a 1905 school census taken in rural areas near Cody, the individuals between 6 and 20 numbered 255, 126 males and 129 females, and only 2 were listed as foreign born, one born in England,

and the other not designated. Under "color", all were "white."

Subjects covered in this study range from geology to early livestock brands with the greatest emphasis on a brief history of each early ranch, lodge and first settlers. Wapiti school in the middle valley is documented and previous schools are listed. The John Yeates ranch on Jim Creek, begun in 1905, and the Johansson Homestead, 1917, are given extensive coverage as prototypes of ranching and of homesteading. Both are approximately midway between the Canyon and the Forest Reserve entrance.

The Civilian Conservation Corp camp and the tragic Blackwater Fire are worthy of separate in-depth study. Pahaska has been covered by W. Hudson Kensel's 1987 definitive study and book, *Pahaska Tepee, Buffalo Bill's Old Hunting Lodge and Hotel, a History 1901-1945.*

Robert Utley, at the Dedication Symposium of Harold D. McCracken Research Library, Buffalo Bill Historical Center, on June 24, 1994, said, "People afford the clearest window for looking on the world of yesterday." Hence, scattered within the factual material on the North Fork are interviews with old timers, folk tales and firsthand memories to give a peek at the past.

Finally, the dude ranching on the North Fork helped to hold on to the culture and drama of the Old West with rodeos, horse back riding, wranglers spinning yarns and tall tales. Seasonally it provided income for the dude ranchers and for the numerous high school young people and school teachers hired during the summer. There were also the actual personal connections with Buffalo Bill and the Wild West Shows, and Colonel Cody's ranches, properties, employees and his relatives.

Looking west up the North Fork from the top of Cedar Mountain. Photo courtesy Cody Enterprise.

NATURAL AND POLITICAL HISTORY OF THE NORTH FORK

The North Fork of the Shoshone River, Park County, Wyoming, is roughly a rectangular area within Range 103 West to 110 West and Townships 51, 52, and 53 North. It is defined as the watershed or drainage area of the North Fork of the Shoshone River, which is made up of several major tributaries between the west end of the Shoshone Canyon and Sylvan Pass. This watershed covers approximately 750 square miles, and the average annual flow from 1916 to 1970 has been roughly 600,000 acre feet.

In 1988, a drought year, the flow on July 1st was 1,155 cubic feet per second (cfs), much less than a normal year. By the 12th of that same month it had dropped to 734 cfs. The maximum flow recorded occurred on a June day in 1981, when the high water peaked at 20,000 cfs and was classified as a "once in one-hundred-years" event. The yearly, daily average is 833 cfs for the years when records were kept. On the average, high water flows at 15,000 cfs', 50 cfs was the minimum recorded on December 16, 1987.

The United States Geological Survey constructs the gauges and collects the data. The first gauge west of the reservoir measured water flow from 1921 to 1926 and from 1979 to 1989, and its cable spanned the river near the Upton place and below the mouth of Trout creek.

Another gauge is near the narrows at Wapiti. A cable firmly anchored on each side of the river permits the metering gauge to be lowered into the water. Sometimes boys tried to cross the river hand over hand on the cable. Young John Yeates once took a break from his job in the Upton hay field and negotiated a hands-on crossing. The exploit proved particularly challenging, especially the return trip, as it seemed to be a very wide river.

This North Fork area is roughly twenty miles wide and forty-five miles long. Jim Mountain dominates and looms over the valley like a benevolent monarch. The more habitable valley floor is adjacent to the river and varies from one mile wide in the lower section to one half mile wide in the upper part. The highway follows the north side of the river from the canyon to where the valley narrows at Wapiti. The road is then carried to the south side of the river by a long concrete span. The two previous bridges were steel truss structures a short distance downstream over this same narrow gorge. From the Wapiti bridge the road follows the south side of the river until well into the forest reserve where it crosses to the north side near Clearwater Campground and stays on the north side as far as Pahaska and from the Middle Fork to Sylvan Pass.

Elevations range from roughly 5,000 feet at the reservoir to 10,000 feet in the Absaroka range with peaks such as Trout Peak, rising to12,244 feet. It is a region of spectacular beauty compressed into a small area.

Geological History

Northwestern Wyoming lies on the edge of a moving tectonic plate. This causes faults, uplifts, and volcanic eruptions of the underlying molten lava. The caldera of the Yellowstone Plateau volcanic field last erupted 600,000 years ago. Geologists expect action again within the next few hundred thousand years. The north-south mountains are part of the economically and politically important "Overthrust Belt" which covers oil deposits.

The streams and glaciers have cut into the elevated volcanic plateaus with further deep carving by extant glaciers. The Pinedale ice cap of 70,000 years ago covered much of the area. There is not much further evidence of glaciation except at the headwaters of the tributaries where they begin as springs or snowmelt at the foot of the peaks and high plateaus.

The lower or eastern portion of the North Fork valley consists of light colored sedimentary rocks. The Shoshone River has eroded through a big slab of Paleozoic rock that was pushed up and over the top of the much younger Mesozoic strata over which the river now flows. Sheep Mountain and Chalk Mountain are parts of these detached Heart Mountain fault blocks which rest on the Wapiti formation.

The tilted, nearly vertical, strata on the upper west side of Rattlesnake Mountain are good examples of palisades and were named "Grand Parade" by early settlers. These are similar to the famous "Flat Irons" near Boulder, Colorado. West from Trout Creek the landscape is dominated by the brown-toned, or maroon volcanic rocks deposited, during the Middle Eocene Era, by activity in the Yellowstone Caldera. Near Jim Creek underlying sandstones are exposed. In this exposed strata John Yeates found and tried to mine a deposit of sublignite type, or "soft" coal. No useable coal deposits have been found on the North Fork.

Geography

One of the earliest maps of the continent of North America, a War Department map copied by Nicholas King in 1806, shows the Big Horn River and Yellowstone River flowing northerly into the Missouri River. No features are described, but the rivers, although geographically vague and inaccurate, are at least already named and placed according to information supplied by Indians.

The north-south mountain range between Yellowstone Park and the Big Horn Basin is called the Absaroka Range from Crow Indian word meaning "big beaked bird." The range has borne other names. Captain W. A. Jones called these mountains the "Sierra Shoshone", and the Hayden Survey called them the "Yellowstone Range." While some old maps show them as the "Snow Range," the United States Geological Survey gave them the name Absaroka Range in 1885 and this has been accepted by the United States Board of Geographic Names.

"Early trappers in the Absaroka Range found this a forbidding land, prospectors who followed them, a barren one." [1] Mountain men transmitted important geographical discoveries among their fellow trappers. Such discoveries could be part of the general knowledge for a few years, then could be lost for years.

Most of the early western maps do not show any geographical features of the North Fork, other than the lower portion of the Stinking Water (Shoshone river) flowing east. William Clark's map (1806-1811) shows the Shoshone River branching west of the canyon and labels Heart Mountain. A map of the West by W. M. Thayer dated 1820 shows this area as vaguely included in the "Great American Desert." Captain Bonneville's 1837 map covering the North Fork areas names only the "Stinking River." An old map displayed in the Buffalo Bill Historical Center dated 1847, "Map of the United States," only identifies Lake Eustis, Fremont Peak and Big Horn River for this area. Other early maps of North America, for 1857, and 1872, add no features. However, an 1874 Wyoming map shows the Stinking River and Heart Mountain, as well as Fremont and Union Peaks. A "Map of Yellowstone National Park" compiled from official explorations and surveys, 1881, shows the Absaroka mountains which are labeled "Sierra Shoshone East Range." The North Fork is labeled "unexplored" and "precipitous mountains." Captain Jones' detailed maps of 1873 had not been utilized. Jones Fork of Passamaria (Stinking Water) is listed but names of many creeks near Yellowstone Park have been changed, such as Gurley, New Cummings, Roy and Mason. See Section on Stream Names for details of naming.

Agricultural Use of the North Fork

Unlike the rivers of the Midwest and East that early settlers were used to, the North Fork was not an avenue for transportation or travel, but a barrier.

The rich bottom lands between the lower branches of the North Fork and the South Fork were inundated in 1910 with the filling of the Shoshone Reservoir. Water is taken from the North Fork by ditches and from eleven streams for irrigation. In 1904 William E. Green built a headgate opposite Big Creek and diverted water into a canal to irrigate his land west of lower Green Creek.[2] The North Fork Valley Ditch now has its headgate just inside the Forest Reserve. In 1904, the only other land owners between Whit Creek and the Forest Reserve, besides Green, were Vinnie Grinder, W. E. Grinder, V. Gifford Langtry, Lee H. Borron and Pat Kelly. Langtry ran an employment office in Cody in 1905.

In 1903 Charles H. Stonebridge settled downriver from Whit Creek. He built a reservoir in the foothills below Table Mountain, and had overflow rights on Whit Creek to fill it and irrigate 40 acres. The reservoir "went out" in 1914, creating a flash flood, Ben Simpers rebuilt and it has held since then.

By 1919, 1,435 acres in the valley were under irrigation. By 1949 this had increased to 2,000 acres and by 1993, to 2,715 acres, close to the maximum that can be utilized (although water rights for some 3,590 acres are allotted). Only a small portion of this acreage was lost with the raising of the dam and the extension of water storage area in 1991. Forest Service statistics show water for 994 acres is diverted from the river, ditches from streams supply the rest.

When traveling westward through the Wapiti valley one notices the region naturally divides into three sections: the lower is from the reservoir to the Wapiti bridge where the valley narrows for a short distance, then the valley widens from the bridge to the entrance of the Forest Reserve at Trail Shop, approximately half-way from Cody to the entrance of Yellowstone Park. Here the wide valley and farmland abruptly end. The last half is canyon-like with forests and eroded masses of the Eocene Wapiti formation.

The upper half is in the Shoshone National Forest and the Absaroka and Washakie Wilderness. The Absaroka Wilderness lies north of the river and the Washakie Wilderness is to the south of the river.

Recreational Use of the North Fork

For thousands of tourists, as well as locals,the main recreational use is sight seeing. Other uses are camping, picnicking, fishing, hunting, horseback riding, hiking, river floating, firewood gathering, birding, and berry picking. Skiing, Christmas tree cutting, and snowmobiling are winter recreations as is observation of wild game wintering at the lower elevation. Wind surfing and boating are enjoyed on the reservoir in summer and ice fishing in winter. Back in the 1930s, Ben Hammond trailered a sailboat back from San Francisco and was the first one to sail it on Shoshone Reservoir. Soon Charles and Thelma Lufkin had a sail boat and eventually there were five. Perhaps it is fortunate this hobby waned, the capricious winds, without warning, can become fierce gales. In January 1993, hang gliding off Cedar Mountain over the frozen reservoir was tried for the first time.

The volcanic mountains are not suitable for climbing. "This miserable climbing rock, formed by volcanic pebbles and boulders, mixed into the molten andesite lavas, like ingredients in a fruitcake, is just about as ready to crumble."[3] Bonney also stated, " The history of the earliest ascents of many of the peaks has been lost in the remoteness of time and the daily life of the herders and sheep hunters to whom it seemed part of the day's work." [4]

Three national highways converge in Cody, and federal highways 14, 16, and 20 draw people to the North Fork. Four places are listed on the National Register of Historic Places: Wapiti Ranger Station, listed in 1963; Buffalo Bill Dam, listed in 1971; Pahaska Tepee, in 1973; and Mummy Cave, in 1973.

Big game for hunting and watchable wildlife include bear—grizzly and black, elk, mule deer, moose, Big Horn sheep, and occasionally mountain lions. Since 1990 bison have come over Sylvan Pass in winter following the packed snowmobile trail. Some remain over the summer.

Small mammals are coyotes, badgers, and the weasel family, including martin. Beaver, hares, squirrels, chipmunks, ground squirrels, bobcats, skunks, and a few river otters have been seen. The raccoon is a recent invasive intruder. In the Forest Reserve there are 72 species of mammals.

There are nine species of reptiles. Rattlesnakes are prevalent from their namesake creek and mountain up as far as Elk Fork. Lonnie Royal remembered the rattlesnakes at Trout Creek when he worked for N.P. deMauriac some sixty years ago, as does this writer from thirteen summers there. Mrs. Emma Kelly pointed out that the rattlesnakes were more numerous on the sunny side of the river and less on the south or shadier side. Bull snakes are few but in the same general area as the rattlesnakes. Water snakes are numerous as far up river as Blackwater. Of the eleven garter snakes found in Wyoming, the Wandering Garter Snake is found all over Wyoming. They rarely bite when picked up but writhe violently and emit a foul-smelling secretion.[5] The Rocky Mountain rubber boa, related to the boa constrictor and python, is a rare, secretive and unique species of small, burrowing snake. It is found around Blackwater and Elk Fork. In 1930, settler George Cles, found one on his Rattlesnake Creek ranch and killed it according to the *Cody Enterprise*. The Forest Service considers this small, docile snake an indicator species in old growth forests, very important for indicating a well balanced ecosystem.

The 230 species of birds are typical of forest and riparian habitats, sage brush and grasslands. Western meadowlarks are seen as far up as Legg's ranch but not at Trail Shop, according to Nina Sherwin. Mountain bluebirds fly along the grassy foothills below Jim Mountain and along Big Creek, and in the fall migrating flocks gather near Lonnie Royal's place on Canyon Creek. Over-wintering robins sometimes survive on juniper berries at June Creek. Yellow bellied sapsuckers drill their even rows of holes in cottonwood trees at Big Game campground and their "plaintive mews" can be heard even when they cannot be seen. Spotted sandpipers patrol the water's edge as violet-green swallows skim the river in the Forest Reserve. Hawks and eagles are not abundant but red-tailed hawks nest and often are heard and seen. European starlings arrived recently. Miss Shawver of Holm Lodge looked each fall for the bald eagle near Hanging Rock, "...it appeared about November at the same place."[6]

The Wyoming Fish and Game Department designates the North Fork main river as a Class 2 fishing stream, which means "very good trout waters—fisheries of statewide importance." Some of the larger tributaries are Class 3 and the smaller ones are Class 4, low production trout waters.

Ninety five percent of the fish are Yellowstone and Snake River cutthroat and rainbow. "The cutthroat remains the one link we have with the pristine streams of our past."[7] Some of the other fish are mackinaw, brown trout, whitefish and suckers. There are a total of nineteen species. The tributaries are critical to the cutthroat and rainbow that migrate out of the Buffalo Bill Reservoir to spawn and in June the dorsal fins of large trout can be seen as the big fish maneuver in the process of spawning in quiet shallows near Big Game campground. Fortunately, this section of the river is closed to fishing until after the spawning season.

There are seven species of amphibians, the most evident are frogs. According to *Wyoming Wildlife,*[8] dark brown spotted frogs are more numerous than any other in the Shoshone National Forest.

Annual precipitation of the area along with the elevation determines what grows. The average annual precipitation between 1907 and 1971 was 11.26 inches at the dam. The mean annual precipitation varies from 12 to 24 inches in the study area, the least at the dam. Temperatures range from minus 40 degrees to 100 degrees Fahrenheit. The overall average for Wyoming is 125 days of growing season. The season is longer near the reservoir and decreases westward with rise in elevation so that from Pahaska to Sylvan Pass frost could occur during any month. Vegetation varies with precipitation, elevation, and soil conditions. It includes alpine, montane meadow-parkland, sagebrush-grassland, riparian, semi-desert, and conifer forests. Wyoming has 2,000 different kinds of flowering plants including twenty-five kinds of willows, more willow species than any other state. Only a few species of North Fork plants will be mentioned.

First, the conifers. In the lower elevations, Limber pine, Douglas fir, and Rocky Mountain juniper grow. What could well be the oldest Rocky Mountain juniper on the North Fork is an old monarch at the northeast end of the bridge over the river at June Creek. This tree has a girth of seven feet and eleven inches, measured four feet above its base. Exposed, charred roots are evidence that it apparently survived a fire. On the north slope of Sheep Mountain a few specimens of the rare and endangered species of Whitebark pine struggle to survive. This primitive pine a relic of eons past, seems to be fighting a losing battle because of global warming.

From 8,500 to 10,000 feet are the dense, even growth of Lodgepole pine that came in after the retreat of the last glaciers. The recent policy of fire suppression has allowed these trees to grow for 80 to 100 years. At this age they become susceptible to Mountain pine beetles, the trees turn brown, fall over and become "combustible matchsticks." After the fires of 1988, a more ecologically sound policy towards fires has developed. Above 10,000 feet the conifers are mostly subalpine fir and Engelman spruce extending to timberline.

Vegetation in the lower valley is semi-desert and riparian with sagebrush, greasewood, some saltbush, cottonwoods and willows. Patches of pink locoweed brightens the beige hills near the canyon in May, along with plains daisies and white phlox. In the middle valley grazing improves with grama, desert buckwheat, and bunch grass. There are also sagebrush and more berry bushes, mainly a scrubby little wild current with distasteful and bad smelling, nonpoisonous berries. This brush adds rusty-red color to the hillsides in the fall.

In the Forest Reserve are gooseberry, wild raspberry, service berry, cowcatcher, red-osier dogwood, quaking aspen and many more. The yellow blooms of silverleaf willows, the understory brush in Big Game and Elk Fork campgrounds, provides a heady pungent odor in June. Among the many wild flowers, rare bitterroot can be found near Elk Fork and the rare and endangered species of orchid, the fairyslipper, grows between Pahaska and the East Gate of the Park. Where the valley ends and the Forest Reserve begins, pink phlox, plains cactus and wild roses bloom in June. A little higher up, the yellow blossoms of arrowleaf balsam root and blue lupine cover the hillsides between Aspen Creek and Blackwater in spring. Mariposa lilies and the many kinds and colors of Indian paintbrush grow from the reservoir to the Park entrance. In the Forest Reserve, where the conifers

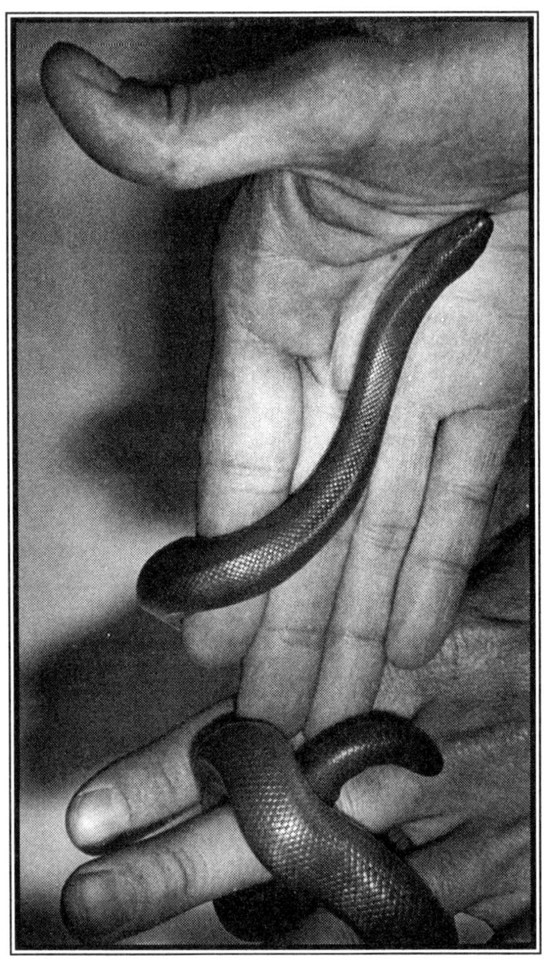

Rubber Boa. Photo courtesy of the Cody Enterprise.

predominate, on open hillsides forbes and grasses—Idaho fescue and bluebunch wheatgrass—provide grazing. Some black sagebrush is found near volcanic rock. The lower valley of irrigated fields produce alfalfa, wheat, oats, and barley. In the middle valley alfalfa predominates, with pasture lands for forage. There is more cattle ranching in the lower valley and more horse pasturing farther up the river.

The white limestone of Chalk Mountain and the dark red volcanic rock of Logan Mountain rise in sharp contrast side by side between Rattlesnake Creek and Trout Creek. West of Trout Creek begin the fantastic eroded volcanics. In 1873, early explorer Captain Jones called them "volcanic ejectaments." The detached, free standing pinnacles are eye catching. The Millers of Trout Creek named their place "The Pinnacles" after these rock towers.

Between Breteche and Whit Creek are the dikes of wall-like rocks or towers, one of which Captain Jones named the "Stovepipe." This eroded dike has one piece of rock that appears to jut out and up from the rest like a small stove pipe. The name did appear on Jones original map but was not generally used.

Another much longer dike, The Chinese Wall stands exposed on both sides of the middle valley. In some places it is thirty feet high, and can be four or five feet wide. On the river bottom, where it is exposed during low water, it has been worn smooth from erosion. Another smaller dike is visible on the north side of the river halfway between Sweetwater and Clearwater bridge. Just inside the Forest Reserve the eroded rock called the Laughing Pig, greets the traveler. J.E. Stimson, photographer from Cheyenne, made a trip up the North Fork in 1903, taking many pictures. His photograph of the narrow road along the cliff just east of the Laughing Pig he called "Dugway and North Fork of the Shoshone River." Fifty feet above the road on the skyline in Stimson's photograph is a tree with sparse branches. Today that lone tree looks practically the same as it did more than 85 years ago.

East of the Holy City, one of the main rock formations on the North Fork, across from Pagoda Creek, is the Goose Rock and around the bend of the Devil's Elbow, named for the way the river curves, the Anvil rock is on the distant north skyline. Devil's Elbow first carried the name El Diablo. A very large block of the cliff on the north side of the river at the Holy City fell into the river in 1933. Farther up the river, near Sheep Creek, the Henry Ford Rock on the ridge across the river makes a memorable silhouette at dusk. Chimney Rock was called the Needle in 1903 when Stimson photographed it. Just beyond that is the Elephant Head, one has to know where to look to catch a glimpse of it from a moving car.

Colonel William Pickett traveled down the North Fork in 1880, and commented on the "fantastical forms." "I saw several cathedrals with tall needle-shaped spires." [9] He further describes the many sculptured rocks resembling people and animals. No wonder the first travelers called it the "Zoo Park Road." Where the breccia of these Eocene Wapiti formations has been eroded, the many pinnacles are often called "hoodoos."

This Rocky Mountain Juniper, with a girth over seven feet, is probably the oldest on the North Fork.

Because they are remote from the highway, the Fishhawk Glacier and larger Borron Creek Glacier, named for William T. "Bill" Borron, are little publicized. Both are receding due to climatic warming. Another phenomenon not visible from the highway is the Blackwater Natural Arch on Coxcomb mountain. It is approximately 240 feet wide, 280 feet tall, and at least thirty two feet thick. It is located at 10,750 feet above sea level and is a world class natural bridge.[10] John Yeates Sr., explored and photographed this arch around 1906. His photographs are the first known to feature a person standing in the arch and of the arch at such close proximity. There has been to date no way to get a picture to portray its size in a photograph taken close by. The access to the Natural Arch is steep and hazardous, making it almost inaccessible. However, it can be seen by climbing the ridge directly north of Rex Hale campground, or from up Libby Creek or any high ridge north of the river.

Political History

The political background and boundaries of the North Fork differ from that of the state of Wyoming because, at various times, Wyoming was divided and fell under different political governments. The North Fork River, on the Atlantic slope watershed, drains into the Big Horn, and on into the Yellowstone, Missouri and finally the Mississippi River. Because of this, the region fell into the area of Spanish Louisiana from 1764 until 1800 when it was secretly ceded to France. Three years later the United States bought it from France as part of the Louisiana Purchase. President Jefferson sent the Lewis and Clark Expedition to explore the newly acquired country, 1804-1806. The members of the exploring party stayed close to the Yellowstone river, but one member of the party, John Colter, a few years later came very close to the North Fork. He most likely looked at it from a distance since he was near the lower reaches of the South Fork and would have observed the North Fork valley.

This northwest corner of Wyoming belonged to France and England from 1603 until 1764. From 1764 until 1800 it belonged to Spain, then from 1800 until 1803 to France and after 1803 to the United States. It was Louisiana Territory from 1803 until 1812; Missouri Territory from 1812 until 1834. For two decades it was designated "Indian Territory;" then Nebraska Territory, from 1854 until 1861; Indiana Territory from 1861 until 1863; and briefly Idaho Territory from 1863 until 1864; then Dakota Territory from 1864 until 1868. Wyoming Territory was created in 1868. The North Fork was never part of Oregon or Utah Territory.

The counties that at times included the North Fork are Carter County from 1867 until 1869; Sweetwater from 1869 until 1884; Fremont from 1884 until 1890; Big Horn from 1890 until 1909; and finally Park County since 1909 to the present. The county seat of Sweetwater County was Green River, a long and difficult journey for the few first settlers on the North Fork. When the North Fork was in Fremont County, it was still a long tedious trip for the six years Lander was the county seat. Most of the above information comes from *The Wyoming Country Before Statehood*, by L. Milton Woods, 1971; *The Worland Press,* Published in cooperation with the Wyoming State Archives and Historical Department.

Three names were suggested for the final county, Beck, Colter, and Park. "Beck" would have been an appropriate memorial for George T. Beck because of his valuable promotional efforts.

The North Fork area fell within the Crow Reservation as promised to the Crow Indians at the Fort Laramie Treaty, September 17, 1851. The original early Crow boundary took in the land west of Powder River to the Yellowstone Park boundary which included all the Big Horn River drainages. The Fort Laramie Treaty of 1868 shrunk the reservation by taking away all Crow lands below the Montana-Wyoming boundary, the same year Wyoming Territory was created.

Early Inhabitants

Previous to Crow claims, Intermountain Native Americans, mainly Shoshone Indians, roamed this region from 1200 until about 1700 A.D. Before that, Western Athapaskan tribes were in the area from 600 until 900. These aboriginal wanderers visited the North Fork valley for thousands of years. A *Clovis* point found near Moss creek would indicate habitation for about 11,000 years. The best dated chronology of one of the inhabitants, besides the archeological finds in many layers of habitation, comes from the excavation of Mummy Cave, discovered by Bob Edgar who helped excavate it. This cave is at the foot of a west facing cliff a few feet from a big bend of the river upstream from what was at one time the site of the Freeman sawmill and downstream from Blackwater, about 35 miles west of Cody.

Excavation of the cave and carbon dating of the 38 culture layers revealed the cave had been occupied for 9,000 years. At the lowest culture layer, 32 feet below the surface, only a single artifact was found, a worked stone tool with curved prismatic blade, possibly a graver. The most exciting find was the mummified body of a buried male, who came to be known as Mummy Joe. He had been buried c. 720 A.D. or 1,230 years B. P.(Before Present). He wore tanned garments made of mountain sheep, the leather pieces neatly sewn together. His teeth and finger nails and long black hair made the body seem more real when compared to the bleached bones found in other burials on the Johansson Homestead and on a rock pedestal close to the ridge east of Moss creek.

Mummy Joe, an adult male Indian, 35 to 40 years old, five feet five inches tall, died and was buried in the late spring, as evidenced by spruce pollen found with him. Since there had been no stream change in the last 10,000 years the cave had not been washed out.

In the cave were pieces of tanned hides, brush and cordage, bark and grass, feathers, basketry, wood tools, a skin boot, and the less perishable and much more numerous worked stone tools. The inhabitants' greater dependence on mountain sheep is evidenced by six times more sheep bone than deer bone. The hide work, sewing, and manufacturing of wood and bone tools indicated the Indians had a hunting-gathering economy. The cordage from the most recent levels-three to seven, was bark cordage, twisted hair cordage, and sinew cordage of two ply twisted strands.

Besides storage pits, there were firepits and hearths throughout most of the levels of the cave. One moccasin cache held a high-top moccasin made of mountain sheep hide (hair side in) with grass pads for an inner cushion.

Researcher Arthur H. Harris said the evidence "does not indicate appreciable climatic-vegetational changes occurring at the cave site during the past 9,000 or so years."[11]

The mostly horseless Shoshone Indians inhabited the upper mountain canyons and mesas. A bundle of twisted sagebrush bark cordage woven into a mountain sheep capture net was made and cached about 10,000 years ago in a limestone cave near the volcanic cap on the western end of Sheep Mountain. This was found by Bob Edgar and is displayed in Old Trail Town. The sheep capture net, being so old, must have been hidden by antecedents of the Sheepeaters. The later

This section of eroded dike, The Stovepipe, is typical of the surrealistic shapes the elements have carved from the rock formations on the North Fork. Photo courtesy Elmor Jones.

Sheepeaters were a subgroup of the Shoshone or Snake Indians and belonged to the Shoshone group linguistically. The Tuku-deka got their name from their chief source of food, Rocky Mountain Sheep. These Native Americans lived in small groups far apart in the Absaroka, Teton, Windriver, Gros Ventre, and Lemhi mountains, and Yellowstone National Park. The tuku-deka are the only tribe known to have lived in Yellowstone Park. Sheepeater Cliffs near Mammoth were later named for their nearby dwellings, and the northern tier of the Park is rich in artifacts.

In the area along the North Fork, many evidences remain of the Sheepeaters, such as their game traps, remnants of chips and flakes from rock projectile point manufacture, and rock blinds. Also, ancient rotting logs of wind breaks and numerous remains of lodge pole wickiups indicate old dwelling sites.

Several portions of trees with horns of a mountain sheep ram embedded in them are still extant. One is in the Dubois museum and one is on display at Shoshone Lodge near the East Entrance of Yellowstone Park. Also, there are place names, the Ramshorn mountain near Dubois and in this area an early location (1885) three miles east of the summit of Dead Indian Pass they called Ramshorn, apparently because a mountain sheep's horns were embedded in a tree. It is surmised Native American hunters placed or hung the heavy horns in the crotch or forks of a tree and through the years the tree grew around the horns, firmly embedding them. According to John Willard's story, "Medicine Tree," he says such trees were known to exist in western Montana with associated stories and legends.[12] The best study of the *tuku-deka*, mountain Sheepeaters, also called *toyani*, Mountain dwellers, is found in "*The Sheepeaters*", by David Dominick.[13]

The Shoshone River was named the Stinking Water by its white discoverer, John Colter, during the winter of 1807-1808. This was the translation of the Crow Indian word "*Mich ka ap pa*," describing the sulfurous smells that issued from the geyser-like formations at the base of the mountain on each end of the canyon. On a manuscript map compiled by William Clark from informants during the period from 1806 until 1811, the Stinking Water is shown in two branches west of the canyon. The North Fork is labeled *Mich ka ap pa*. The Shoshone Indians under Chief Washakie called the Stinking Water *Pa sama ri.* Another possible Indian name is given by Father DeSmet and described in his 1851 trip from Fort Union to Fort Laramie, "near the source of the

River Puantc is a place called Colter's Hell." Was this the geyser formations of Colter's Hell at the east end of the Shoshone Canyon, or was Yellowstone?

Early Explorers

Jim Bridger is the earliest explorer associated with the North Fork. In a biography of Jim Bridger, J. Cecil Alter writes, "Bridger seems to have led his curious trappers through Sylvan Pass to the Canyons of the Yellowstone River."[17] No doubt Bridger traveled the valley, but it could be questioned if he went due west up the Middle Fork over what came to be called Sylvan Pass. The main game trail and Indian trail followed the North Fork as it turned north, then west up what came to be called Jones Creek, and over Stinking Water Pass. This trail was an important link with what in later years came to be called the Bannock Trail, which was heavily used from 1838 to 1878. The Stinking Water trail joined the Bannock Trail at the mouth of Cache Creek in the Lamar valley of Yellowstone Park.[15] There was a route from the head of the Stinking Water past Stinking Water Peak that joined the Sunlight-Clarks Fork trails.

Jedediah Smith, one of America's greatest explorers, crisscrossed the West from the Upper Missouri to the deserts of the far Southwest. In 1829 he and his men passed through the Yellowstone National Park area, across Stinking Water Pass, down the North Fork into the Big Horn Basin and into the Wind River valley.[16]

Joe Meek, "The Merry Mountain Man," was in the Jedediah Smith-William Sublette Party on this late

Above, the "Chinese Wall", in some places rises thirty feet high. Photo courtesy of Elmor Jones.

Middle, J.E. Stimson, early photographer of the North Fork. (Photo courtesy of Wyoming State Archives, Museums and Historical Department)

Bottom, a Stimson photo of a horse and buggy "Dugway and North Fork of Shoshone River. (Photo courtesy of Wyoming State Archives, Museums and Historical Department)

1829 trip. While out hunting in Yellowstone Park he was cut off from the main party by Blackfeet Indians and wandered for four days before being found by two trappers of the group. After three more days they caught up with the main party in the Sierra Shoshone Mountains (Absaroka Mountains). With great difficulty they broke a trail over Stinking Water Pass (Jones Pass). They "made only a few hundred yards a day," but "at last, without the loss of a man, the brigade came to the forks of the Shoshone River."[17] However, one hundred head of horses and mules died in the ordeal, mainly getting stuck in snow drifts. As was the custom of the trappers and explorers, horses that "gave out" were utilized for food.

"In 1864, splinter groups from the Stuart expedition traveling into the Big Horn and Stinking Water (Shoshone river) drainages of Wyoming, returned to Montana through the present park..." [18]

In his journal, Osborne Russell refers to the Stinking Water. He remembered during his trapping travels that he started up the North Fork on July 24, 1835. Russell described it as "dense piles of mountains, granite, slate and sandstone."[19] This would be the lower drainage, just above the canyon of the river. He travelled the North Fork game and Indian trail, then the "Frost Lake Trail" into the Lamar River valley.

"Woman with Bustle" formation is an example of a "hoodoo." Photo courtesy of Elmor Jones.

His next reference is in 1837, when he and other trappers drifted in and out of the head of the North Fork from the 9th to the 12th of August, 1837, crossing over Sylvan Pass and then moving into the headwaters of the Clarks Fork and Sunlight Basin.[20]

Aubrey Haines states that "Norris discovered Sylvan Pass in 1881." [21] Another writer says, "It is said that Colonel Cody on his second trip to this country in 1896 discovered the eastern entrance to the Park." [22]

The most detailed account of early exploration of the North Fork is in Captain William A. Jones' report of his 1873 reconnaissance for the United States Army. At the time of the trip he was a lieutenant. By 1875 he had advanced to Captain of Engineers, the same year his book-length report was published. Coming north from Camp Brown (near present Fort Washakie), on July 26th he made his 32nd camp just west of the mouth of Rattlesnake Creek. He states the latitude 44 degree 30'-16", longitude 109 degree 14'- 4". The camp was "near a large spring raised two or three feet above the ground with an abundant flow of blackish water, strong sulphurous smell."[23]

Rattlesnake is the first stream draining into the North Fork just west of the Shoshone Canyon. For the next five days Jones described his trip up the river, and finally up the tributary, later named after him, and over Stinking Water Pass into Yellowstone Park. He had 66 pack and saddle mules, one pack master and ten packers. He chose camping locations for water, wood, and open areas or meadows for the mules. Although he does not specify, the Shoshone Indians would have had their own livestock and camp supplies. His guides were some of Chief Washakie's Shoshones. Narkok, a petty chief, was one of the guides and John LeClaire, a French half-breed, was "one of the most intelligent of our guides," wrote Jones. He had ten Shoshone Indians as scouts accompanied by their families.

On Jones' second day on the North Fork, he started out from his Rattlesnake Creek camp, which he ascertained to be 5,273 feet altitude, and moved up river. He noted evidence of Indian rock construction and wrote, "The best example of an undoubted sepulcher was seen near the trail, two miles beyond Camp 32 on the left bank of the North Fork...." This consisted of a low mound of loose stones lying nearly east and west, with an irregular and broader heap extending a few feet

Blackwater Arch against Ptarmigan Mountain. (Photo, Dewey Vanderhoff. © 1993,1995.)

John Yeates Sr. in Blackwater Natural Arch, 1906. Believed to be the first white person to explore and photograph the landmark. Photo Courtesy Yeates' family.

northward from eastern end. "Our Shoshone Scout Narkok said it was a burial place of a Blackfoot warrior."[24]

After traveling 14.7 miles Jones observed "the mouth of the canyon, upon either side stand two lofty and slender peaks of similar form which I have named The Sentinels." Today these two peaks guard the entrance of the present Forest Reserve and have been renamed Signal Peak on the north and Flag Peak on the south side of the river. On Jones' excellent maps his 33rd camp was located just west of the mouth of today's Big Creek at 5,845 feet,latitude, 44 degrees, 28'-48", and longitude 109 degrees, 30'-34".

Earlier, as Jones traveled around Carter Mountain, he had observed the well-known landmark Heart Mountain, and he described a "mountain with many cedars," which he named Cedar Mountain, but he labels Sheep Mountain "Cedar Ridge." He is the first to name the dike with its eroded pinnacles west of Sheep Mountain "the Stove Pipe." The formations at the head of Big Creek he called "The Three Palaces," but none of these places retained those names.

From Big Creek, on July 28th, the expedition marched up the river 9.1 miles. The trail became very difficult for them after they entered the present Forest Reserve. "To avoid a huge precipice which reached quite into the river, unfordable through the canyon, it (the expedition) made a detour to the right over the most difficult hill met with on the trip. It did not seem possible for animals to climb it, and the mishaps to the pack train were quite numerous."[25]

Jones wrote, "It was necessary to ford the river repeatedly—no easy matter— . . . . Today and thence forward it was necessary to send a pioneer party from the escort ahead of the main body to clear and make the trail."[26]

The scouts returned and reported they had been following the fresh trail of two white men with two "led horses." The scouts again went ahead and found the two men who proved to be prospectors from Clarks Fork. These two travelers were greatly relieved when they found the Indians were friendly.

E. S. Topping in *Chronicles of the Yellowstone* wrote that "His (Jones) course lay along the wagon road made by the Big Horn expedition of 1870, till he arrived at Stinking Water river. He went up the north fork of this stream for sixty miles, on a large elk trail which led through a pass in the high range between this river and the Yellowstone."[27]

Topping explains that he and Nelson Yarnall had started out from Bozeman to prospect on the Stinking Water. Zigzagging back and forth they had gone up the Yellowstone to the "Clarke's Fork" mines where they were joined by Pat O'Hare [sic] and the three "went down Clarke's Fork to the prairie."[28]

Pat O'Hara was greatly handicapped by being near-sighted. He sometimes thought herds of wild game were bands of unfriendly Indians. Pat O'Hara left his companions at the foot of the mountains. Years later he returned to this spot and for awhile settled on what is today known as Pat O'Hara Creek. Topping and Yarnall crossed the divide to the Stinking Water, probably Skull Creek divide. They traveled to the forks of the Stinking Water where they were chased for two miles by a war party of Arapaho. They went up the North Fork branch prospecting along the way to the "pass across the Sierra Shoshone, then rounded back on their own trail." When they were about halfway down the river they had the tense and jittery encounter with the scouts from the Jones expedition and were relieved they weren't unfriendly Sioux or Arapaho. The prospectors parted and went on down the river, then spent a month prospecting on the South Fork without any luck, so, went "over to the Yellowstone Lake and down to the settlements."[29]

On the way to Camp 34, Jones made a mountainous detour north of the river and badly used up the pack animals. They made camp at Clearwater, latitude 44 degrees, 28' -6", longitude 109 degrees, 39'-14", and laid over a day to rest up. Then they moved 14.5 miles up the river and made Camp 35, latitude 44 degrees, 28'-11", longitude 109 degrees, 52' - 13", at present day Libby Creek. Jones found the trail extremely difficult and had to ford the river seven times. In one place it was so dangerous that even the Indians dismounted. According to Jones, Indians stick to their ponies in the "most unheard of places rather than dismount."

Above Camp 35 he had to turn north to follow the main stream. Between Camp 35 and 36 Jones named the mountains to the west Giant Castle and Soldier and Sailor Peaks. These names remain today on many maps. Camp 36, latitude 44 degrees, 33'-46", longitude 109 degrees, 59' - 15", is known today as Sam Berry Meadows. Here, on Thursday, July 31st, the Indian guides told Jones he could make one "big march" to the divide or two easy ones. He chose the easy marches. Jones climbed Sailor mountain on August 1st to view the country. He wrote, "The trail leads through perfectly lovely country" and they camped "in a spot that was absolutely perfect." The location of this last camp of the North Fork, number 37, was latitude 44 degrees, 32' -45", longitude 110 degrees, 10'- 46".

Leaving such perfection he crossed Stinking Water Pass at an elevation of 9,444 feet and left the study area on August 2nd, 1873. Jones described the pass which would later bear his name: "Stinking Water Pass is a narrow opening between two high points on the divide between the North Fork and Yellowstone Lake.[30] Jones wrote, "The Sierra Shoshone range is probably the most remarkable one in the entire Rocky Mountain chain."[31]

Jones' trip disproved Nathanial P. Langford's contention that Yellowstone was only accessible from Montana.

Another early visitor to the North Fork left a written account of his visit. In July, 1878, Scout

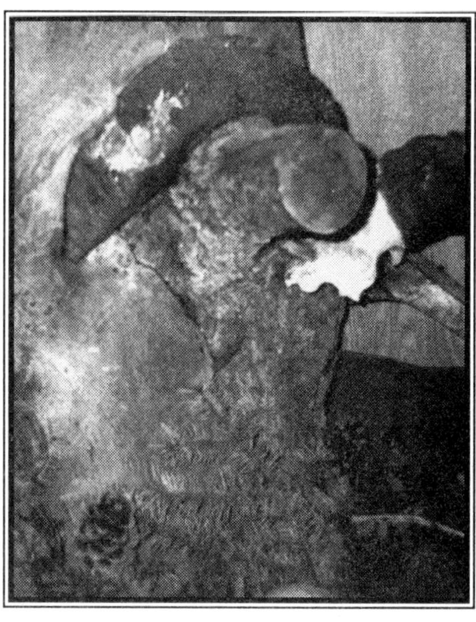

Above Left: Petroglyph in Sandstone. Photo courtesy of Mary Williams

Above Right: Rams horn grown into tree from Dubois Museum.

Below left: Wickiup at Lava Creek, photograph taken in 1992.

Below right: Rams horn grown into tree, on display at Shoshone Lodge, North Fork.

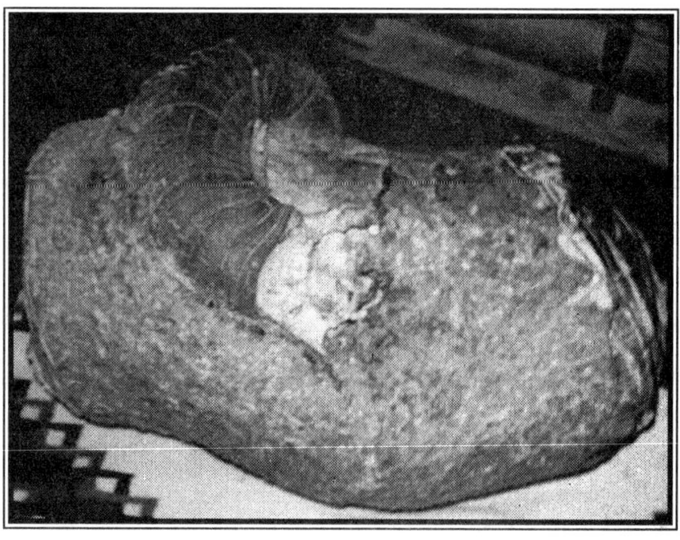

Man on horse petroglyph Photo courtesy of Mary Williams.

Luther S. Kelly, employed by the United States Army, was ordered by General Nelson Miles to check on the wandering Bannocks and prospectors south and west of the boundary of the Crow Indian Reservation. At this time the Montana-Wyoming boundary was the southern boundary of the Crow Reservation, but was not officially surveyed and marked until 1879-1880 by Engineer Reeves and party.[32]

Kelly left Fort Keogh (present Miles City, Montana) with two companions and three pack horses and proceeded through Pryor Gap into the Big Horn Basin. Kelly wrote, "I had spent many years in Montana and Dakota, but the region of country west of the Big Horn Mountains was still an unknown quantity, and at that day was used mostly by the Mountain Crows and the Arapaho as a hunting ground."[33]

Kelly was a well-liked, intelligent and handsome man with long dark hair, clean shaven except for a moustache. He traveled up Trail Creek, east of Rattlesnake Mountain, and found prospectors but they were off the Crow Reservation. He rode to the top of Rattlesnake Mountain and looked upon the valley of the North Fork and later wrote in his memoirs, "From our point of observation the vista stretched up the north fork of the Stinking River and was altogether lovely, wild, and picturesque. The sharp, pine-clad ridges sloped gently to the valley, the dark green foliage of which was dotted with groves of the brighter tinted aspen and cottonwood."[34]

After checking on the prospectors, Kelly took the easiest trail over the top of Rattlesnake Mountain, the one going westward from near the head of Trail Creek. Here he watched a black bear raking frozen grasshoppers out of a snow bank, and said the melting snow water carried other grasshoppers into the streams for hungry trout.

There were a number of other men in the area in 1878. Besides the prospectors on the east side of Rattlesnake Mountain, Kelly and companions ran into an officer and his guide from Fort Washakie on the west side. They were part of a party of cavalry camped "near the forks, about a mile distant where the valley opened out to form a little park above the narrow canyon."[35]

Kelly tried to take a short cut back to his camp on the east side of the mountain by striking a "bee line over the mountain which like most short cuts in a wild country involved double the labor," consequently his party had to camp out another night. He regretted they hadn't gone to the cavalry camp and enjoyed the hospitality there instead of "toiling over the rocks."

Finally, they were ready to start for Yellowstone Lake. He wrote, "Winding along the north fork of this mountain stream was a pleasant diversion, for here the game trails led ever upward . . . "[36] He never mentions the type of difficulties Captain Jones suffered on this same trail five years earlier.

Other writers attested to the unexplored character of this area. William A. Baillie-Grohman, an English gentleman/traveler, visited Wyoming in 1880. He scanned the landscape from a mountain top in the Wind River Mountains and wrote, "Our vision is very extended: in the few places where intervening mountain chains do not obstruct the view the diameter of the circle we overlook is scarcely less than 400 miles, perhaps more. To-day [1880] the country we see is decidedly the most secluded portion of the Rockies, for those portions of the landscape over which our vision is unre-

stricted there is not a single white-man's settlement and probably there were not more than half-a-dozen human beings, aside of Indians, abiding in it."[37]

In 1962 Richard A. Bartlett wrote about the same area, what we call The Greater Yellowstone Ecosystem. "Today, this region includes Yellowstone National Park and Grand Teton National Park. But in 1871, when Hayden led the first official government expedition into the area, it was still a virtual terra incognita—almost the last such area within the continental boundaries of the United States and its territories."[38]

Above, Ptarmigan Mountain, west of Table Mountain. Photo courtesy Elmor Jones.

Below, "Indian Grave Rock," east of Moss Creek is the site of an Indian Grave found in the early 1930s.

Two years after Yellowstone Kelly's trip, Colonel William D. Pickett traveled down the North Fork and documented it in 1908 in an article, "Memories of a Bear Hunter." it was included in *Hunting at High Altitudes.* [39]

In the early fall of 1880 Colonel Pickett started out from Bozeman accompanied only by friend, experienced mountain man, George Herendeen, and a "Swedish boy as cook and camp keeper."[40] They planned to seek out Lieutenant Jones' 1873 route over the Absaroka Mountains. Apparently they chose the wrong game trail and came down Crow Creek, the drainage between Middle Fork (Sylvan Pass) and Jones Creek. They didn't discover their mistake until they "were too far down the mountain to turn back." Colonel Pickett wrote, "At last we came to a ledge of rock in the trail which required a jump down of three feet . . .[41] Only Herendeen's expertise got them safely off this ledge. They camped a little farther down. The next day they moved camp 14 miles down onto the main stream, possibly near Eagle Creek. Here they camped for a week, Colonel Pickett always on the alert to kill bear.

On October 21st they moved camp seven miles downstream, probably to Newton Creek, well protected by timber. Opposite the river the cliffs rose 100 feet vertically from the water's edge. On a reconnaissance climb from this camp Colonel Pickett first saw the Blackwater Natural Bridge on Coxcomb mountain.[42] This world record natural bridge is 240 feet wide, 280 feet tall, 32 feet thick, and is located at an elevation of 10,750 feet.

They next moved another seven miles down to Elk Fork and camped two miles up that stream. Elk Fork was named by Colonel Pickett on October 29, 1880. There were many antlers shed along this heavily used migration route from the Thorofare to the south, up Open Creek and over Rampart Pass. Pickett called it Elk Horn Creek and later just Elk Creek.

The little party moved out of the main North Fork area, around Sheep Mountain onto the South Fork. Here they were delayed until November 22, 1880, before leaving the South Fork and starting for their winter quarters in Bozeman. By this time they were running a little short of flour but they were able to obtain some from the Judge William Alexander Carter outfit near the mouth of Carter Creek. Pickett erroneously recalled it was "Dr. Carter" and in another reference "Captain Carter" who gave them the flour. Actually, Judge Carter never set foot on his northern cattle range. He had sent his foreman Peter McCulloch north with the herd and McCulloch built the cabin Pickett visited.

Pickett also visited the only other ranch in the area, seven miles up river, Captain Belknap's run by John Dyer.

Colonel Pickett came well prepared for cold weather camping. He had a twelve by fourteen foot wall tent with a waterproof tarpaulin floor, he had a small stove, robes and blankets, and his own fur-lined sleeping bag.

Colonel Pickett returned to the North Fork in 1881 and 1883, and on October 30, 1883, he visited the Jay Bradley ranch. Their cabin was a few miles above the Shoshone Canyon, below the mouth of Rattlesnake Creek. Colonel Pickett persuaded Jay Bradley and wife to move over to Pickett's ranch on the Greybull and work for him. By 1883 people were moving into the North Fork. Andy Chapman had built a cabin about a mile up Trout Creek, and there was a cabin at the mouth of Rattlesnake Creek.[43]

The West from the Census of 1880, reported Wyoming had a population of 20,788, up from 9,118 in 1870. The authors stated, "The northern half of the Territory, which is fertile and well watered, and possesses a milder climate, besides being almost inaccessible, has from time immemorial, been occupied by the Sioux Indians . . ."[44] Hardly had these words been printed before the situation rapidly changed and settlers started moving in and the Indians were long gone.

In 1882 Colonel William F. Cody and party traveled by train to Cheyenne and from there went north by horseback and pack mules to the Big Horn Basin. The party ventured into the area just above where the two forks came together but they did not penetrate very far up the North Fork.[45] Cody recognized and appreciated the unspoiled wilderness of the northwest corner of Wyoming, and later in life sympathized with his Indian friends in their loss of hunting territory and homeland.[46] He set his heart on a piece of the paradise by filing on land for a lodge on the north side of Carter Mountain, also the TE Ranch on the South Fork and lastly built a hunting lodge on the North Fork at Pahaska near Yellowstone Park.

Like many of his contemporaries he had ambivalent feelings, a desire for development and the love of unspoiled wilderness. Cody believed in development and conquering the wilderness. He participated in establishing the town of Cody and developing canals and irrigation projects. He had farm land on the Irma Flat and near Marquette, later submerged under the reservoir.

Cody's friend General Phil Sheridan subdued the Indians and conquered the West but he wanted to save the game animals. If his proposal had been accepted it would have had a most profound effect on the North Fork area.

Ecologically, Sheridan's plan was sound and would have included much of the area and biodiversity of the Greater Yellowstone Ecosystem. Sheridan's plan came from his 1882 trip through Yellowstone Park, when he entered the Park through the south and exited the northeast corner over an unexplored route across the Beartooth Plateau to Billings, Montana. In Sheridan's final report he wrote, "I would like to see the government extend this park to the east as far as a north and south line through Cedar Mountain; this would be due east about forty miles, at the same time placing the southern boundary of the park at the 44th parallel of latitude, which would be due south ten miles. This would increase the area of the park by 3,344 square miles, and would make a preserve for the large game of the west, now so rapidly decreasing."[47]

He further made an appeal to all the sportsmen of this country and to the various sportsmen's clubs to assist in getting Congress to make the extension for a game refuge. His proposal was not accepted, but the idea hung on and surfaced later in another plan for a game preserve. Sheridan wanted the military to police the Park, and from 1889 to 1916 soldiers did police the Park.

An interesting and detailed hunting trip in the lower North Fork valley in November 1889, was written by William T. Hornaday, Director of the New York Zoological Park, and published in *Scribner's Magazine* 19 years later. The hunting party set out from Fort Custer near the mouth of the Big Horn river in Montana. Lieutenant Robertson, Lieutenant Barber and Win Brisbin of the

First U. S. Cavalry were accompanied by Hornaday. They had Sergeant Fleming as their packer and cook and two Crow Indian scouts, Poor-Face and Forked-Gun. They traveled well equipped with two four-mule wagons, eight saddle horses, two Sibley tents and a cook's tent. Hornaday's article pointed out that poaching was a serious problem for stockmen since the meat hunters greedy slaughter of game forced the stockmen to hire their own game warden. This little military expedition came through Pryor's Gap and crossed what was then called the "Forty-Mile Desert," and reached the main crossing of the Stinking Water, called Corbett. Hornaday wrote, "In a blinding snowstorm we plunged down the steep bluff road to Green's Ranch and stage station, which is called Corbett, and camped in the willows on the river bottom just below it. Mrs. Green, the ranchman's wife, told us that she had not seen a white woman in two-and-one-half years."[48]

The group continued their trip, traveled around Cedar Mountain and set up camp above the canyon. These army hunters had just begun serious shooting when J. W. Sharrock rode into their camp. He was the "official and effective game warden for the Northern Wyoming Game Protective Association, Colonel Pickett, president." Sharrock, "sandy-haired and square-jawed, riding a tough little cow pony and leading a pack horse,"[49] didn't have time to socialize.

Ironically, Colonel Pickett, the most prolific of bear exterminators, was the founder of the Wyoming Game Protective Association. Otto Franc of Meeteetse wrote to the Billings *Gazette* in 1889 reminding all meat and skin hunters the GPA was still strictly enforcing the Wyoming game laws.[50]

Hornaday describes an early resident they encountered near their permanent camp:"A quarter of a mile from the mouth of the impassable canyon we made our permanent camp. Quite near by, up on the level floor of the valley, was the cabin of William Whitworth, an old-time hunter and trapper, and a human document dating back to pioneer days. I pay [sic] him several visits, and always found his cabin neat and clean, his earthen floor swept and garnished. He spoke in a low, even voice, and told me many interesting things. I realized with a feeling of sadness that he represented a fast vanishing type, which soon will totally disappear, and be known no more in the history of the wild West."[51]

Years later, Whitworth moved up the North Fork about 14 miles and settled on a creek which bears his name, Whit Creek. Once a month he rode his mule into town to collect his Civil War pension and spend it.[52]

Hornaday was much impressed with the impassable canyon and the sulphur springs near both the entrance and exit of the canyon. Not only did the scenery impress Hornaday but also the excellent hunting. On November 16, 1889, he experienced an exhilarating hunt and wrote, "One of the greatest days of my life was that on which I pursued and killed, alone, amid the grandeur of the Shoshone Mountains, my first big Mountain Ram."[53] This was on the crags of Rattlesnake Mountain, north of the canyon.

After Hornaday and Lieutenant Robertson had photographed the mouth of the chasm, "We returned to camp and held an indignation meeting . . .we all voted unanimously that it was a burning shame that an unsullied mountain stream . . . should longer remain under the libelous handicap of such a name as 'Stinking Water!'"

What did they do? "...we resolved that the stream should be renamed and called the Shoshone."[54] What was the next action? "When again in Washington, I went to Mr. Henry Gannett, of the U.S. Board of Geographic Names and filed the protest of the party."

Mr. Gannett informed him that any change of this kind must be asked for by the residents of the region affected. Hornaday assured him the residents wanted it. In parentheses he names the residents: The Greens at Corbett, Charles Marston and Sharrock. Hornaday in all fairness added this, "I do not know how much or how little our action had to do with the result; but at all events, it has come about that the name was changed...".

Dee Linford in *Wyoming Stream Names* and Mae Urbanek in *Wyoming Place Names*, state the

The "Needle" Cody, WY Gateway to Yellowstone national Park. Photo by J.E.Stimson courtesy of Wyoming State Archives, Museums and Historical Department.

Wyoming Legislature changed the name in 1901 (Linford), and 1902 (Urbanek). Both agree Shoshone means "abundance of grass" and "grass lodge people" and both quote Wilson O. Clough, *Some Wyoming Place Names.*

The first official survey of Township 52, North Range 103 was in 1883. Of the five cabins designated on this first map, only the Chapman cabin on Trout Creek and the Bradley cabin near the mouth of Rattlesnake Creek were identified.

In the next decade railroad surveyors covered the North Fork seeking a practical outlet through the mountains, mainly for opening up the Stinking Water Mining region which lay between the headwaters of Sunlight creek and the North Fork. The Billings *Gazette*, for September 1, 1894, quoted an article from (Red Lodge) *Pickett*, "George Van Camp who represents large varnish works at Cleveland, Ohio, returned from Stinkingwater Asphalt mines. He has leased the asphalt property and intends to develop it."

This mining activity generated a newspaper (of which, no extant copies have been located) which is mentioned in the Billings *Gazette* during the year 1891. It went by the name the *Stinking Water Prospector* and the editor was Shelby Eli Dillard. It consisted of a "seven column folio issued at Red Lodge."

Of the prospectors mentioned in connection with this mining area in 1891, the names of T. P. McDonal, Frank A. White, Thomas Fisher, and Frank Chatfield are listed. Frank Chatfield's wife, Kitty, gave her name to Kitty Creek on the North Fork.

One last 19th century plan, proposed but never fulfilled, would have profoundly affected and altered the history of this area. It was promulgated 15 years after General Sheridan's 1882 plan for enlarging Yellowstone National Park as far east as Cedar Mountain, and was recorded in the Billings *Gazette* for March 30, 1897. The plan proposed a 50,000 acre game preserve on the North Fork of the Stinking Water. The promoters belonged to the "Lambs" Club of New York City and included Archibald Rogers, John W. MacKay, and Theodore Roosevelt. The plan included a $50,000 clubhouse, and all to be surrounded with an eight-foot high woven wire fence. Men would be employed to maintain the fence. The article said twenty men had agreed to each subscribe $5,000 toward this project and no game were to be killed for five years. The motive came from the spirit of conservation, just coming into popularity, but the ecological results were not considered nor understood. For one thing, the long elk migrations would have been sorely disrupted. Fortunately, this proposed plan fell through.

Another wildlife conservation plan relayed to the *Wyoming Stockgrower and Farmer,* April 1907, by C.H. Stonebridge of the North Fork, described a plan William T. Hornaday and seven others, including Stonebridge and A.A. Anderson of New York, suggested to "Perpetuate the Bison." The plan would gather some of the remaining buffalo of the "Vanishing Herd," and establish a game preserve on the Pryor Mountains for them. Annual dues were $5 for members and $1 for associates.

By October, 1908, the *Wyoming Stockgrower and Farmer* noted Hornaday's "American Bison Society" had secured funding and land for a refuge near Moiese in northwestern Montana.

Besides hunters other notables visited the North Fork. The first political visitor on the North Fork was the governor of Wyoming. "Governor Hoyt visited Yellowstone National Park on horseback in the summer of 1891. His party of 16 men included an army escort of seven men . . .They entered the Park by way of Togwotee Pass and left by way of Jones' Pass and the North Fork of the Shoshone."[55]

In the fall of 1901 the Stock Growers Protective Association, headquarters at Marquette, Wyoming, "held a meeting to halt the invasion of sheep(men). It was determined to establish a dead line to halt the invasion of sheep at all costs." The sheepmen respected the deadline and no confrontations occurred. (There were problems elsewhere).

The Carey Act of August 1894 profoundly affected the destiny of the Marquette bottom land settlement and eventually severed the oneness of spirit of the North Fork and South Fork. The Act gave federal and state aid to irrigation projects. The Shoshone Dam was built between1905 and 1910 and the reservoir flooded out the settlers in the Marquette area. The Bureau of Reclamation provided a road through the canyon so that North Forkers now had a shorter route and did not need to share the road south of Cedar Mountain with the South Fork ranchers. The flooding of the valley drove out the little ranchers, but the Reclamation paid them for their property and improvements. The money provided them with a nest egg to start a business or buy other land.

The other event that profoundly opened up the North Fork was the building of the road to the East Gate of Yellowstone Park to connect with the Park's internal road system. This went forward from 1901 to 1903 and 1904, and when the Park allowed automobiles in 1915-1916 that further benefited Cody and the North Fork.

NOTES

1. Orrin H. Bonney and Lorraine Bonney, *Guide to the Wyoming Mountains and Wilderness Areas*, (Denver, Colorado: Sage Books 1960), p. 240.

2. Surveyor C. E. Hayden's map of Green's Big Creek Ditch, North Fork, 1904, courtesy of John Housel, Attorney-at-law, Cody Wyoming.

3. Bonney, and Bonney, ibid p.240.

4. Bonney, and Bonney, ibid p. 245.

5. *Wyoming Wildlife*, May 1995.

6. Mary Shawver, *Sincerely Mary S.*, (Casper, Wyoming,Prairie Publishing Company, no date), p. 73.

7. *Wyoming Wildlife*, June 1992, p. 2.

8. *Wyoming Wildlife*, May 1995.

9. Colonel WIlliam D. Pickett, *Memories of a Bear Hunter, Hunting at High Altitudes,* George Bird Grinnel, editor. (New York: Harper and Brothers, Publishers, 1913) 163.

10. *Cody Enterprise*, June 19, 1991.

11. Arther H. Harris, *The Mummy Cave Project in Northwestern Wyoming,* by Harold McCracken et al. Published (Cody, Wyoming: Buffalo Bill Historical Center, 1978) p. 146.

12. John Willard, *Adventure Trails in Montana,* "Medicine Tree", John Willard Publisher, Billings, Mt. 1964, pp. 93-94

13. David Dominick. "The Sheepeaters", *Annals of Wyoming* Volume 36, October, 1964.

14. J. Cecil Alter, *Jim Bridger*, (Norman, Oklahoma: University of Oklahoma Press, 1962) p. 77. Alter based his research on Charles G. Coutant's *History of Wyoming.*

15. Aubrey L. Haines, *The Bannock Indian Trail,* (Yellowstone Library and Museum Association: 1964) p. 7.

16. National Park Service, *Exploring the American West, 1803-1879* (Washington, D.C.,U.S. Department of Interior, 1982) p. 51.

17. Stanley Vestal, *Joe Meek*, (Lincoln: University of Nebraska Press, 1952) p. 69. All researchers depend on Mrs. Frances Fuller Victor's *The River of the West* (1870) in which she interviews Joe Meek. Unfortunately, he does not go into detail about the arduous trip. Another brief reference is from The Ashley-Smith Explorations 1822-1829, by H.C. Dale. Harrison Clifford Dale, *The Ashley-Smith Explorations 1822-1829 and the Discovery of a Central Route to the Pacific* (Glendale: Arther H. Clark, 1941) p. 293. H.E. Tobie, "The stink ing River led them to the Bighorn, where to their great joy, the trappers found Milton Sublette." H.E. Tobie, *The Life and Times of Joesph L. Meek,* (Portland,Oregon: O.E. Binford and Mort for the Oregon Historical Society, 1949) p.16.

18. Charles W. Cook, David E. Folsom, and William Peterson, edited by Aubrey L. Haines, *The Valley of the Upper Yellowstone,* (Norman: University of Oklahoma Press, 1965) xxiii.

19. Osborne Russell, *Journal of a Trapper,* edited by Aubrey L. Haines, (Lincoln: University of Nebraska Press), 1955 reprint 1965) p. 26.

20. Osborne Russell, pp. 66-67.

21. Aubrey Haines, *The Yellowstone Story, Vol.1*, (Yellowstone Library and Museum Association with Colorado Associated University Press, 1977)p. 249.

22. Albert E. Straub, Jr. *The Oldest National Forest*, Hayden Scrapbooks, p. 75-76, Park County Archives, Cody Wyoming.

23. Captain William A. Jones, *Report Upon the Reconnaissance of Northwestern Wyoming,* (Washington: Government Printing Office, 1875) p. 296. At the time of the trip Jones was a Lieutenant, by the time the report was printed he had been commissioned a Captain.

24. Jones, p. 267.

25. Jones, p. 1.

26. Jones, pp. 18-19.

27. E.S. Topping, *Chronicles of the Yellowstone* (St. Paul Pioneer Press: 1883) p. .96

28. Topping, pp. 97-98.

29. Topping, pp. 98-99.

30. Jones, p. 151.

31. Jones, p. 44.

32. Ester Johansson Murray, *"Original Survey of the Montana-Wyoming Boundary 1879-1880,"* unpublished manuscript.

33. Luther S. Kelly, *"Yellowstone Kelly", The Memoirs of Luther S. Kelly,* edited by M. M. Quaife, (New Haven: Yale University Press, 1926) p. 213.

34. Kelly, p. 218.

35. Kelly, p. 218.

36. Kelly, p. 219.

37. William A. Baillie-Grohman, *Camps in the Rockies*, (New York Charles Scribners Son's, 1882) p. 196.

38. Richard A. Barlett, *Great Surveys of the American West,* (University of Oklahoma Press, Norman, 1962) p. 36.

39. Colonel William D. Pickett "Memories of a Bear Hunter", *Hunting at High Altitudes,* Boone and Crocket Club, 1913, George Bird Grinnel, editor.

40. Pickett, p. 157.

41. Pickett, p. 161.

42. Pickett, p. 167.

43. *First Government Survey Map of Township 52, North Range 103,* July 2 1883.

44. Robert L. Porter, Henry Gannett, William P. Jones, *The West from the Census of 1880,* (Chicago: Rand McNalley and Co., 1882).

45. Helen Cody Wetmore, *The Last of the Great Scouts*, (Lincoln: University of Nebraska Press 1899- Bison Book reprint) pp. 235-237.

46. Wetmore, 235 "It is the Ijio (heaven) of the red man." The Eithity Tugala," Indian word for the Big Horn Basin. It is not clear which tribe, possibly the *Arapaho.*

47. General Philip H. Sheridan, *Report of an Exploration of Parts of Wyoming, Idaho, and Montana in August and September, 1882*, p. 17 and 18.

48. William T. Hornaday, *"Diversions in Picturesque Game-Lands, Golden Days in the Shoshone Mountains,"* Scribners Magazine, Vol. XLIV No. 5, November 1908, p. 576.

49. Hornaday, p. 577.

50. *Cody Enterprise*, March 22, 1989.

51. Hornaday, p. 579.

52. Martha Marston's "Memoirs" Park County Archives.

53. William T. Hornaday, *Hornadays American Natural History*, (New York: Charles Scribner's Son's, 1904) pp. 107-108.

54. Hornaday, *Diversions,* p. 259.

55. T.A. Larson, *History of Wyoming,* (Lincoln: University of Nebraska Press, 1965), p. 131.

TRIBUTARIES OF THE NORTH FORK OF THE SHOSHONE RIVER

How the Creeks and Streams were Named

Starting at the Buffalo Bill Reservoir each stream will be identified on both north and south sides of the North Fork, crossing back and forth, moving westward up-stream. The main tributaries will be identified and it will be explained how or for whom they were named, except in obvious cases such as a "Lake Creek," or an "Icy Creek." In other sections an in-depth study is made of the earliest settlers on each creek, and of lodges and summer homes on the streams within the Forest Reserve. In December, 1829, men of the Rocky Mountain Fur Company, the Sublette-Smith group, came out of what is now Yellowstone Park and traveled to the Big Horn Basin via the North Fork of the Stinking Water. Although this is the first recorded trip no recorded place names remain.

However, Lieutenant Jones (he was made Captain right after the trip) on his 1873 United States Expedition named several prominent mountains and rock formations, some were later renamed, apparently no streams were named.

There are few Native American names on the North Fork. Wapiti is a Shawnee word for American Elk, meaning "white rump." Pahaska is a Lakota-Sioux word for "long hair," the Indian name given to William F. Cody, "Buffalo Bill." Absaroka is the Crow word for "bird with long beak." Shoshone river was first called the Stinking Water which was a translation of the Crow word, mich ka ap pa. The Shoshone word was Pa sama ri. Shoshone translates "abundance of grass" or "lodge grass people."

The first government survey map of the area was in 1882, and shows Rattlesnake Creek and Trout Creek which were already named. On the 1893 government survey map most major streams were named. M. O. Newton and William T. Borron, temporary rangers, c. 1900, named streams that had not been named. Some names appearing on early maps have been changed, and if named after early settlers, will be covered in the section on Early Settler

From north: *Rattlesnake Creek*, first stream west of Rattlesnake Mountain, named from prevalence of snake. Tributaries are: *Iron Creek*, named for its mineral content. *Canyon Creek*, there is a steep trail up Canyon Creek over the mountain to Cody.
Logan Creek, named after George Logan.

Trout Creek, named for the excellent trout fishing. Was named by 1882. Tributaries are: *Big Creek; Sheephead; Fly; Robbers Roost*, old horse thieves cabin there, later used by Martinss for cow camp cabin. *Agee*; named for Fred B. Agee, Deputy Supervisor of Forest Reserve, "a most efficient Clerk, very rapid and did not object to working long hours." *Singing Brook* and *Laughing Water*, probably named by Bill Borron, he had a poetic nature. *Stockade*, possibly old Sheepeater Indian stockade. *Burnt Timber*; *Gunnysack; Weber* - after John P. Weber who worked at sawmill on Rattlesnake Mountain; *Murray creek*, after Jack and Smith Murray who bought Trout Creek ranch from Wesley Bloom.

From south: *Post Creek,* there must have been a post there.

Breteche Creek, always pronounced "Brittisher" Creek. Named after Count Paul Breteche of the French Colony east of Rattlesnake Mountain. He ran cattle and horses on the North Fork in the 1880s. He had the Crown brand, not to be confused with the Crown brand of Fred Morris of later date.

Slack Creek, named after George Slack who homesteaded there in 1896, father of Frank Slack.

From north:*Dry Pat Kelly "Creek"*, occasional spring runoff and storm drainage. Johansson Homestead on far upper end.

Jim Creek, first named Robie Creek on 1882 U. S. Survey map and 1901 Rand McNally map. By 1915 it was called Jim Creek, possibly after Jim McLaughlin, according to Martha Marston's memoirs. According to what Ned Frost recalled, it was named after Jim Baker. Baker and William Whitworth camped on the river in the 1850's.

Dunn Creek, another mainly dry wash. Possibly named after Methodist minister, Rev. Wallace B. Dunn who performed a 1910 wedding at Pat Kelly's. A recent folk tale gives it a name, a considerably less polite variation of "Dung" Creek.

From south:*Whit Creek*, named after William Whitworth who moved up there from his cabin near confluence of North and South Forks when settlers began moving into those bottomlands.

Rand Creek, named after early Marquette resident Dave Rand, probably planned to homestead.

From north:*Wall Creek*, after Chinese Wall, a volcanic dike formation that extends from South Fork across the North Fork valley and into Sunlight Basin.

From south:*Arnsberger Creek*, the spelling varies, but J. W. Arnsberger was clerk of school district No.23 in 1897, Marquette, Big Horn County. Rand and Arnsberger homesteaded in the area. This creek does not flow into the river.

Green Creek, after William Green, early settler. Before 1904 it was called Cabin Creek.

From north: *Big Creek*, called Crag Creek on the 1893 Survey and on geological survey maps for 1899 and 1904.

Spring Creek;*Half Mile Creek*, is a half a mile from the Forest Reserve boundary.

From south: *Canyon Creek*, early ranger station there washed out in 1923 giant cloudburst.

All of the following tributaries of the North Fork are within the Forest Reserve.

From south:*Lost Creek*, has no beginning or end.

Nameit Creek, when creeks were being named, a name couldn't be chosen. So it was written in pencil, "Nameit" and so it was called.

Clocktower Creek, named on 1893 map. Large rock formation resembles a clocktower, not seen from road.

From north: *Grizzly Creek*, good source of cedar posts.

From south: *Pagoda Creek*, for rock formations which resemble Chinese pagoda; named on 1893 map.

From north: *Horse Creek* horses pastured there.
Sweetwater Creek first named on 1893 mapn amed from mineral springs. Oil was found seeping out there in 1908. Tributaries: *Peanut; Turret; Wilson*, after prospector William Wilson, but could memorialize Ed "Kid" Wilson a later owner of Sweetwater Lodge.

From south: *Elk Fork*, for awhile it was called Wapiti River. First named Elk Horn by Col. William Pickett on October 29, 1880, because of many shed antlers. Tributaries: *Grace*, named for Grace McMullin Borron, early teacher at Marquette who married Bill. *Couger Creek*, five lions were caught on Elk Fork in 1921. *Frost Creek*, after early guide and outfitter. *Borron Creek*, formerly called Somber Creek,after William T."Bill" Borron.The large Borron glacier-at head of creek. Tributaries: *Elizabeth Creek*, after Elizabeth Hollister. *Cabin Creek*, a trapper's cabin there in early 1900's.
Blind Creek; Icy Creek; Swede Creek, Irma Flat Swedes hunted and camped up Elk Fork. *Burned Timber Creek*, and *Lake Creek*, *Rampart Creek*. The trail goes up over Rampart Pass and down Open Creek into the Thorofare. A main elk migration route.

From south: *June Creek*, some of the largest and oldest Rocky Mountain Juniper trees grow near the river here.

From north: *Clearwater Creek*, on 1893 map. Location of the Civilian Conservation Corp camp. Also Captain Jones camped there in 1873.

Aspen Creek, beautiful stand of aspen trees.

Moss Creek, Maude and Jessie Newton named it when the family was camped there in 1902. They played on its mossy banks.

From south:*Blackwater Creek*, on 1893 map. Worst tragedy on the North Fork was the Blackwater Fire in 1937.

From north: *Newton Creek*, named after M. O. Newton family who spent the summer of 1902 nearby.

From south: *Sheep Creek* Mountain sheep still lamb on the surrounding cliffs.
Mesa Creek, starts on side of Sheep Mesa.

From north: *Gunbarrel Creek*, on 1904 geological maps this was called Gothic Creek. The Earl Martins and Tracy Hill bought the lodge there from Earl Crouch. Earl Hayner was part owner one time. Earl Martin was called The Third Earl of Gunbarrel by Caroline Lockhart.

From south: *Fishhawk Creek*, as early as 1893 and1899 it was called Fishhawk. On a 1901 map it was called Cannon Creek. The trail goes up Fishhawk, over a pass and down Mountain Creek into Thorofare.
Fishhawk Glacier is not well known and is receding due to global warming. Tributaries: *Ruth Creek*. ?? *Norris Creek*,after Philatus W. Norris, Superintendent of Yellowstone Park 1877-1882. *Eyrie* and *Avalanche* testify to the steep terrain.

From north:*Chimney Creek*, named for Chimney Rock.

Goff Creek, after Johnny Goff who rode down from Yellowstone Park in June 1906 and set up a hunting camp there.

Libby Creek, after Arnold P. Libby, early Cody and Powell resident. Aron "Tex" Holm built Holm Lodge there, the second dude ranch in the Forest Reserve.

From south:*Kitty Creek*, named for Kitty Chatfield, wife of Frank Chatfield who mined on the far upper reaches of the North Fork in 1891. They were pioneers in 1885 in Sunlight Basin. Kitty was wounded in her arm from a shotgun blast and died in Cody 1909. She was sleeping in an upstairs room at the Cody Hotel when erratic gunshot from drunks in the bar below struck her.

From south:*Eagle Creek*, on a 1901 map was called Masons Creek. The trail goes up over Eagle Pass, down North Fork of Mountain Creek into Thorofare. Tributaries: *Cloudburst Creek*. *Neva Creek*, named for Neva Hill Crouch (Mrs. Earl). *Crouch Creek*, after Earl Crouch prospector, who started the lodge on Gunbarrel Creek. *Cabin Creek*, named for another trapper cabin.

From north: *Mormon Creek*, named after Mormon road builders and their families from Otto-Burlington area who camped there 1903.

From south:*Canfield Creek*, named for Sherman Canfield, foreman for logging crews and partner of Wallop-Moncrieffe logging/lumbering firm. Also for the father, George Canfield, secretary for Buffalo Bill.

From north: *Grinnell Creek*, named for Joe Grinnell, surveyor for mineral and mining outfits, mainly in upper Sunlight Basin.

From west: *Middle Fork of North Fork of Shoshone*, the route chosen for road between

Yellowstone Park and down North Fork to Cody. Here the main branch of the North Fork comes in from the north. Sam Berry and Walter Braten built first cabin and ran a road ranch. Berry poached game. Braten soon moved to Cody. In 1905 S. H. Berry advertised as "guide and scout".
From west: *Crow Creek*, for Crow Indians. The trail goes over into Yellowstone.

Jones Creek, after Lt. Jones of the U. S. Corps Engineers who led 1873 Expedition up North Fork into Park. The main Indian trail went up Jones Creek over Stinking Water Pass into Yellowstone. *Bear Creek,* still a favorite habitat of bears.

*Red Creek, f*avorite trapping area of 1920's. A trail goes over into Lamar Valley.

Torrent Creek, Camp Monaco was near mouth of Torrent Creek, famous 1913 hunting camp.

Hughes Creek, after "Dad" Hughes, early prospector who had a cabin in Silver Tip Basin between the North Fork and Sunlight.

ORIGIN AND DISTRIBUTION OF THE NORTH FORK OF SHOSHONE RIVER

The main source of water for the North Fork river is high mountain snow banks and springs, a lesser source from seasonal precipitation with immediate runoff. The North Fork and South Fork of the Shoshone river are the only contributors to the Buffalo Bill Reservoir. In 1990 the North Fork contributed 603,500 acre feet or 68%, and the South Fork 32% or 282,600 acre feet, to the reservoir. The South Fork also supplied 59,980 acre feet to the Cody Canal and 54,180 acre feet to the Lake View Irrigation Ditch. The total supplied to the reservoir that year was 886,100 acre feet. It is interesting to note on River Flow Table -l, the North Fork alone in 1925 supplied 889,069 acre feet to the reservoir. Smaller diversion ditches supply water to ranches up stream on both rivers. The North Fork with its 44 constant and/or intermittent tributaries drains about 750 square miles, mostly in the National Forest.

The headwaters of the North Fork are located in Silver Tip Basin on the northwest side of Sunlight Peak. Land Mountain on the north divides the drainage between the North Fork and Sunlight Creek which flows into the Clarks Fork of the Yellowstone River. To reach Pahaska the stream flows in a semi- circular pattern from west to south for thirteen miles. From Pahaska the river flows east for 35 miles to the Buffalo Bill Reservoir, thus the North Fork is fifty miles in length with a fall of 4,447 feet from the headwaters of Hughes Creek at 9,840 feet to the reservoir at 5,393 feet, or roughly from 10,000 feet to 5,000 feet.

Because of ever increasing and conflicting demands for water in the west, accuracy in measuring and distributing has developed into an exact science. It is the snow pack that holds the information for next summer's irrigation water. The science of measuring snow depth and determining its water content has evolved from manual on-site measurement to remote automatic telemeter (snotel) station. The earliest manual snow measurement station on the North Fork was in 1937, a quarter of a mile inside the East Entrance of Yellowstone Park. Records kept for 51 years showed an average of 45 inches maximum snow depth.

The immeasurable value of the North and South Fork water, besides supplying both river valleys, supplies water for 93,450 acres in the Garland, Frannie, Willwood and Heart Mountain divisions of the Shoshone Irrigation Project. The Buffalo Bill Reservoir can store over 650,000 acre feet of water since enlarged in 1992. This water flow supplies three hydro-electric power plants with a combined capacity of 26.5 megawatts and produces an average annual output of 90,400 megawatt hours.

The North Fork, of all the near-by area rivers draining into the Gulf of Mexico/Atlantic watershed, is most similar to the free flowing Clarks Fork to the north as to volume and seasonal fluctuation in cubic feet per second. The North Fork drains approximately 745 square miles, while the Clarks Fork drains a larger area of l,l54 sq. mi.

The North Fork is free flowing until the Buffalo Bill Dam, but not unutilized. The North Fork Valley Ditch diverts the most water into a ditch at the Forest Reserve boundary for irrigating 994.24 acres in the middle valley. Water is taken out of Trout Creek to irrigate 525.7 acres, from Rattlesnake Creek, 474.3 acres. Water from Canyon, Big, Green, and Jim Creek is taken out in amounts from 322 to 220 acres. The three smallest contributions from Rand, Arnsberger, and Logan Creeks varies from 46 acres to 3 acres. Total amount of water rights for 3,590.62 acres is allowed, but probably not much over 2500 acres is cultivated. Inside the Forest Reserve, a ditch takes water from Elk Fork in an amount to irrigate 10.5 acres of hay meadows near the Wapiti Ranger Station.

Complete statistical reports with accompanying graphs and tables compiled by John A. Yeates are available at the Park County Archives.

Upper Wapiti Valley

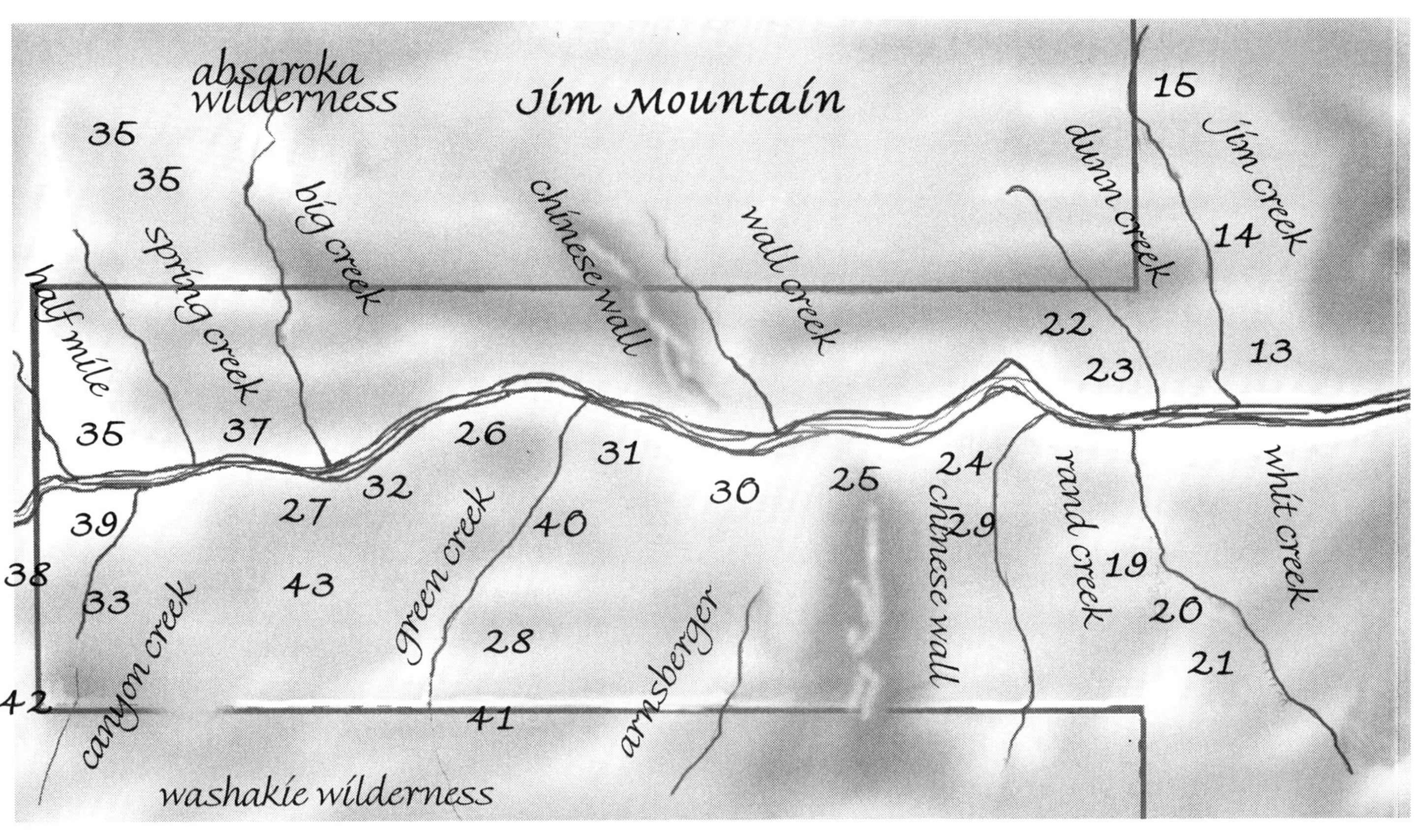

24.. Lee H. Borron
25.. W.H. Grinder
26. W.E.. Greem
27. Vinnie Grinder
28. Langtry
29. Elizabeth Hollister
30. Frost and Richard
31. J.F. Kelly
32. Elizabeth Hollister
33. James Osborne /- Jack Spicer / Lonnie Royal
34. L.C.Freeman
35. Dad Edwards -/- Hardy Shull
36. Phil Hardifer / Bud and Chella Hall
37. Claude Shull
38. Wiley Sherwin
39. Jenkins / Montgomery
40. Hal Everts / Montgemery
41.. Sullivans
42. Earl Martin
43. Jim Legg
44. Dwight Hollister

scale : approx. 1″/ 1 mile

Lower Wapiti Valley

numbered chronologically from earliest settlers

1. Chapman
2. Slack
3. Wesley Bloom
4. Smith & Jack Murray
5. R.G. Miller
6. N.P. deMauriac
7. Charles Thurmond
8. John Thurmond-Shanbacker
9. Mary & Fred Morris – W.B. Nuckols
10. Napoleon B. Nuckols – W.T. Borron – Henry Dahlem
11. C.E. Stonebridge – Jim Corder
12. Charles McClain

N.P. deMauriac

13. John Yeates
14. Oscar Montgomery
15. Lawrence & Pete Nordquist – Olive Fell
16. Pat Kelly
17. Carl Johansson
18. Ed Holmquist
19. Wm. Whitworth
20. Pat Kelly
21. Ben Simpers – F.O. Sanzanbacker
22. Brooks Borron – Henry Westerman
23. Geraldine Coy

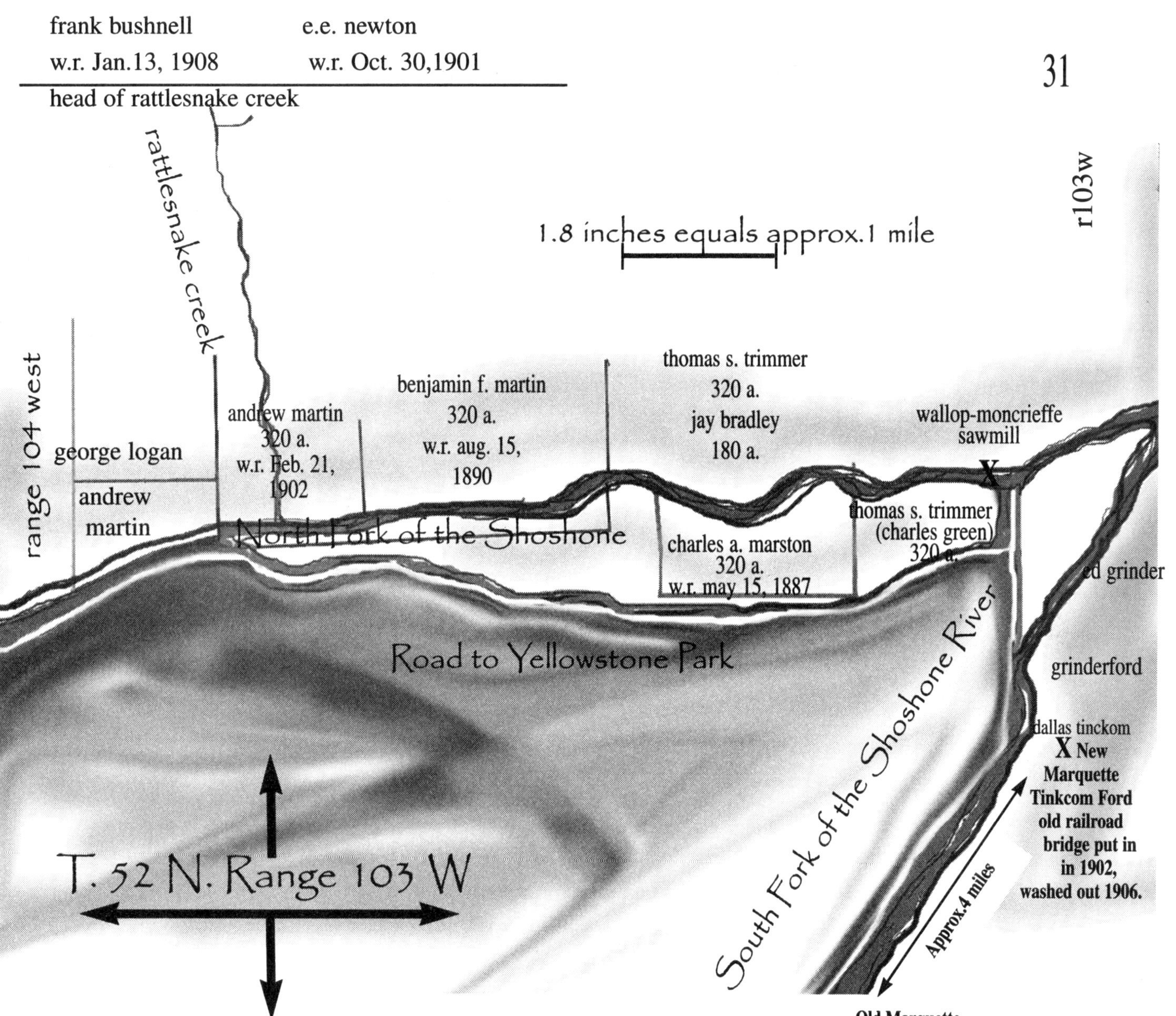

Earliest Homesteaders on the Lower North

George Marquette. Photo courtesy of Park County Archives.

Old Marquette

When this part of the country was still in Fremont County, George Marquette had homesteaded on the creek that came to bear his name, in the early 1880s. He later sold this property to A. C. Newton. From there he moved to the location about a quarter of a mile below present Cody canal headgate. Uncle George had been calling this area of the Big Horn Basin home for ten years before he established a post office at his home on April 8, 1891. He handled the post office until 1899, when Frank L. Houx became postmaster. Sarah Barbee was appointed in 1901, and held the job until old Marquette post office closed in April 1903.

Uncle George, best known for his fiddle playing, was in great demand in the late 1800s and early 1900's to play for dances. This strong, stocky, pioneer had a full head of hair, bushy beard and heavy moustache. He gained many friends from his affable, helpful nature. He was a good carpenter, which meant in those days he built log houses. It would be interesting to know how many of the first log homes in the 1880s to early 1900s George Marquette built . Like many of the old timers in his age group he had fought in the Civil War. He was a Notary Public and because of his age and wisdom gained the title "Judge", besides being affectionately known as "Uncle George".

George Marquette found work along the Greybull river and at the first settlements of Corbett and Arland. In 1880 or 1881 he built the first log home for Captain Belknap on Belknap Creek. In 1882 he built the big, log house for Richard Ashworth of the Z-T. He conducted the inquest on Philip Vetter's death in October 1892. A bear killed Vetter as he was getting water from the Greybull river near his cabin just below Otto Franc's Pitchfork Ranch.

George Marquette first homesteaded on Marquette Creek. He later moved over on the South Fork River, and built a long log building that served as a dance hall and he lived in one end of it. Here in a grove of cottonwood trees along the east side of the river were a cluster of

George Marquette and horse Pete. Photo courtesy of Park County Archives.

buildings. Besides the long dance hall were the barns and corrals, and the log building occupied by the Houx family. Frank L. Houx married Ida Mason Christy at Marquette on December 21, 1898, almost two years after the well publicized Jordan wedding. Ida's seven-year marriage to Walter DeGarino ended when DeGarino died, and she left Lynnville, Iowa, for Wyoming to marry Houx. Ida was 35 years old, five feet four inches tall with reddish-gold hair and blue eyes.[1] Frank Houx, Cody's first mayor and one time acting governor of the state, operated the dance hall. Perhaps the best documented dance and social event in the "Old" Marquette dance hall was the wedding of Mr. and Mrs. Hillis Jordan on January 22, 1897. A photograph taken at the wedding shows the forty friends and neighbors and everyone's name was recorded.

On the west side of the river was the Charles E. "Ed" Martin ranch, childhood home of Mary Martin Ebert, whose family bought land from Marquette in 1900 and George also helped them build their log house. In fact, they moved the log dance hall across the river and it became part of the Martin's home.

The "Old" Marquette Post Office ran from April 8, 1891, until March 31, 1903 with George Marquette the first postmaster. Then the post office was transferred to "New" Marquette four miles north, down the river. Here Edd C. Payne was first postmaster. This new post office absorbed the Irma Post Office that had been in existence from June 21, 1898, to April 7, 1903.

Another post office in the vicinity, a little to the north and east on Poverty Flat was the Tinkcom Post Office that operated only from July 16, 1898, until June 30, 1900.

Marquette's home came to be called Marquette Flat, and it was here the ditch camp for the workers building the canal for the Shoshone Land and Irrigation Company was located. Frank I. Rue ran a saloon and barbershop at old Marquette, "in the ditch camp days of rag houses," Rue later recalled.[2]

"Uncle" George Marquette moved several miles up the South Fork when he bought the John Thompson place. Mary Martin Ebert remembered when she was six years old Uncle George had promised to teach her the "two step". However he died before this could be accomplished. He loved to fish in the South Fork, but one time his favorite river went on the rampage in July of 1905, when a cloudburst coupled with high water, caused the river to overflow its banks and flooded through his place causing some damage.

Marquette's home on the South Fork later became known as the "Ed Carter" place.[3] The Ed Carter place is now numbered 1557 on the location markers along the road. From his last location Uncle George had a good view of Castle Rock, a local landmark.

George Marquette died on November 26, 1906, of "apoplexy". After a funeral service in the Cody Episcopal Church, his body was shipped to Arlington, Ohio, for burial.

By 1896, Buffalo Bill had fallen in love with the area along the South Fork of the Shoshone river. His interest lay in starting an irrigation project, taking water out of the South Fork and carrying it in a canal to irrigate the level plain he called Irma Flat, named after his youngest daughter. Buffalo Bill Cody organized the Shoshone Ditch Company to build the canal. Freighters brought supplies from Billings to the store at old Marquette, a large shipment of merchandise arrived in April of 1896. It took the freight outfit nine to twelve days to make the trip from and back to Billings.

With the ditch only partly completed Cody set about getting settlers for this project. Cody, a good promoter, had quite a number of European immigrants in Chicago signed up by March of 1896. These people came to start a colony, which could be designated as the "German Colony." At this time W. E. Hymer managed the Shoshone Land and Irrigation Company, but was replaced by George T. Beck the end of March. Colonel Cody assisted these settlers in every way. Horses were driven to Billings from the Black Hills, and Cody purchased twenty brand new Studebaker wagons and sets of harness from Yegen Brothers of Billings. Approximately seventy persons arrived by train from Chicago, comprising fifteen German families (probably German-Bavarians) accompanied by four parish priests from Chicago. The number of families vary, but some newspaper accounts speak of as many as fifty families, which is probably an overestimation.[4] On May 5, 1896 this cavalcade left for the proposed new settlement of "Irma," led by Buffalo Bill and Peter Yegen and guided by U.S. Marshall Frank Grouard. Grouard rode along as a special safeguard "against an Indian attack," as they crossed the Reservation. Yegen chose a route across the new toll bridge that Billings businessmen had built in 1895 at Blue Creek, then south over the Blue Creek Hills, through Pryor Gap, across the 40 mile desert to Corbett. Two days later, on May 7, the group arrived at "Irma."

The first plans called for eight log houses built in a group in a star-like pattern. Each family had eighty acres to farm. The parish priests returned to Chicago and in the grandiose plans of the times, hoped to bring 65 more families within three or four weeks. Unfortunately, this colonizing project failed and the colonists left in September.[5] Seventeen families left, the only substantial house built by the colonists was the log house that the J.D. Buchanan family later moved into. Buchanan was a relative of Jack and Smith Murray, also of Iowa.

J. D. Buchanan came out in 1897 to look over the prospects of moving out here, and Wesley Bloom guided him around. The first night Buchanan stayed at Old Marquette and the second night with Wesley Bloom on Trout Creek. Apparently Irma Flat looked the best, and he moved into the house vacated by one of the German colonists.

May Ballinger remember when the Nordquists came to Irma Flat they saw the shacks left by the earlier residents. She said her family pitched a tent inside one of the flimsy shacks to live in until their house was built.[6]

Joe Vogel was the only one of the colonists who stayed,but he did not remain on Irma Flat. Instead he moved to a place east of Cody.[7] Joe Vogel gained notoriety as one of the twelve jurors empaneled for the Spring Creek Raid trial in 1909 in Basin, when five cattlemen were tried for killing three sheepherders, burning their wagons and killing thousands of sheep near Ten Sleep. Big Horn County had not yet been divided, so they chose several jurors from this area.

The Irma Post Office was finally established by the second wave of settlers, on June 21, 1898, with the first postmaster, Ellen Buchanan, but was transferred to new Marquette April 7, 1903.

NOTES

1. Information on Ida Houx is by Shauna Barling Gibbs, *First Ladies of Wyoming,* 1869-1990, edited by Mabel Brown, (1990).

2. Rue moved over to Basin and became County Clerk of Big Horn County in 1906.

3. This Carter had no connection with William Alexander Carter of Fort Bridger, who sent Peter McCulloch into the area in 1878 with a herd of cattle, and after whom Carter Mountain is named.

4. *Billings Gazette*, May 5, 1896.

5. *Billings Gazette*, September 22, 1896.

6. Interview, May Nordquist Ballinger May 1993.

7. Gladys Andren has written up the account of the failed German colony in more detail on page 4 of *Life Among The Ladies Of The Lake,* telling about this interesting, but short-lived project that faded away with scarcely any record of its short existence.

Poverty Flat ...

New Marquette

Because of settlers moving into the lower river valleys they closed out the old Marquette Post Office and established the new Marquette Post Office four miles down river on April 8, 1903. Edd Payne served as postmaster at new Marquette until 1907, when C. Peter MacGlashan became postmaster. This post office absorbed the Irma Post Office. Felix Alston, a Texas cowboy came north in 1892 on a cattle drive. He established a road ranch, a stopping place for travelers, on the banks of the South Fork before he had the post office. "It was said the store consisted of a grocery department, dry goods, and irrigation department—the saloon". [1] At this spot it was possible to ford the river, except during high water, and they called it the Tinkcom Ford because the Dallas Tinkcoms lived just to the east. In 1902 the county obtained an old railroad bridge for a safer crossing but it washed out in the high water of 1906 and was never replaced. Edd Payne, a brother-in-law of Alston helped run the mercantile business because Alston served as deputy sheriff of Big Horn County in 1903. Later Alston was elected sheriff of Big Horn County in 1906, and ably conducted the investigation of the case of the cattlemen who killed three sheepherders in April of 1909 at the Spring Creek Raid near Ten Sleep. The jury found the cattlemen guilty.

In January 1902, the main building burned to the ground at an estimated loss of $5,800. It was insured for $4,100, and by the end of February the building had been rebuilt. Alston sold to C. Peter MacGlashan who advertised in the *Wyoming Stockgrower And Farmer* in 1906: "Will buy your butter, eggs, chickens, grain, hides, and pay the limit—Cash or Trade. We handle the finest groceries, flour, and feed, the Konantz and Clark Saddles and harness, Stetson hats, Mayer shoes, Gatzman Shoes and cowboy hats. Ferry's seeds. Don't be a clam—you try this store. If you don't like it quit..." In the 1990s, Mary Martin Ebert still remembered the store as "Alston and MacGlashan."[2]

MacGlashan came West from Georgia and had been trained as an auctioneer. Mac had a shock of brown hair and strong features, and gained a reputation as a personable and astute business man. After he left Marquette he continued to have many interests, and went into real estate in Powell and Cody, later becoming editor and manager of the *Park County Enterprise*. From there he became Deputy Secretary of State. He resigned to go into banking and owned the newspaper in Big Piney, Wyoming and served as the first mayor of Big Piney. In April 1910 he married Grace Hesser. He died in an automobile accident in September 1917, on the Lander-Big Piney road.

During 1907, MacGlashan apparently had a partner named Mc Keller, but when they dissolved partnership MacGlashan became sole owner. By January 1908, he accepted cash only, because time was running out—the reservoir would soon be filled. But there had been many profitable years when workers were building the Shoshone Dam and new road through the canyon. Marquette was closer to the workers on the west side of the canyon than Cody. Besides the farmers and ranchers on Poverty Flat, Marquette Flat, and Irma Flat, settlers were moving farther up each branch of the Shoshone river.

The filling of the reservoir flooded out the landowners but the United States Bureau of Reclamation compensated them for the loss of their land. According to Beryl Gail Churchill, the land owners were paid from $45 per acre for alfalfa fields to $3.50 per acre for rough grazing land with no water right.[3] An interesting expression arose after the residents moved and the reservoir was filled. For awhile it was called Shoshone Lake and descendants of those residents often said their parents/grandparents "used to live under the lake." Betty Bates Lufkin said her grandparents Stevens "lived under the lake." Clyde and Libbie Huffman moved away in the spring of 1910 because their place would soon be "under the lake." Gladys Fenex Andren remembered her schoolmate Marion Scholes telling her, that her grandparents, the Dallas Tinkcoms had "lived under the lake."

When plans for the Shoshone Dam got under-way they needed a large supply of lumber for scaffolds, forms for cement, various buildings, platforms, and many other uses. To meet this need, Oliver H. Wallop, Malcolm Moncrieffe, Sherman Canfield, all of Sheridan, and George T. Beck of Cody and formerly of Sheridan formed the Shoshone Lumber Company. [4]

They had a crew of men cutting timber on Grinnell Creek, east of Yellowstone Park, and they planned to float 1,000,000 board feet of logs down to Trimmer's Ford, located a few miles north of "New" Marquette, where a log boom was constructed to hold them. The company bought a steam sawmill from Hud Darrah in September 1905, and set it up near the Trimmer's Ford where the company had leased the necessary land. George T. Beck represented the company in Cody. To facilitate moving the lumber down to the dam they built a bridge. According to Maud Murray's memoirs, "a long, wooden, ramshackle bridge crossed the North Fork near the Tom Trimmer ranch." Beck sold to Wallop-Montcrieffe about 3,000,000 board feet between 1903 and 1906 at $5.06 per 1,000 board feet. In 1906 Wallop-Moncrieffe bought out Beck's Sawmill.

Floating logs down the North Fork from Grinnell Creek to the log boom at Trimmers, where they were held for the sawmill, was difficult and hazardous. John Rice drowned on the log drive in July 1905. In 1906 there were eleven men in a boat directing the log drive and at Devil's Elbow the boat capsized and five of the men drowned. Frances Shull Witzleban's father Hardy Shull came out to the area in the early 1900's. He cowboyed on the local ranches, was a good friend of George Marquette, and took a job working on the log drives. He developed rheumatism in his legs from the long hours working in the cold river water according to Frances.

The terrible accident of the 1906 season did not deter the Company from going ahead with the 1907 drive. A Cody newspaper reported in May 1907, "The Wallop-Moncrieffe company received two large boats they called pirogues and sent them up the river to be used with the log drive." The pirogues were hauled up the river by team and wagon. That same season, during high water, on July 4, 1907, record floodwaters hit the saw-boom, flooded it and the logs escaped.

Years later, in August of 1927, Oliver Wallop, the Earl of Portsmouth, visited in Cody and reminisced, "My logging operations in Cody, which I carried on in quite an extensive way, were doomed to failure however, the Shoshone river went too fast and most of my logs went on down the river and were put to good use by settlers down in the Lovell section."[5]

Enough logs were cut and sent down river each year to supply the needs of building the dam and to supply the Wallop-Moncrieffe lumber yard in Cody. To facilitate moving great quantities of lumber more efficiently than by horse drawn lumber wagons, the Wallop-Moncrieffe Company ordered and had shipped to Cody a large traction steam engine to pull loads of green lumber to their lumber yard in Cody.

In February 1907, the Wallop-Moncrieffe traction engine made its first trip from the sawmill at the Trimmer place to Cody bringing 20,000 feet of green lumber. They traveled the old route south around Cedar Mountain. *The Wyoming Stockgrower and Farmer* February 28, 1907, stated "it handled the job easily without bringing into action the 30 horsepower auxiliary engine under the lead truck." Racks to hold the logs were built at the F. C. Scholes blacksmith shop in Cody. Mr. Moncrieffe came to Cody to see how the machine operated and was pleased with its performance.

When the dam was completed they dismantled the sawmill and stored the steam engine in the Wallop-Moncrieffe lumber yard, where the present Elks Club in Cody is located. One time they activated the traction engine and drove it to the city waterworks pump house on the river, just above the early bridge to the depot. Here it furnished power for pumping water for the city waterworks while the electric plant was out of commission. From then on until 1925, the great machine sat idle under a protective roof in the W-M lumber yard. J. H. Vogel and Henry Dahlem assembled a sawmill on Grinnell Creek and purchased the traction engine and took it up the river. It was so heavy it broke several wooden bridges on the trip. The historic engine should have been preserved, but the Forest Service had a policy to tidy up the forest and considered these old artifacts unsightly

Wheels from Wallop-Montcrieffe steam tractor used to shore up bridge to ski run near Grinnell Creek.

New piroque for Wallop-Moncrieffe timber in front of Irma porch on 12th street, loaded on wagon for trip up to Grinnell Creek, May 1907. Photo courtesy John Yeates.

and they ordered it removed.[6] During World War II, Lee Woodruff dismantled it and hauled it to Powell, where it was cut up for scrap. However, some of its massive iron wheels stayed at Shoshone Lodge, where they were used to shore up the supports under the river bridge from the lodge to the ski area. Later, floodwaters washed the wheels on the north side away, but, as of May 1993, the huge wheels under the south end of the bridge were still in place, the only remnants of the Wallop-Moncrieffe tractor engine.

NOTES

1. According to Hauns Schnackenberg, Cody student who wrote about Marquette and won the 1994 State Young Historian Award.

2. Interview with Mary Ebert, May 1995.

3. Beryl Gail Churchill, *Dams, Ditches and Water*, Rustler Printing, 1979, p. 18.

4. Michael A. Amundson, "The Rise and Fall of Big Horn City", *Annals of Wyoming* summer 1994, p. 25, states "...Big Horn and Little Goose Creek Valley were forever altered by the arrival of three remittance men: the Englishman Oliver H. Wallop; and the Scots, Malcom Moncrieffe and his brother William Moncrieffe." In the 1905 era "remittance men" were as the dictionary states, "men paid to remain abroad" so as not to embarrass or annoy their family. The money usually was remitted to a caretaker, bank, dude ranch, or whoever. Apparently in the 1990's the word has taken a benign meaning.

5. *Park County Enterprise*, August,1927

6. Interview with Betty Dahlem.

William T.Borron "Bill" in hat and his father John Arthur Borron in cap. Robert Holbrook Borron "Brooks" between them. Bill has his arms around Glen and Theodore. The grandfather was visiting from Missouri. Photo courtesy of Borron family.

Earliest Settlers

The earliest settlers on the North Fork of the Stinking Water river chose the fertile bottom land west of the canyon which was easily accessible to the Big Horn Basin by skirting the south side of Cedar Mountain. These pioneers arrived on the heels of Peter McCulloch who brought the first herd of cattle into the Big Horn Basin for William Alexander Carter of Fort Bridger in 1879. McCulloch started the Carter ranch on Carter Creek. That same year Captain Henry Belknap claimed a location on a tributary farther up the South Fork. The first government survey map shows that in 1880, Andy Chapman, Jay Bradley, and William Whitworth had cabins on the lower North Fork. Chapman built on Trout Creek, Bradley and Whitworth closer to where the North and South Forks joined.

Charles Marston knew John Chapman in Eastern Oregon, John settled on Pat O'Hara Creek. John claimed no relationship to the brothers Hank and Andy Chapman who also moved to Wyoming from Oregon. According to folk tales, Hank Chapman was the first white man to travel through the Shoshone Canyon. Marston moved from Maine to the far West around 1875, first to California where he learned horsemanship and riding skills the Spanish way, then on to eastern Oregon where he worked for John Chapman. He raised hay on Slough Creek in Yellowstone Park and that spot is still known as Marston Meadows. The hay was sold to the soldiers at Fort Yellowstone (Mammoth). There is also a Marston Fork up the South Fork of the Shoshone River honoring Charles Marston.

In 1880 Marston guided the surveyors for the first land survey above the Canyon. His water right on the North Fork dates from May 15, 1887, and his land patents are July 1, 1893, and February 3, 1898.

Among other early pioneers were George Marquette and William T. Borron, both here by 1881, the same year as the first roundup organized by the Board of Live Stock Commissioners of Wyoming to supervise cattle grazing on the open range on the Stinking Water. The last cattle roundup for this particular area came twenty two years later in 1903.

Other early inhabitants were the Grinders, Ed, Bill, Frank, and one sister, Vina, called "Vinnie." The Grinders were Pennsylvania Dutch. Ed and Rice Hutsonpillar and their widowed sister, Anna Hutsonpillar Holman came to Marquette from east of the Big Horns. Anna brought her three sons, Art, Blen, and Evan, and her daughter May. All of the boys grew up to be bronc -busters. Anna Holman married Ed Grinder. Later another relative, Olive Watt, whose mother was Alice Hutsonpillar Watt, came from the Buffalo area and worked for Hollisters and married Lawrence Nordquist.

Bill and Frank Grinder were bachelors, but Vina married Walter Stephanson. Her second husband was named Charron. Frank and Bill and Vina moved up the North Fork and took up land in the middle valley by 1905. Vinnie was a full bodied woman who liked her booze and was a bit of a kleptomaniac. She died in March of 1910.

The southeast area of this new river bottom farmland came to be called Poverty Flat. The Thompson family lived on the South Fork side, they had two boys John and Gus, and five girls, one of whom married Wesley Bloom and drowned in crossing the North Fork river.

H.K. and Sallie Barbee came in the 1890s. Their children were Ella Barbee Thompson, Myrtle Barbee Wilson, and James Barbee who died in Denver, April 3, 1919 of influenza.

The Nuckols brothers were Mel, Napoleon Bonaparte, "Pol", and N.B."Ben", who was one of the many victims of typhoid in 1905. None of the Nuckols stayed around, either selling or moving away. N.B. Nuckols moved to Mountain Grove, Missouri.

The Eugene Wilder family lived on Poverty Flat, the children were Alice, Lillian, Winifred and one son. The family came west from New England and brought with them a little money and "aristocratic habits." They had hired help to do the ranch work and a cook, but their hospitality and friendliness assured them community acceptance. Mary Ebert remembered Eugene Wilder was sort of "laid back" and relaxed by smoking a pipe.

John Ruff, a Texas cowboy, won the hand of their daughter Alice. Later, the Ruffs had a son and the Cody paper couldn't resist the news item noting "Mr. and Mrs. John Ruff and the little ruffian made a visit to Cody."

Charles L. Green had patents to land closest to the canyon dating from April 25,1894 and May 20, 1897. He sold land on the North Fork to Thomas S. Trimmer. Trimmer had the 360 acres of Green's land on the south side of the river, plus 320 acres of land on the north side just across the river from Charles Marston's 320 acres.

When the Benjamin Franklin Martin family moved to Marquette from east of the Big Horns, it increased the population. Benjamin Franklin was a distant cousin of Christopher "Kit" Carson. Martin's family included Andrew, Mary Martin (Glasgow), Dorothy "Dolly" Martin (Timmer), Edith Martin Brundage, and Christopher Elias, all coming in 1890. Elias never married. He was affectionately called "Old Elias" although he was only forty-six years old when he died. His obituary noted he had a keen sense of humor and a ringing laugh, besides being a crack shot and an expert roper.

The Brundage family came also in 1890 with son Ben, born in Big Horn Wyoming. Seven more children were born while the family lived near Marquette on the South Fork side.

In May of 1903, Elias Martin met his aunt Maud (Benjamin Franklin, "Frank" Martin's sister) her husband Ben Brown and daughter Amelia in Toluca, Montana. The B.F. Martins were from Bedford, Iowa, and the Browns also came out from Iowa. They traveled by train whereas the Martins had made the trip from Iowa to Big Horn, Wyoming, by wagons. The Browns lived with the Martins for awhile. Maud and Amelia cooked for the engineers and foremen during the construction of the Dam.

Just north of the Marquette post office in 1902. William F. Cody had 160 acres of "poor crop land" near the cottonwood flats. There were other settlers, the Dallas Tinkcoms, and Stilley Riddles, the latter came from southern Oregon and were related to the Frank Riddles. Frank a miner, had married a Modoc Indian named Wi-ne-ma, but called Tobey Riddle. (She had earned a $25 a month pension from the United States for courageous negotiation in the Modoc conflict of 1873.) No doubt other settlers who had lived "under the lake" have been inadvertently left out. All these settlers had to sell their land to the government because soon the reservoir would fill and flood their property after the Dam was completed in 1910.

RATTLESNAKE CREEK

A.C. Newton came to Cody and bought a ranch on Trail Creek from Baron Paul Breteche, who had bought out the French Syndicate. Soon his brothers, M.O., L.L., E.E., and sister S.D.(Darlene) Newton Ingraham came West. Earle Newton and F.A. Ingraham bought property in 1901 at the head of Rattlesnake Creek. The Ingrahams called their place the Springdale Ranch.

Earle Newton married Eliza Bushnell, April 23, 1902. She was a mail order bride, an adventurous young lady from Cherokee, Iowa. Their happy marriage ended with her death in 1945. Earle married Martha Marston whose first two husbands had died.

Esther Newton was born on the Springdale ranch February 11,1903, and Dan Ingraham, April 12,1903. Earle's water right dated from October 30,1901. Earle's brother-in-law, Frank Bushnell, took up a homestead nearby and his water right dated January 13, 1908. Earle Newton and Frank Bushnell each filed on additional homesteads in the vicinity in 1917. The Newtons and Ingrahams moved to Cody in the early 1900s. According to Court House records, Frank Bushnell sold to David Dickie who sold to Mae Price and then the property went back to David Dickie.

Lloyd and George Coleman bought the Newton ranch and with Jim Winsor started to build up a dude ranch. They built five cabins, had a polo field, and drove a team of white mules. By 1923, David Dickie, rancher from over on Gooseberry Creek, foreclosed the mortgage he held on the Coleman's Flying W Ranch. Anna Lucylle Moon acquired the ranch after the foreclosure and came to settle there in 1926. She changed the name to Mooncrest ranch with a brand of a crescent moon. Originally she planned to continue operating a dude ranch but changed to a cattle operation. She soon met Elmon T. Hall at a dance at Mountain View lodge and they were married on horseback in a meadow at Mooncrest by Reverend Arthur Beaty. Lucylle held a bouquet of Indian Paintbrush tied with a leather thong.

Elmon "El" was a carpenter and built a cabin or two. There was a gypson outcrop on the lower part of their property, so they burned the gypson to make a cement-like caulking to use between the logs of the cabins.

One of the adventures Anna Lucylle Moon Hall had while living on the ranch involved hunting cattle that had wandered afar in a blizzard. Lucylle went looking for them, heading up over the mountain towards Trail Creek. She had to climb the precipitous "Steep Trail", so the custom was to tie the horse's reins to the saddle horn, hang on to the horse's tail and ascend the trail. Her horse spooked and got away from her and left her afoot with only her dog. On top of the mountain she was led astray by following some vague snow-covered tracks that turned out to be elk tracks. A mountain lion kept her company for awhile, this made her abandon the hunt and hurry home. Going back down the "Steep Trail", she sat down, dug her heels in the snow-packed trail and tobogganed off the mountain. At the bottom of the trail she had another mile to slog through the snow. When she got to the ranch her runaway horse stood at the corral but he had become entangled with a six foot evergreen branch—snagged on the saddle horn, and brought that home with him.

All was not married bliss at the Mooncrest ranch. Elmon, an alcoholic, often went on drinking binges. When drunk he became a wife-abuser. One time he attacked Lucylle, knocking her down and striking her repeatedly while cussing out her "damn Scotch relatives". She managed to get to her feet and ran to one of the cabins where she found a fireplace poker. When the enraged man came after her she recalled, "I laid two poker blows to the side of his head, I gave him everything I had." She later realized these could have been death blows, but he finally came to and crawled into bed in his cabin. After he slept off his drunk and got up he seemed to have forgotten the gory details of the near-death altercation.

Lucylle and El had one daughter, Chaska. Sometimes Lucylle rented a log cabin at Montgomerys on Green Creek so Chaska could attend Wapiti School. When Chaska was in fifth grade Lucylle moved to town, she spent close to twenty three years as owner of Mooncrest before selling. Lucylle and Elmon were divorced and Elmon told some friends he received alimony in the settlement.

JOHN HENRY MARTIN DRAW

At the time the Shoshone Dam was being built the long draw on the southwest side of Rattlesnake Mountain was called the John Henry Martin Draw, after the man who was for a time manager for Buffalo Bill's business interests in Cody. He was no relation to the Benjamin Franklin Martin family. John Henry Martin died in 1910. This draw later carried the name of Neland, sometimes called Porcupine Pete Neeland, who had a still and whiskey-making operation there. Bartel G. Neeland was born in Norway and was listed as age 53 in the 1920 census. He had several run-ins with the law.

Peg Garlow, Fred Garlow, Elaine Rhoads, Cack McClellan. Photo courtesy of Park County Archives.

RHOADS RANCH

Dr. C. J. Rhoads, father of Willard, grubstaked Art Reese who homesteaded the land just north of the Andrew Martin place at the mouth of Rattlesnake creek.

Rhoad's water rights date from October 28, 1903, 1908, 1916, (2), and the last February 16, 1921. The 1908 water right was a permit for the "Reese Ditch."

One anecdote Willard recalled told how Arthur Reese got the ditch dug. He hired some of the foreigners who had been imported to work on the dam construction to help him build the ditch. While digging the ditch Reese told them about the wild Indians living back in the hills and added colorful stories of scalpings and raids. When the workers were finishing the job they were terrified to see a horseman galloping his pony over a nearby hill. The rider brandished a spear and gave blood-curdling warhoops. The men dropped their shovels and took off for the safety of the barracks at the canyon, never even waiting to get their pay—which was the whole point of Art Reese's masquerade.

Willard said, "The old road used to go between our cabin and Old Elias Martin's cabin. Elias was a ''loose rope artist,' a kind of Robin Hood type, he would take from one person and give to another and he couldn't stand to see an unbranded calf. My mother was a real good friend of Dolly Martin Trimmer (Mrs. Thomas), she had been invited down to Dolly's and was served turkey. Mother asked Dolly, 'Where did you get the turkey?' and she answered, 'Elias gave it to me.' Elias didn't have any turkeys, but the Rhoads had turkeys. That sort of thing is hard on neighborly relationships. Elias was a fine old gentleman, he just loved kids. My sister Helen and I used to go down there and we loved to eat his sweet biscuits. He put a lot of sugar in his biscuits. Old Elias used to put on all the clothes he had to ride a bucking horse, so if he fell off it wouldn't hurt him. He had epileptic seizures too, and he had an old horse named Ted trained so that if he fell off, his horse would wait for him. You have to understand we settled right in the spring range of the Martins and Trimmers and there was quite a bit of conflict and we kids were part of that conflict. My Dad was a dentist and he was building up this ranch and I was his cowboy for the operation, I was responsible for those cows, I was his eyes and ears. By watching Old Elias Martin in the early days and Jimmy Tuff in the later days I got suspicious of everybody."

In all fairness, a member of the Andy Martin family said the Rhoads didn't pass up a chance to put the DND brand on any handy unbranded calf they encountered.

Elaine NeVille and Willard Rhoads were married June 26, 1935, and spent 38 years ranching on Rattlesnake Creek. Before her marriage, in 1925, Elaine was one of the first to wear the crown of "Miss Wyoming". After her marriage she devoted herself to the ranch work, at one time raising 150 bum lambs. During World War II, ranch help was hard to get, so Willard handled the irrigating and haying and Elaine took care of the cattle. When their son Howard attended Northwest Community College, Elaine ran his trapline. The Rhoads ran straightbred Herefords and were among the first to use artificial insemination to upgrade their herd.

When Willard was interviewed in the summer of 1983, he recalled his life on Rattlesnake Creek. "It took my father his whole lifetime and Elaine and me our whole lifetime to put together all our holdings in one working unit, and when we got too old to ride the windy ridges we had to sell. The first thing the buyer did was to subdivide. It just makes you sick. You spend two lifetimes to put a place together and then they subdivide just to make a dollar. It is a sad story."

CLEAS PLACE

Virginia St. Denis came from Iron Mountain Michigan in August 1912, to spend a vacation with the Art Reeces. Later she came out to Rattlesnake Creek to teach an early school there. She found a piece of land up the creek and homesteaded it. She went down to Powell and married George Cleas, according to Willard Rhoads, "A kind of overall farmer, but she made quite a place up there. She was a plague in my side and really taught me water laws. She had a junior water right and I had a senior water right. We fought over these water rights for years and years." George Cleas was listed in the 1920 census as age 30, and born in Iowa.

Perhaps in no other North Fork area were there so many years of conflict over water rights and range-land grazing rights. One time Anna Moon Hall said, "The Rattlesnake valley was a paradise until Jimmy Tuff moved in. He was like Satan entering paradise." Willard Rhoads probably felt that way about Jimmy Tuff and the Cleas. According to Willard, "In the beginning all of Trout Creek Basin was shared rangeland by Andy Martin, Rhoads, and Cleas. Newtons ran sheep in one part of the range and there were posts with old signs marking the boundaries saying, 'No sheep beyond this point.' Anna Moon's range was separate. Her stock didn't mix with the rest of ours."

JIMMY TUFF

In the early 1900's a wiry little bronc buster rode into the North Fork from Canada about "three jumps ahead of the Mounties." His real name was Norman Price, but he went by the name of Jimmy Tuff, and looked every bit the bowlegged cowboy with big Stetson, high heeled boots and friendly smile. He liked to ride a "pacer" with its smooth, weaving gait. He ran horses and had a little permit on the side of Rattlesnake mountain which was always called the Jimmy Tuff pasture. He ran a fence on two sides and there was a steep trail over the mountain called the "Jimmy Tuff Trail" according to Willard Rhoads. Jimmy never worried too much about the legality of what he did and ran his horses on Ed Heald's sheep range. When Clifford Spencer was the ranger he finally took him to court and got this trespassing stopped. According to Willard, Jimmy Tuff got Ed Hayes to take up some land for him. "This is a very deep and long intrigue and cannot be covered quickly."

During World War I, Jimmy went back to Canada and enlisted in their army, and it wasn't until after 1926 he became a United States citizen. All through the 1920's the officers carefully watched him. In 1923 he changed the W. R. Coe brand of 7J into a 3 reverse B, which was the Tuff brand. The Coe outfit continually had horses stolen and from time to time horses on the North Fork, and other near-by areas, came up missing.

According to the *Northern Wyoming Herald* for July 9, 1919, Jimmy married Mrs. Esther Giffen of Big Timber, Montana. He later had a wife known as "May", also a bronc rider.

In February of 1923 Jimmy broke his arm and set it himself. He was one tough hombre. In October of 1923 Jimmy divorced May. He married Elsie Strause in Idaho Falls, October 2l, 1939, joined the First Baptist Church, and the couple had seven children. Ironically, after surviving innumerable horse-related accidents he was killed in a tractor accident on October 23, 1963, at the age of 72.

LOGAN CREEK

The next source of creek water west of Rattlesnake Creek is Logan Creek, a small, short stream named for Uncle George Logan who got his water right on it on August 15, 1890.

Logan was born in Pittoe, Nova Scotia, around 1830, travelled west to Kansas in 1852. There in 1865 he married, but sadly, his wife and child died in 1867. Logan had been badly crippled in a Kansas cyclone. He came West in the 1880s, built a log house on Logan Creek, and piped spring water into his house. His gentle horse had been trained so Logan could open and close gates without dismounting. Uncle George Logan ran cattle and had registered three different brands.

In 1908, Logan sold his farm land that would be flooded by the filling of the reservoir, to the United States Bureau of Reclamation, for which he received $35 an acre. He moved to Thermopolis, where he died February 14, 1911. His obituary stated he was known as a man of "beautiful character and many splendid traits."

A pensioned Civil War veteran named Billy Boyer lived with Logan and helped him with the work.[1]

Harry Thurston, a nephew of Logan's came out to teach the Marquette school in 1902. He had sixteen pupils and earned $50 a month for the five month school term. It was said that Thurston had tuberculosis. Often in that era the treatment was to suggest the patient go to the dry western climate. Thurston took up land between Trout Creek and Logan Creek but later relinquished his filing.

Lawrence Wagoner and wife Vivia, sometimes called Vivian, came to the North Fork from Taylor County, Iowa, as did the Jack and Smith Murrays, and some of the Martin family. Vivia Johnson (Wagoner) came by stage from Red Lodge in 1901; Lawrence also came in 1901 and worked for George Logan. Their son Don was born at Logan's place. They later moved to New Marquette where Vera and Carl were born. When the dam was completed the family moved to Whit Creek, in March of 1911.

After the Wagoners, the C.J. Huntington family lived for awhile at Logan Creek. The Huntingtons had three sons, Carl, Cecil, and Don, and one daughter, Dorothy. The Huntingtons were from Lovell and related to Mildred Huntington who married Wylie Sherwin. The Sherwin family moved to the North Fork in 1922, and Mildred died in 1927.

Henry Westerman took up a homestead on a small spring that fed into Logan Creek. Frank Morris homesteaded a plot in 1938 and Fred and Margaret Richard bought it in September 1949 and spent their last years on Logan Creek. Fred's son Jack Richard and wife Doris lived there from 1966. At two different times, for short periods, they held school at Logan Creek.

THE UPTON PLACE

Clyde R. Huffman and wife Libby were the first to take up land that Uptons bought and also land later sold to Fred Morris. When Colonel William F. Cody was negotiating to buy the Carter Ranch he hired Clyde Huffman to run that ranch for him, so Huffman left the North

Fork. Huffman was born in Utah and came to Cody in 1898.

The Upton family typifies the westward movement of the nineteenth century. Elizabeth Passage was born in New York state on March 20, 1844, the one daughter among the four sons in the family, which moved west to Clinton County Michigan. Here Elizabeth grew up and married Roswell E. Upton in 1863, and son Lee was born in St. John, Michigan on May 6, 1865. The family moved west and after only five years of marriage, Roswell died. Elizabeth and Lee moved several times, out to California, and back to Wyoming to the Sherman Hill area east of Laramie. Lee attended school in Laramie. At one time they lived in Big Timber, Montana.

Before moving to Cody, in 1902, they ranched near Riverton, Wyoming. In 1903, they bought property from Clyde Huffman on the south side of the North Fork river across from Trout Creek, the first ranch up-river on the south side.

For twenty nine years Lee and his mother, fondly known as Grandma Upton, worked patiently and industriously on their ranch. Lee ran fifty head of cattle, and his hay fields were irrigated with water from the North Fork, carried from a headgate for a mile in a narrow ditch along the steep river bank. Both Elizabeth and Lee had water rights on the North Fork dating from January 2, 1904, and Lee acquired additional water rights on October 15, 1910. Lee also had a water right to a spring on Table Mountain, acquired April 15, 1907, for watering stock on summer range, and they had water rights to two springs on the side of Sheep

Lee Upton homestead with unidentified woman. Photo courtesy of John Yeates.

Mountain, both acquired in September of 1904. Elizabeth had a big garden, planted fruit trees and berry bushes, and was "famous for her gooseberries" in 1908, as reported in a Cody newspaper. One year she brought four varieties of her apples to the Park County Fair, she was growing Jonathons, Wealthys, Rambos, and Crabapples.

For some twenty years, friends gathered to celebrate Grandma Upton's birthday with a party. *The Wyoming Stockgrower and Farmer* for March 25, 1909, reported thirty two people came to celebrate Mrs. Upton's sixty fifth birthday. A fat lady's race and lean lady's race were run. A prize of fifty cents went to Mrs. McLaughlin, winner of the fat lady's race, Miss Reif won the thin lady's race and received $1.

Grandma Upton's presents included an oil painting by neighboring artist, E. Farrington Elwell. Other presents were spreads, a book, a table, linen and rugs. On her sixty eighth birthday friends gave her a writing desk and bookcase.

At one time, the Uptons also raised hogs for market. In 1912, the newspaper reported Lee had sold a wagon-load of dressed "porkers" for eight cents a pound. By 1913 Lee invested in a Model T Ford, and their last car was a 1926 Dodge.

In April of 1932, Grandma Upton was in her eighty eighth year and not well. When she required nursing care, several of her North Fork friends took care of her in rotating shifts. She died on the ranch, June 10th, 1932. Three years later, on March 7, 1935, Lee Upton died after thirty two years on the North Fork. John A. Yeates recalls, "Lee was a man of generosity, creativeness, kindness and good humor. In the 1920's he installed a pelton wheel in the small water line from high on Sheep Mountain and operated a Twenty eight volt DC generator which provided electric lights in the house and charged the batteries of his home-built radio set. The radio probably was the first one built and operated on the North Fork. One time he ordered from a catalog Zeiss binoculars and enjoyed having his friends look through them at far away objects and would slowly comment, 'They'll — bring — a — sheepherder — up close enough — to hear him cuss.'"

Lee's pelton wheel could belt-drive a grindstone making it easier to sharpen sickles for the mowing machine. He could also belt drive a grinder wheel to grind apples for cider which he generously shared with his friends. He owned a unique hay stacker called a "Jayhawk".

When Lee died, the Presbyterian minister conducted the funeral from the Upton home and appropriately read the poem, "A House by the Side of the Road", by Sam Walter Foss.[2]

TROUT CREEK

Due west of Logan Creek is the fairly large stream, Trout Creek. Andy Chapman settled there in the days of the open range, but didn't stay long, in 1891 Andy headed for the "mineral strike" at Kirwin. Wesley Bloom took up a homestead on Trout Creek and his water right on Trout Creek dates from May 25, 1889. He originally came from Wisconsin to Wyoming in 1880. His first wife was a Thompson daughter from Poverty Flat, the two older children were John W., born 1886, and Lena S., born 1888. Mrs. Bloom and a baby died when the family was trying to cross the North Fork with a load of hides and furs during the high water at the end of June 1893. Wesley later married Malissa Lovina Slack on April 19, 1897, she was sixteen, born in Portage County, Wisconsin, July 20, 1881. They had a daughter, Flossie E., born in 1899. While Wesley Bloom was owner of Trout Creek he was arrested for stealing cattle. He was sentenced for five years in the state penitentiary and a $669.80 fine on August 11, 1900 for grand larceny and receiving stolen property. He was pardoned after one year and came back to run his ranch. He died in Pinedale Wyoming, April 23, 1909, at the age of fifty years old.

Bloom worked as a guide, hunter, and trapper. When J. D. Buchanan came out west to look over land in 1897, he hired Wesley Bloom to drive him around. Buchanan chose land on the Irma Flat of the South Fork area.

In 1896, Frank and his wife, Emma Lafferty Slack, born in McCook, Nebraska, February 2, 1875, and Frank's parents, George and Kate Slack, came from Sioux county, Nebraska, by wagon to the North Fork. On a previous trip west they had worked for Charley Webster, father of Clyde and Bud Webster, in Montpelier, Idaho, and it is probably through that contact they came to the Big Horn Basin. According to Emma, they built a "snug, windowless cabin, with only hard-packed dirt for a floor," near the mouth of Trout Creek. Here, in 1899, their second son, Lawrence, was born, and in 1901, they moved over on the Greybull river, northeast of Meeteetse.

In February of 1902, Wesley Bloom sold his 250 acre ranch to Smith and Jack Murray for $9000. Jack Murray first brought out a load of household goods and was later followed by his wife, Maud and one-year-old, Margaret.[3]

Briefly, in 1903, F. H. Welch, a clerk at the Irma Hotel, bought some land "up the river from John T. (Jack) Murray," according to the *Wyoming Stockgrower and Farmer* for October 20, 1903, Welch shortly after moved to Red Lodge.

Tragedy again struck the residents of Trout Creek. In June of 1903, Mrs. Smith Murray drowned herself in Trout Creek. The *Wyoming Stockgrower and Farmer*, stated, she, "for some time had showed signs of being of an unsound mind." Tom Trimmer, senior, went to town to notify the coroner and Smith, who was in Cody when it happened. Smith had already started home from Cody traveling over the Rattlesnake Mountain trail, since the water was high and the rivers difficult or impossible to cross. Because of this high water, the body could not be taken to Cody for burial, so it was interred west of Trout Creek. No marker was erected and all traces of location of the grave are lost and it is believed some of the ranch sheds now cover the burial spot. Henry and Retta Westerman worked for deMauriacs for many years and lived in the Mess House. Henry said Mrs. Smith Murray was buried "behind the Mess House".

The Smith Murrays had two children, Marland , age five at the time of his mother's death and Lovena, age four. In September of 1903 the two children went back to Illinois with Smith's mother, but the 1910 census lists the children with their father.

Smith Murray remarried in 1904, his second wife named Florence, helped him build a large log house on the east side of Trout Creek. This building was later moved and/or dismantled.

Soon Jack bought out his brother and Smith moved over to the South Fork. Jack built a four room log cabin on the west side of Trout Creek. The kitchen had a door to the east. Off the kitchen to the north was the dining room. A door on the west side of the kitchen led to the living room and from the living room a door to the north opened to the bedroom. Another door from the living room opened onto a long porch to the south. In later years a bell hung outside the kitchen door that was rung one half hour before meals to alert the ranch hands. It was rung again on the hour of twelve and six to announce "time to eat".[3]

In July of 1910 they sold the ranch to Ralph G. Miller, a lawyer, for $5000 but had to bring suit to collect the money. Ralph G. and Lucy B. Miller were a wealthy Catholic family from New York City, with two young sons, one named Samuel Bond was five years old, however, information on the other son is not available. The Millers travelled extensively, to Massachusetts, Florida, Colorado. They called the place The Pinnacles Ranch .

The Ralph G. Millers had Trout Creek a brief six years, but they built a very large ranch house of trimmed logs, painted white, designated The Big House, on the east side of Trout Creek and the Jack Murray residence henceforth became the foreman's home, and since the foreman's wife often cooked for the ranch crew the log house became known as the Mess House.

The large log house had ten rooms and three bathrooms, and probably Fred Gail built it. It was designed in a U shape. The south wing consisted of the help's bedroom and bath, the help's dining/living room, then the kitchen, with a door to outside porch where the ice boxes were located.

The only telephone on the ranch hung on the kitchen wall next to the back door. This was the Forest Service telephone line, and the ranch had the first connection on the river so the number was 6F2, and consisted of two rings.

From the kitchen a door led down stairs into the large basement where the furnace heated water for the steam registers, here also were wash tubs and numerous storage rooms and a coal storage room. Back upstairs in the kitchen, a sink with running hot and cold water was too small for dish washing, so they washed dishes in large pans on a zinc-covered table. The cook prepared meals on a large coal burning stove and cupboards holding every conceivable cooking utensil lined the walls. In later years the deMauriacs installed an electric range next to the old stove, which they kept for heating and backup. Between the kitchen and the main dining room was a butler's pantry with cupboards for dishes and work counters. A swinging door separated the pantry from the dining room which had one of the four fireplaces in the building. The dining room had luxurious china cabinets, one cabinet held such valuable pieces of china it was always kept locked, there was a massive buffet also. After the deMauriacs bought the ranch and spent their summers there, Mr. deMauriac always mixed their pre-dinner cocktails at this buffet. A wide entrance from the dining room led into the huge living room with high vaulted ceiling. This room was filled with the mounted trophies of the Miller's successful hunts, including owls and hawks suspended from the rafters, and the floor covered with fine Oriental rugs and four or five bear rugs. The Millers brought west thousands of books, many of them very old, rare editions, and rows and rows of book shelves lined three walls of the living room. They also had an upright piano. Mr. deMauriac had a pool table built and installed in the middle of the living room and covered it with an elk hide, and in the center stood a huge cloisonné punch bowl. Neither the pool table or punch bowl were ever used.

A large fireplace dominated the east side of the room opposite the front door that opened out onto a large porch always referred to as the 'piazza'. The deMauriacs later had the porch screened.

A door on the north opened onto a long hallway, the west end formed a small room called the 'office'. Next, off the hallway was a nursery-type bedroom with blue decor used by the younger Miller boy. It had large music boxes, sets of miniature toy families and animals, left in place by the next owners, it also had a fireplace. Farther down the hall was a bedroom in yellow tones, used by the older Miller boy. This room had a large bookcase with books suitable for youths, including many dog and horse stories and a set of Book of Knowledge encyclopedias. Two large bathrooms separated this bedroom and the one at the end of the hall, another large, attractive room with windows to the north and east, and south-facing French doors leading to the open space between the two wings of the house. They never used these doors.

The Millers did not go into cattle ranching, but enjoyed the sport of hunting. Huldah Borron told the story about the Miller's pet bear they had acquired when it was a cub. It was very popular at that time for anyone who could to obtain and raise a "pet" bear, always kept on a chain. Later this became illegal. Miller enjoyed wrestling with the cub every day, but the time came when the bear had grown so big Miller could no longer break its"bear hug." While gasping for breath, Miller told his wife to get a gun and shoot the bear, which she managed to do, thus saving his life.

Norman Parsons deMauriac, from Bedford, New York, was hunting with Joe Jones of the Majo ranch at the head of the South Fork, when he learned the Miller ranch was for sale. He immediately bought it on September 1, 1916. At this time the infamous Sam Berry was caretaker.[4] Berry, in by-gone years had practiced the trade of an outlaw and paid for it by spending over five years in the state penitentiary. Later, no longer a "hired gun," he hired out as a winter caretaker for various places. In 1912 he had been caretaker over at the Rumsey-Ferguson ranch on upper Sage Creek.

The Millers moved out taking nothing with them except their clothing and guns. In 1917, the deMauriac family first came west to enjoy their property. In 1919, Henry and Bertha Dahlem moved to Trout Creek and they ran the ranch for deMauriac until 1921, followed by Oscar and Ethel Montgomery, whose first child, Jimmy, was born in the Mess House.

In 1928, Dewey Riddle was foreman for a short time, and one winter Carl Johansson stayed at the ranch. That may have been when they built the lambing sheds.

For awhile the ranch was called the KE ranch, brand K lazy E, but soon became known as Trout Creek ranch. deMauriac made a great deal of money playing the stock market. In 1925 deMauriac decided to go into sheep raising and hired Roy Glass from Emblem to be sheep foreman. Roy had married red-haired Margaret Newcomer, adopted daughter of the Newcomers of Emblem. Roy and Margaret lived in the Shanbacher house with their adopted son, Bobby.

In the spring of 1927, Mrs. Ben Simpers took the deMauriac's bum lambs to raise, and in 1928 deMauriac built a modern lambing shed south of the highway on the east side of Trout Creek. He ran some of the sheep across the river on the east slopes of Sheep Mountain and had a shearing operation on Spring Creek. Dutch Hartung herded the sheep and kept his sheep wagon so meticulously clean he didn't want anyone stepping inside, not even the camp tender.

In 1928, a year before the stock market crash, deMauriac bought A. J. Martin's herd of short horns, for $40,000, including grazing rights in Trout Creek basin. Austin "Scoot" McCoy, one of their later cow foremen,from 1934 through 1944, said the dividing line between deMauriac's cattle range and Rhoad's range was Robber's Roost Creek. Also included in the sale with the Martin cattle was their pig eye brand , sometimes known as the hog eye brand. They hired tall, mustached Texas cowboy Johnny Kirkpatrick as cattle foreman. Kirkpatrick was fifty eight and getting rather deaf at the time. Another Texan succeeded him, short, good natured Bert McCracken and his two horses, Comanche and Kid. Bert always wore a brown, genuine beaver cowboy hat, until they were no longer available.

They soon phased out the sheep, and upgrading and registering white-faced Hereford cattle became the main aim of the ranch operations. Famous herd bulls of the Domino line were bought from the Wyoming Hereford Ranch near Cheyenne, as well as from top breeders of Bozeman, Montana, and from Colorado.

In 1933, fire destroyed an old cow camp cabin in Trout Creek Basin. Scoot McCoy said he had heard a fellow called the Three Fingered Swede had built the cabin. In 1934, deMauriac hired a talented young Swedish carpenter, Marten Martenson, who had first worked as a tie hack near Dubois, Wyoming. Martenson, never having been on a horse, rode off into the mountains and built an elaborate three-room log cabin containing large storage cabinets and closets, and extra bunks in the main room as well as on the south facing porch. He built a heavy slab door, pine tables and chairs with laced rawhide backs and seats.

Despite the Great Depression, deMauriac continued to make money and poured it into expanding his range, upgrading all the property, and acquiring modern equipment. A landowner could acquire more land by having a person take up a homestead and then sell it to him. This happened when Roy Glass, sheep foreman, received a patent from the United States on December l0, 1934, and on December 15, 1934, sold this property to N. P. deMauriac.

Jack and Maud Murray's log house continued to be the Mess House. The two-story log barn was enlarged with addition of a state-of-the art dairy barn. A graduate of the College of Agriculture, University of Wyoming, William Rice, was hired to manage the dairy operation. The dairy operation did not pan out. At first, though, Bill and his bride, Emma, moved into the Shanbacker house south of the lambing sheds, as did Marten Martenson and his bride, Marie. Marie Mayland from Emblem Bench had been hired to do the "second work" for the deMauriacs and met Marten on the ranch. Their's is but one of the numerous romances that developed between men and women employees on the North Fork ranches. Brooks Borron and Huldah Hogland met while working on the North Fork. Thelma Obenaur, who came out from San Francisco to look after Maury and Lucy Hammond, met and married Charles Lufkin who also worked on Trout Creek ranch.

Trout Creek, top: Big House built by R.G. Miller. Portable house to the right. Garage near Creek.

A Kohler electric light plant supplied electricity for the ranch. Rural Electric Administration lines were not strung on the North Fork until the 1940's. No longer did the chore boy have to hand crank the ice cream freezer every Sunday morning. Martenson soon modernized the freezer with an electric motor, and fixed up sprayers for painting the big white house. A new frost-free cement cellar served as a commissary for the truckloads of food staples stored there. A combination lock secured the underground store room, the number was 1215, (the date of the Magna Charta). Since practically everybody on the ranch knew the combination, candy bars and dried fruits didn't stay on the shelves long. Ranch youngsters learned to enjoy German semi-sweet chocolate bars lifted from the commissary.

Norman Parsons deMauriac and Alice Bergen deMauriac had only the one daughter, Alice, called "Babsy" by her parents. One time when traveling in Europe, Alice met Bennett Hammond, a descendant of Daniel Boone, and they were married in Athens, Greece. At first the Hammonds planned to live in Mt. Kisco, New York, but soon decided to manage the Trout

Creek Ranch. deMauriac built a new home for them a few hundred yards north of the main house. It had a similar U design like the "big house," but with simulated logs and also painted white. The small living room proved inadequate, so Marten Martenson cleverly designed a way to enclose the space between the two wings and provided a large living room furnished with Molesworth furniture. Stone masons used red and blue granite from the Shoshone canyon for the fireplace in the small front room.

Shortly after deMauriac bought the place from Miller, he had a prefabricated house shipped west and assembled northwest of the big house and closer to the creek. This five room brown house was designated as the Portable House, and used both as a guest house and for housing the help. After the completion of the Hammond's new house, the old Portable House's usefulness was over and they burned it.

Ben and Alice had two children, Norman deMauriac "Maury" and Lucy, various nurses and nannys cared for the children and Friedel Mees (Mrs. Hollis) was one of the first. Thelma Obenaur (Mrs. Charles Lufkin) from San Francisco later cared for the children and there were numerous other nannys. Hulda Johansson cooked for the deMauriacs for thirteen summers, When her daughter Ester, was old enough, she was hired to do the "second work".

Big House view from north.Below: Moving band of deMauriac sheep across North Fork River, 1929.

The deMauriacs continued to come out summers and often brought guests. During this time the ranch expanded, but it was never a profitable operation, Scoot McCoy said it probably cost deMauriac fifty or sixty thousand dollars a year to run the place. Scoot recalled the ranch did make a profit of $15,000 one year when he ran the cattle. Alice gained a reputation as an unusual person, headstrong, flamboyant, and promiscuous, given to extramarital affairs. Eventually Ben divorced Alice and returned to the East where he pursued a successful career working for modeling agencies, sometimes modeling Arrow shirts and McGreager sportswear. He became a familiar figure in Life and

Time magazine ads.
In November of 1941, ranch manager Cy Williams lived in Alice's home. Alice and her two children had moved into the Big House. Ethel Montgomery and her daughter Ruth, also lived there helping with the cooking and house work. Alice decided to start a fire in the dining room fireplace, unused since the time of the Millers. The fire escaped from the crumbling masonry and three hours after the blaze started the $50,000 home had burned to the ground and only the five chimneys were standing. Ranch foreman, Ray Wilde, lived on Jim Creek and drove down river each morning, about 4:00 a.m. to work. He was the first to see and report the flaming building.

Alice spent an incredible amount of money in a run for Congress in later years. She also tried various ways to earn a living. A political change brought hard times to deMauriac's stock market income. They became financially impoverished and sold their property in the east and moved to the ranch. Again, a prefabricated house was built on the ruins of the white log house and the deMauriacs lived there until Mr. deMauriac died, and Mrs. deMauriac moved to town.

Other homesteaders who took up land and requested water from Trout Creek included Thurston, who took up a homestead

Ester Johansson at Trout Creek mess house, 1935.
"Boots" and pony cart at Trout Creek with Thelma Obenaur (Lufkin) and assorted ranch children, including Lucy and Maury Hammond and Virginia Westerman (Thompson).

between Logan and Trout Creek but soon relinquished it. John W. Thurmond's water right dated from March 23, 1894, he had been living on Poverty Flat but sold and moved when the reservoir filled. Elias M. Thurmond was the elderly father of John and Charles and Annie Thurmond Sweney. Annie always spelled her name with one "e", but everyone else spelled it with two "e's". In 1909 Charles built a two story log house on their homestead east of Trout Creek, surrounding it with a cement and stone fence. By 1911 they had a big new barn and gave a dance in it. The Thurmonds were quite an extended family, Mrs. Charles Thurmond's father and mother and brother, the VanEverens were mentioned in the newspaper during the years the Thurmonds lived there. Charles Thrumond sold to Delbert V. Early in 1919 and D.V. Early sold to Floyd Early in 1929. C.J. Huntington, lived there 1920 through 1922, apparently the Farmers State Bank of Powell held a mortgage for many years. deMauriac bought the place in the late twenties and with it's productive hay fields it fit perfectly with his operation. Wesley Newton and family lived in the Thurmond house when Wes was cowboying for deMauriac.

In 1956 a small plot of ground where the Thurmond's house had stood became home to Bob Rumsey. Hans Snortland, an excellent log carpenter, built him an attractive house close to the small spring, and Rumsey lived there until his home was struck by lightning and burned completely to the ground.

Another parcel of land between the lambing sheds at Trout Creek and the mouth of the creek was sold by John Thurmond in 1917, to Frank Shanbacker who planned to run sheep, but who did have a "bunch of cattle" at the time of his death. After he and his bride bought the property he built a white frame house on the east side of the creek. This house had a kitchen, large living room, two bedrooms and a bath. On the north and east sides it had an unroofed board porch, and there never were any trees or gardens around it. In 1919, on a visit back east to see his parents, Shanbacker died of pneumonia, leaving a widow and baby. Before he left on his trip he "took out all the insurance he could carry", according to Huldah Borron. deMauriac soon bought this property that complimented his holdings.

Murray creek, a tributary of Trout creek, flows into it several miles upstream. In 1913, Earl Linde, (pronounced Lindy) a young remittance man, who came out from Philadelphia and lived with the Morris' for a number of years, planned to take up a homestead in a pretty spot on Murray creek. (School Census lists Earl as age seventeen in 1913, the only year he is listed). He had to travel through the property of the Millers to reach his place. Miller ordered Linde and his cousin, Ernest Rueger, not to trespass, but they did not obey. An altercation occurred resulting in the arrest of Miller on charge of assault, he then pressed charges of criminal trespass against Earl. It came to the court of William Foster, Justice of the Peace, and the case against Linde was dismissed. Another time Miller was involved in a legal dispute, in 1915, when Hardy Shull had to go to court to collect $2,000 owed him for pasturing Miller's horses.

MORRIS RANCH

In 1904 Fred Morris bought property from Clyde and Libby Huffman west of Trout Creek. The Morris ranch was not situated on any stream, but north of the river. They acquired a Libby Huffman water right on Trout Creek that she had obtained February 28, 1906, and carried the water by a ditch to their ranch. Fred Morris came from England where he served an apprenticeship in ship building, then worked in West Philadelphia in the ship yards. He was a big man, genial and hearty, and well suited to running the dude ranch he had going by the

Above, main lodge at Fred Morris Ranch.In 1929 a swimming pool was built north of the lodge. Photo courtesy of Park County Archives. Below, Leonard Morris wearing white angora chaps. Photos courtesy Park County Archives.

summer of 1908. His wife, Mary Cody Morris, a short lady, came from Dublin, Ireland, she was called "Maggie". (She and her sister Delia were Catholic. Delia Cody married Hardy Shull, another big, friendly man. These Cody girls claimed they were no relation to the William Frederick Cody family.)

They had big plans for their dude ranch, many of which materialized. The living room thirty-two feet by thirty-two feet had an impressive fireplace, other plans were also mentioned in the Cody newspapers such as the dining room of fifty-five feet by twenty-two feet and a kitchen of twenty-two feet by twenty-two feet. Some of these were completed by 1912. Fred's brother, Jack, an expert plumber came from Philadelphia to install the water and heating system. There were plans to build a billiard room forty-four feet by twenty-four feet, and ten log cabins plus two larger cabins for guests.

The Morris ranch is noteworthy because they built the first outdoor swimming pool on the North Fork, it was seventy-one feet by thirty feet, with depth from two and one half feet to eight and one half feet. Fred Morris returned to Philadelphia in World War I to take charge of the Philadelphia shipyards,and again during World War II, when he was again in charge of the Consolidated Shipyards.

The Morris' only child, Leonard, was born in Philadelphia in 1905, and he first came West with his mother c.1909. When he was seven and school age his parents were instrumental in getting a school at Wapiti.

The Morris ranch succeeded and became a busy, active place. In May of 1911 the *Park County Enterprise* stated Fred Morris had booked twenty-two wealthy Philadelphians for a stay of four months at his dude ranch. In those times vacations seldom lasted less than two weeks and the guests often spent an entire summer on a ranch. The next year Fred had a horse-related accident in Yellowstone Park. While riding bareback he got bucked off and broke his left shoulder, "when he failed to roll out of the range of the horse's heels". He received medical treatment at Fort Yellowstone (Mammoth) and had to return to the ranch.

Bucking contests had been popular entertainment at New Marquette in pre-reservoir days. Morris continued the event at his ranch and on August 6, 1913, Henry "Hank" Goodman won first prize of $50 put up by Morris. This may have been the first dude ranch rodeo on the North Fork.

By 1917 young Leonard attended a convent school in Philadelphia. Other schools he attended were St. Josephine Academy in Baltimore, Roxbury School in Connecticut, and Brown University. He excelled in athletics, football, fencing and javelin throw. He did so well in fencing and the javelin throw they considered sending him to the 1928 Olympic Games in Holland.

In 1926 Fred built a three room cabin across the river. Perhaps he was homesteading a piece of river bottom land there, since this location would be difficult to reach part of the year. Later Leonard built a bridge across the river.

Lillian Balder from Fromberg started working at Morris' during her summer vacations when she was fourteen and worked seven summers, until 1937. Mr. and Mrs. Morris ran the dude ranch with scarcely any help. When Lillian first started working there Soofoo, a Chinaman, with thick black brows and quite large ears, did the cooking. Meals were hearty with big roasts of pork or beef at night. The dining room table held twenty four people and they served the food family style. The help ate in the kitchen. Mrs. Morris was a thrifty overseer. Once Barbara Evans assisted in the kitchen and served up big portions of canned peaches in dishes for the help and Mrs. Morris made her take back a couple from each dish.

Lillian recalled, "When I first started working for the Morris' I did everything except cook. The more I did the more they piled on me, and the more I had to do the earlier I got up. The old Chinaman used to say to me, 'Lilly, you get up too early'. I had to clean the dining room before serving the breakfast, then go do the cabins and the laundry. I did the ironing, everything had to be ironed in those days and I did it with old sad irons. When I got caught up with the stack of ironing piled in the laundry room, Mrs. Morris had me hemming flour sacks for tea towels. I hemmed 47 tea towels that summer."

For a few years Soofoo did the cooking in the summer and stayed on as caretaker in the winter. He was just the kind of employee the Morris wanted. He didn't waste anything. In the winter he stood by the corral and watched the horses so they didn't waste any hay. After he left Morris ranch he came to town and worked as a swamper in the bars. He worked for the Log Cabin for years.

For a few years the Morris' ran a little filling station on the south side of the highway some distance east of their gate. There was also a homestead cabin near the highway. Lillian recalled, "When they let Soofoo go, Mrs. Evans came up to cook at Morris ranch and her daughter Barbara was to help me so I wouldn't have so much to do. I always had excess energy. So when we got done work at night, occasionally we would go down to Mary Morris' homestead cabin and 'prove up on the homestead.' Sometimes we would make a batch of fudge and spend the night, but then we had to get up at four the next morning to get back and get ready for breakfast."

One year Lillian had to go home because of illness in her family. They hired young Ellen Jensen (Waggoner), now McNeice to fill in. Ellen was in her early teens and one time she and Dottie Morris rode calves for the ranch rodeo. They were such good sports the ranch wranglers rewarded Ellen with a pair of cowboy boots. They made her a pair of spurs with her initials inlaid in silver. A silver spoon from the dining room happened to disappear at this same time.

Nineteen thirty five was the last year Fred and Mary Morris ran the ranch. During that summer Mrs. Morris knit bathing suits,and sold them for $75 each. She also made face cream. Lillian recalled, "She had this formula and made a real heavy cream which she used herself. She didn't have a wrinkle on her face. Sometimes she had me come in and help her put the cream in jars for sale. She was always drumming up business."

Nineteen thirty seven was the last summer Lillian worked there. She had met Everett Dixon who worked on the neighboring Trout Creek Ranch and they were married in February of 1938. They moved into the Shanbaker house and were there until fall, when they moved up to the Hollister place which was owned by deMauriac, and lived in a little house there for fourteen years.

About 1935 Leonard and Dot sold their lodge on Nameit Creek and took over the Morris ranch. Leonard put in a cable swinging bridge across the river. Paul Stock would come out and they would trap shoot across the river. Life got livelier with cocktail parties before dinner, and dancing parties. They put in a Kohler electric plant.

After Mrs. Evans, Edna Bjordahl from Red Lodge cooked at the ranch. Leonard hired more help than his parents believed necessary.

POST CREEK

Across the river from the Morris Ranch a small stream flows from the west end of Sheep Mountain into the river. Mary Helen Dahlem married Roy Daly December 9, 1931. They met at the Red Star Lodge (now Shoshone Lodge) when Roy worked for Ranger Clifford Spencer as a fire guard checking campgrounds and lodges. Roy went to work for the Dahlems and homesteaded on Post Creek where they ran sheep. Fred Morris had taken out a water right on a tributary of Post Creek February 28, 1906.

BRETECHE CREEK

During the days of open range, Baron Paul Breteche of the French Colony, near Trail Creek, ran horses and cattle in the area of the creek which today bears his name. North forkers always pronounced Breteche "Brittisher." Napoleon B. "Pol" Nuckols patented his homestead on Breteche Creek March 15, 1898. Perhaps he sold this homestead to W. T. Borron. On December 5, of 1900, William T. Borron who lived on Poverty Flat acquired a water right on Breteche Creek. Borron had come to the area in 1881 and homesteaded on Poverty Flat, receiving his patent May 20, 1897.

Bill's half brother Lee came to the North Fork later and worked for Dwight Hollister and ran the post office for a few years. Lee was fifteen years younger than Bill. Lee took up a homestead near Rand Creek. Lee sold his property to the Hollisters, he also worked for them many years.

Grace McMullen taught at the Marquette school in 1897, she married Bill Borron in 1897 or 98. Her sister, Maude McMullen, married William E. Green. Grace came west from Nebraska and was twelve years younger than Bill. They had four boys, Robert Holbrook, the oldest, Glen a year younger, Theodore was born c.1901 and John A. born about 1905. They lived on Breteche Creek, probably from 1900 through 1905, in that year the Borron Brothers had pamphlets printed advertising "Take a Midsummer Vacation. We Tell you how." Bill had been on the school board while living on Poverty Flat. When they moved up river schooling became a problem and James Dickson taught the Borron children on Breteche Creek for three months. Huldah Borron said Dickson wrote a "beautiful hand", he moved to town, married, had a candy and fruit store on Sheridan Avenue and later he committed suicide.

William T. Borron received his patent to his Breteche homestead on May 18,1911. The

Borrons may have had the earliest guide licenses. Members of the Borron family still have the guide license to Yellowstone Park, with the number "1". Bill and Lee obtained the licenses by writing to Wyoming Representative Mondell, who wrote on January 21, 1902, to the Secretary of the Interior, who forwarded the request to Major Pitcher, acting superintendent of Yellowstone Park, and he sent W. T. Borron the "desired license" on March 21, 1902. This gave Borron permission to enter the Park with his pack train by way of Mountain Creek, to Upper Yellowstone, to Bridger Lake and return the same way.

On March 24, 1903, Major Pitcher sent W. T. Borron and Lee H. Borron, Irma, Wyoming, renewals of license, and the same for 1904.

According to the 1910 Census, the W. T. Borrons were living over in the remote Sunlight mining area. An April 1910 issue of *Wyoming Stockgrower and Farmer* reports that "W. T. Borron left the North Fork for Painter, Wyoming." The Winona mine in this remote Sunlight Mining District was at this time a hot spot.

Bill Borron had a propensity for drink and a weakness for gambling on hitting a productive mineral strike. Shortly after this move the Borrons separated and Grace took the four boys and moved to Old Mexico to teach school. Mexico's dictator Diaz had turned the rich natural resources of the country over to foreign capitalists. By 1910 there were 50,000 Americans living in Mexico. During a change in the power structure of Mexico, Carranza and Villa became antagonists. Villa shot a number of Americans, and Americans fearing for their lives moved out. Grace took her family and moved back to Virginia, but the oldest boy, Brooks, had already headed back to Wyoming, he was only fifteen but worked his way north, after many adventures he arrived safely in Cody.

Borron family folk tales include stories about Bill having to ride to Lander to pay his taxes when Poverty Flat was in Fremont County. Later, he had to ride to Basin to get his marriage license when the north part of Fremont County became Big Horn County. Bill also wrote to Borden Milk Company and suggested smaller condensed milk cans would be handier for pack trips, the company acted on his suggestion.

The Henry Dahlems lived on lower Breteche Creek in an old cabin for awhile, later moving to Trout Creek when Henry was foreman there. When Henry Dahlem was elected sheriff they lived in town in the sheriff's quarters—combination jail and Mary Helen was born there in the "jail house".

Farther up Breteche creek Jud and Pearl Weston took up a homestead in 1916 and one in 1917. Pearl Weston received her patent on a homestead in 1918. They ran some cattle and raised a little hay. Jud was a tall, skinny man, and Pearl was small in stature and of ornery nature according to Huldah Borron. Pearl always call Jud "Mr. Weston".

Jud Weston drove the mail for years. Mrs. Weston was very jealous of her husband, and sometimes she would go down to the Dahlems with field glasses to spy on Jud and see who was riding with him. According to Morris Simpers, a neighbor of Westons, Jud Weston chewed tobacco and spit the juice through his teeth. One time Ben Simpers and son Morris were out riding for cattle and Ben said, "I see Jud Weston has been riding here ahead of us." At regular intervals there appeared a brown streak in the snow beside the trail.

Morris Simpers said, "The first 'No Trespassing' sign I ever saw was on a gate to the Weston Place. Mrs. Weston had nailed up the end of a box and written 'No Trespassing', but someone had come along and turned the sign over and nailed it back so it read, 'Keep in a Cool Dry Place'."

But true to the spirit of the west, travelers were as welcome at Westons as any other ranch on the river. Morris remembered staying overnight one time when he was out looking for cattle, they made him a bed on the floor. Pearl divorced Jud Weston in June of 1931.

Johansson homestead.

JOHANSSON HOMESTEAD

Across the river from Breteche Creek is Dry Pat Kelly Creek. The Johansson homestead was at the head of this draw. In many ways this homestead is a prototype of a holding in the middle Wapiti Valley.

Carl Johansson felt optimistic when he filed on the 640 acres, more or less, that lay along a narrow dry wash running from north to south, high above the North Fork of the Shoshone River. Except for a new road, the area has changed little over the years. Jim Mountain, 10,425 feet, rises to dominate the view to the west. The government land Carl chose is fairly steep, with varying altitude around 7,500 feet, and it is two thousand feet above the river valley. On the north the divide is the boundary between the homestead and Shoshone National Forest. The Cannonball Trail went from the river up the dry wash, over the low pass into the Trout Creek basin country.

Johansson's legal document is called Homestead Entry No.08034 for Lots 9-20-18-19-23-24-25-33, Section 6, Township 52 N.R., 104 West. Eventually, the Johansson property totaled 14 lots. Carl filed on it April 19, 1916, and on January 13, 1922, before Clerk of the Court George S. Russell, he gave proof, with witnesses Lawrence Nordquist, W. O. (Oscar) Montgomery, Peter Nordquist, all of Cody, and Earl Linde of Morris, P. O. Actually, all the witnesses lived on the North Fork. Earl Linde (pronounced Lindy) a remittance man from Philadelphia, had taken up a homestead over on Trout Creek. Lawrence and Pete Nordquist took up land bordering Carl's on the west, on Jim Creek and started building log cabins for their new dude ranch called the P Bar P. Oscar Montgomery homesteaded lower down on Jim Creek.

After the solemn court procedure they all marched down main street to a pool hall where Carl bought the drinks of finest bootleg whiskey, discreetly supplied to the place by Jack Spicer later of the North Fork.

In May of 1920 Carl set to work on his log cabin home. Since the Cannonball Trail was

Middle: Hulda and Ester Johansson in door of homestead 1920-1921.

Below, Sara Murray in doorway of Johansson homestead cabin built by her grandfather 75 years earlier.

too easily washed out, he improved the grade of the road that took off from the highway and climbed the treeless foothills. On the grassy bench west of his land the road forked. The old branch led west over to the P-P and a new track led to his cabin. He cut a dugway through the clay and gumbo hill north of the little flat where the cabin would be, so cars could circle round and drive down to the cabin site. This road had a tendency to wash out, or in winter, would drift in with snow. Most of the time he had to park their gawky Model T 1917 vintage Ford pickup on the top of the bench to the west.

With the logs he had cut and snaked out and a few hundred dollars worth of nails, framed windows, flooring and sheet rock for inside finishing, he spent most of the summer building the cabin. During this time his wife, Hulda, took their year old child, Ester, and traveled by train to visit relatives in Snohomish, Washington.

Hulda came back in the fall and moved into their brand new home. This was not the best time to be settling in for a session of homesteading. Perched so high above the Shoshone river valley the panoramic view from the cabin was its greatest asset.

Besides the isolation, the down-drafts and updrafts in this mountain cleft created a breeze that whistled and howled around the cabin with the loneliest sound imaginable.

The square, three room cabin had a ten by twelve foot kitchen connected to a bed room the same size. Parallel to those two rooms was a twelve by twenty foot "sitting room". The one outside door faced west and opened into the kitchen from which one door led to the bedroom and another door to the big room.

They couldn't afford many furnishings. They bought a second-hand cook stove from

Carl's brother, Leonard. Carl used left-over lumber to build a small kitchen table and a wash stand with enclosed cupboard underneath, and they had a few chairs. A double bed and a cot fit into the bedroom, along with Hulda's Stanley sewing machine she bought for $25.00 from the Red Cross after World War I. The sitting room had nothing to sit on nor other furnishings, but provided lots of storage space. Forty feet west of the cabin stood a small, one-hole outhouse. Wood wasn't much of a problem but water was very scarce. A couple small ponds close by, fed by seepage, provided water for wildlife, but was not fit for people to drink.

After finishing the cabin, Carl next fenced on the south and west sides where there were no natural barriers. One time to break the monotony, Hulda took the toddler and started to walk to where Carl was fencing. Somehow, she lost her way and in climbing up along the sandstone ledges she got onto a high ledge and could neither climb up nor down. She had gotten "rimrocked." Luckily, Carl heard her cries for help, hurried to reach her, lifted the toddler off the high ledge and assisted Hulda off the outcrop.

After 1922 the family never again lived there. They hid the key between the foundation and a log on the east side. From time to time they would drive up, pull out the key and check the place. The cabin, snug and tight for a number of years, began to show its age when pack rats started nesting above the kitchen ceiling. The aging logs weathered to grey and settled into the landscape.

On September 4, 1936 N. P. deMauriac bought the homestead for $3500 it tied in with his grazing permits on forest land in Trout Creek basin. In its beautiful location without a dependable supply of water, the homestead had limited usefulness.

The Johansson homestead.

SLACK CREEK

The next small stream flowing into the river from the south and just west of Breteche Creek is Slack Creek named after George Slack, father of Frank. George took up a homestead there but relinquished it when he moved over on the Greybull river near Meeteetse, around 1898.

There was a logging road up Slack Creek that dropped over into Breteche Creek. Eddy Dorrance had a homestead in the area. High up on the foothills of Table Mountain, the panoramic view of the Wapiti Valley is spectacular.

STONEBRIDGE PLACE

Charles H. Stonebridge came west and by August 16, 1901, had a water right on Whit Creek for taking water by ditch to his place on the river, he had two more water rights, one for September 27, 1901 and June 20, 1904. Like Morris's ranch, Stonebridge was not situated on a stream. Stonebridge started the North Fork Cattle Company in 1905. He had the rocking chair livestock brand, also a his horse brand of T over reverse C. He planned a "model ranch" and briefly, Dwight Hollister was his manager. Stonebridge built a dam on upper Whit Creek and built a reservoir. He diverted this water via ditch to this place. In an interview in the *Wyoming Stockgrower and Farmer* for November 17, 1903, Stonebridge said he was laughed at and called a tenderfoot when he built his dam . In 1908 Stonebridge was renting his place to Massachusetts artist, E. Farrington Elwell family. They had two daughters, Alice May who was nine years old and Grace Irma who was six. Elwell had years before first come to the TE ranch through the courtesy of Buffalo Bill. Elwell and Stonebridge were now into raising horses and running some dudes. Elwell, Stonebridge and Findley Goodman (nephew of Buffalo Bill) took fourteen New Yorkers to Yellowstone Park in 1908. While Elwell planned to live full-time on the ranch and continue his art career, Stonebridge returned to New York in the winter.

By the fall of 1911 Stonebridge had hired John Thurmond and George Inman to build a five room log house with Fred Gail doing the finishing work. Legal records reveal he borrowed $5000 from Park Loan and Trust Company.

One year later Stonebridge ran a big ad in the paper to sell his 320 acre ranch and 70 head of horses. The ad said, "High Class Ranch for Sale at a Bargain."

By this time Elwell had moved back East. Horse raising wasn't doing so well with the advent of the automobiles. The *Northern Wyoming Herald* ran a notice in 1917, of foreclosure by Jennie Minor against Charles H. Stonebridge and Adelaide Stonebridge for $5000 plus another $1000 mortgage dated October 3, 1911. Stonebridge had also borrowed $7000 from A.O. Salter.

Stonebridge did not leave a good memory when he left the country. He ran up quite a few bills around town. One time he came back and paid up all his debts. He got on the train and when the train stopped in Frannie, he sent a telegram to his bank in Cody, stopping payment on all the checks. That was his last visit to Cody.

Stonebridge was also remembered by the old timers on the North Fork for being an inventor. He invented a folding lantern consisting of a small flat 4 inch square with four pieces of ising glass sides hinged to this base and folded flat on it, when unfolded it provided ising glass protection for a candle. By a strange coincidence, Morris Simpers saw one in a museum in Lead, South Dakota, crediting Stonebridge as the inventor.

Jim Montgomery tells of another of his inventions, the Stonebridge Special - grizzly bear trap. There were so many grizzlies on and around Table Mountain in the early days and the ordinary bear traps were ineffective so Stonebridge invented one with sharp prongs, or "teeth". These teeth were later outlawed.

The Jim Corders lived on the Stonebridge place in 1912, and the Simpers family moved there in 1914 for two years. In 1914 the Stonebridge reservoir "went out" from a deluge caused by a cloudburst. Ben Simpers repaired it and it has held ever since. After living on the Stonebridge place two years the Simpers moved west to the next creek in 1916 and bought the place from Pat Kelly, in partnership with deMauriac.

John Bloom's homestead on Dry Pat Kelly Creek, 1917. Land was formerly homesteaded by Ed Holmquist. Photo courtesy of Mark Simpers.

The McClains called the Stonebridge place home for awhile. Sometime in 1918, Charles McClain,his second wife Louesa, with their daughter Audrey, Charles' son Ed, and Louesa's two boys, Cecil and Bill, came by automobile from Lolo, Montana, near Missoula. Their belongings came on the train. The McClains probably bought the place from A.B. Minor, as far as Audrey can recall. Records show McClain paid $10,500 for it. The children started going to the Wapiti school, sometimes they traveled in the family buggy. Audrey remembered young Dwight Hollister (Bucky) was the school yard bully, always picking a fight with her brother Bill.

Audrey remembers with fondness visiting the Pat Kelly place where the children from across the river were welcomed with special treats. Audrey particularly enjoyed the canned pineapple. The Kelly's player piano provided amusement for the children. Mrs. McClain helped deliver Jimmy Montgomery when he was born in the Mess House at the deMauriac ranch. One time Mrs. McClain had yellow jaundice and spent some time in Cody under the nursing care of Mrs. Tex Thomas. During this time their neighbors, the Borrons, came and stayed at the ranch. Audrey stayed in Cody country when the rest of her family returned to the Missoula area of Montana. After Audrey married Ray Wilde they bought the Al Clarke place on Jim Creek where they lived for some years while Ray worked at Trout Creek.

Art and Margaret Pickard Royce lived on the Stonebridge place. In August of 1933, while driving home through the Canyon, Art and his three year old daughter Elizabeth Ann ran off the road into the canyon and were killed. Margaret's sister Emily Pickard married Austin "Scoot" McCoy in 1945, he had been cow foreman at Trout Creek.

New Yeates home on northside of river on Jim Creek. Photo courtesy of John Yeates.

JIM CREEK

The Mountain, the Creek and the Homesteaders

Jim Mountain, rises impressively to 10,425 feet, on the north side, half way up the Wapiti valley. Geologically, its twin, Table Mountain, directly south across the valley is about a thousand feet lower. Looking eastward the valley residents were familiar with the profiles of Rattlesnake and Cedar Mountains, cut apart by the Shoshone river canyon and their road to town.

Jim Creek originates from springs and snow banks. On an 1883 map the creek was called Robie Creek. There is no clue as to where this name originated, but by 1915 maps it is called Jim Creek. Martha Marston believed it was named for Jim McLaughlin, early trapper in the area.

John Yeates, from long and close association with Jim Creek, appreciated its reliability but also its variability and said heavy rains or cloud bursts could raise the water in the channel two to three feet for a few hours.

Peter, and Lawrence Nordquist took up homesteads at the top of the foothills below the cliffs of the mountain. Oscar Montgomery homesteaded directly south downstream and the John Yeates ranch bordered both sides of the mouth of the creek as well as land directly across the river.

The Yeates Homestead Ranch

John Yeates of Idaho Falls, Idaho, son of original homesteader John Yeates, grew up on the family ranch and attended Wapiti school, and contributes the information for this account.

In September 1904, his father, John A. Yeates, newly arrived in Cody, left town on foot, hiked up and over Rattlesnake Mountain on a very steep trail, and walked up the North Fork of the Shoshone River. Although preparations were underway for construction of the Shoshone Dam, (later renamed Buffalo Bill Dam) there was no road then through the Canyon. Preliminary work went forward for the road being built to Yellowstone Park.

Yeates scouted out the North Fork, liked what he saw, and applied for a homestead of 163.4 acres, forty of which lay on both sides of the mouth of Jim Creek and the rest bordering the south side of the river across from Jim Creek. However, only that portion of the forty acres west of the creek was flat and tillable. Yeates had grown up on a Missouri farm and he planned to raise livestock and grow crops. His first crop came from a field of red potatoes. He built a twelve by fourteen foot log cabin with gravel roof and dirt floor on the south side of the river.

John Yeates recalls his father fulfilled the requirements of the Homestead Act and received Patent No. 234127, officially authorized by President William H. Taft on November 13, 1911. Another Act of Congress, The Sale of Desert Lands, March 3, 1887, permitted Yeates to buy 162.45 acres of "partly tillable, partly native pasture and partly arid land directly north of the Pat Kelly ranch." This was approved by the Office of President Woodrow Wilson on March 26, 1919. Prior to this time the Jim Creek water rights for the lower Pat Kelly ranch, one mile east, had lapsed due to lack of use. Yeates applied for this unused water and legally acquired it.

By 1910 the government was paying for a new section of road because much of the older road had been covered by the reservoir. Yeates donated the land for the road through his ranch property. The government also paid for a new one lane, steel truss bridge with timber deck to cross the river where it passes through a narrow defile. This bridge crossed the river a short distance west of the Yeates homestead and made it much easier to get back and forth to the separated plots of his land.

During these years little cash flowed in from ranch operations. Yeates found summer employment driving spring mounted horse drawn carriages transporting tourists between hotels in Yellowstone Park.

Romance entered John Yeates bachelor life. The Yeates family and Taylor family of St. Louis had close friendships going back to neighboring farms in Kentucky in the 1830's. John Yeates began writing of the charms of the North Fork to Roxilettie Taylor, a St. Louis music teacher and church organist, enclosing pictures of the western scenery. She succumbed, took the train to Billings, Montana, where John met her and they were married on July 11, 1917. They happily moved into the tiny bachelor cabin but when Roxilettie's furniture arrived from St. Louis it completely filled the cabin space and plans for a bigger home across the river got underway.

First, logs had to be stockpiled. Yeates selected tall, ten inch thick Lodgepole pines from the Pahaska area thirty miles west. He cut these by hand, loaded them on his stripped down wagon and hauled them to the Green Creek sawmill where they were slabbed (cut flat) on one side. It took a week for each load and many trips to get enough logs. Roxilettie rode along on several of these trips, enjoying the fantastic scenery and the adventure of camping.

Yeates located his new house 200 yards north of the road with Jim Creek flowing through the front yard. The house had six large rooms and hallway, all with ten foot ceilings. Yeates liked to look out to the mountains from the picture windows on the east, south and west sides. Finished inside with lathe and plaster it provided a comfortable setting for the stone fireplace in the living room. Uphill from the house an underground concrete reservoir provided piped in water for kitchen and bathroom. In the kitchen water circulated through a water jacket in the fire box of the Majestic range and the heated water was piped to sink and bathroom.

They moved the old homestead cabin to the north side of the river and used it for a toolshed and no buildings remained on the south side of the river.

The worries of managing the final days of pregnancy in the wilds of a Wyoming winter caused Roxilettie to return to St. Louis where their son, John junior, was born January 8, 1919. It was a joyous reunion in the newly completed home when baby, mother, and aunt Eva Taylor arrived just as spring was greening the hillsides.

Meanwhile, John senior, had to get his allotted portion of Jim Creek water to his newly acquired "desert" land. This involved miles of digging a ditch, dropping the water over a 13 foot sandstone ledge and down old dry gulches to the forty acre field to be planted in alfalfa. The three and half mile ditch was inefficient and much water was lost through seepage and washouts, but by carefully tending the irrigation and "changing the water", they got two good cuttings of hay each year. Some years oats, barley, or wheat were planted and harvested by a three horse operated grain binder.

John A. Yeates takes a ride, Jim Mountain to the North. Below a neighbor, may be Plamantier and his two sons who lived on Marston Ranch, around 1906. Photos courtesy John Yeates.

Like other small North Fork ranchers, the Yeates family ran a few white face cattle. Young John Yeates remembers this well because as a teenager he had the job of cowboy, helping with the stock. He said success in raising range cattle in semi-arid Wyoming depended on natural pasture for spring, summer and fall, and an adequate crop of alfalfa hay to feed during five months of winter. And always that need for adequate irrigation water to produce the hay and sustain limited seeded pasture.

The natural pasture consisted of a Forest Service grazing permit on Table Mountain. The Yeates had a permit for 25 head of cattle, this meant one bull and 24 cows with spring calves could graze from June 15 until snows in October ended the grazing. Yeates remembered June 15 date was set because early blooming, poisonous larkspur would no longer be a threat for sheep and cattle.

It took a full day to drive the herd of cows, calves and herd bull over the foothills, up the Whit Creek trail, to the top of Table Mountain.

Cattle needed salt to thrive. Within two weeks after putting cattle on summer range, someone had to pack in three 50 pound bags of salt on a packhorse and deliver to several salt licks. In later years, salt blocks were used.

Meanwhile, during the summer, irrigating and haying provided alfalfa for the hay stacks to feed the cattle during winter. In the fall when the deer came down, the Yeates found

especially annoying the nightly visits of mule deer to their hay stacks. Yeates said they didn't actually eat that much, but would jump on the stacks and nibbled the hay leaves. "Their jumping and stomping produced an eight inch layer of bare stems mixed with deer hair and droppings. The cattle would refuse to eat such an unpalatable mix and each day this worthless layer had to be thrown off the stack before loading good hay on the hay rack, from the lower layer to feed the cattle."

Yeates Ranch on Jim Creek, Above John A. Yeates, Jr. and below John Yeates Jr., on "Zulu." Photo courtesy of John Yeates.

John Yeates remembered the many ways they produced income. Roxilettie had graduated from a St. Louis music conservatory and she was determined to maintain her piano skills. Her Steinway piano had been shipped out from St. Louis and hauled by wagon to the ranch. She often practiced before breakfast and gave a few lessons to children of the valley for 50 to 75 cents per lesson, and in later years gave lessons in Cody. Audrey Wagoner (Kelso), daughter of Don Wagoner, one of the pupils at the first Wapiti school, took piano lessons for thirteen years in Cody from Mrs. Yeates.

For awhile five to seven cows were milked, the cream separated by a hand-cranked centrifugal type separator, and at times, some weeks, they took ten gallons of cream to the creamery in Cody. The monthly "cream check" of $20 or so, was often the only cash income. They bucket-fed skim milk to a few "skim milk calves" or processed it for cottage cheese. Sometimes in summer tourists stopped to buy whole milk at fifteen cents a quart.

With summer tourist travel the need for overnight lodging increased. The Yeates built a rental log cabin and set aside two rooms in the house to rent. If requested, they served the tourists breakfast and evening meals. Probably this could be the first "Bed and Breakfast" on the North Fork.

The Yeates home was one of the few on the North Fork equipped with indoor plumbing, and since it was less than a mile from the Wapiti school it provided an ideal location for the Wapiti school teacher to room and board. This they did for $30 a month.

John Yeates recalls that as a boy he drove the hay stacker for neighbors during the haying season for a dollar a day plus the substantial dinner at noon. As a teenager he irrigated alfalfa fields, mowed, raked and stacked hay at home or sometimes hired out to neighbors, even loading wagons with threshed grain and peas. "For this I received the standard wage of $3 per day and noon dinner," he recalled.

Another source of cash income is described by Yeates: "The Valley Ranch boys and girls horseback trips traveled up the North Fork a day apart with their horse-drawn supply wagons, chuck wagons, cooks, wranglers, and thirty or so riders with guides and counselors in each party. The head guide would strike a deal with my Dad to have him furnish two butchered beeves for camp use, to be delivered to a campground near the East entrance of the Park. After butchering, the carcasses were cooled over night, loaded in the back seat of the Model T Ford and delivered. The occasion provided an outing for our family."

Winter trapping could bring in a good income for the professional trapper setting out traps in the forest from a winter camp. Some of the ranchers did a little trapping on the side. John Yeates carried out a time-consuming preparation of setting a trap line that masked any human odor or telltale tracks. He sometimes caught twelve or fourteen coyotes during the winter. He skinned them, scraped and stretched their hides and brushed the thick grey fur. Average pelts brought from $7 to $9 each, and an especially thick furred hide could bring $12.

One time some beaver started a colony at the mouth of Jim Creek, and began cutting down the cottonwood trees. John Yeates caught a few, the hides sold for only $3 or $4, but he did discourage the beaver settlement and they moved on and the trees were saved.

Another rather unusual but supplemental source of income involved bartering. Every two or three weeks during the summer Roxilettie Yeates sent a bag of garden produce and a pie to Caesar Querish, sheepherder, who would in return give them the fresh hindquarter of young mutton. Caesar herded sheep for a South Fork rancher who had summer sheep range on the high foothills of the north side of Table Mountain.

The horseback trip to the sheep camp took two hours and Caesar always insisted the riders stay for lunch, for which he would fix a fresh batch of delicious, fluffy biscuits, along with mutton chops. These trips provided a diversion and break from ranch work, on one visit Caesar had nailed to a tree the hide, flesh side out, of a large black bear that had attacked his sheep and he had killed with his .30 - .30 rifle.

OSCAR MONTGOMERY HOMESTEAD

Oscar Montgomery took up 607 acres of grazing land just north of the John Yeates place and south of the P-P on Jim Creek. Oscar built a cabin on the west side of the creek, sheltered and shaded by the many cottonwood trees. For a couple summers, Geraldine Coy, a Chicago social worker, and her guest stayed in the cabin. Geraldine was anxious to have her own place, because she loved lots of sunshine she found the creek side location of the Montgomery cabin too shady. Geraldine bought several acres of land farther west on the north side of the river. In 1923 the Montgomerys sold their homestead and bought the Hal Evarts place on Green Creek.

In 1926 an Arkansas lady, Mrs. Gula Jackson and her rowdy young son Billie, lived in the cabin. Gula thought there would be money in raising chinchilla rabbits so she had some hutches built, ordered breeding stock; and furs from the first litter skinned out and sold. One night a pack of roving dogs broke into the hutches and destroyed the chinchillas and hopes for future income from them. The neighbors were relieved when Mrs. Jackson and unruly Billie moved away in 1928.

In March of 1931, Alfred H. Clarke, a civil engineer from "back East" with an independent income moved in. He kept a few horses, bought hay for them and improved the cabin by adding a dining room and a front porch. He added to the local bootlegger's income and he and his cronies socialized with drinking parties.

Captain Watkins and wife Marjorie rented a cabin at Mountain View lodge from the Montgomerys who had bought the business. Watkins was associated with the Civilian Conservation Camp at Clearwater. A life-time resident of the North Fork, Jim Montgomery recalled Marjorie was the "southern belle type" and Watkins a "dapper military man." Marjorie and Al Clarke developed a relationship and when Watkins learned of it he told Marjorie she had better go ahead and marry Clarke. The Watkins divorced, she married Clarke and moved to Jim Creek.

Marjorie and Al had a rocky marital relationship. Young John Yeates recalled, "One day, about midmorning, Marjorie walked the quarter mile down to the Yeates ranch, arriving in a state of agitation and disarray. She both pleaded and demanded that my father immediately drive her to town because Al was drunk and had beaten her severely. My Dad held a dim view of people who could not handle their own problems and he resented having to waste three hours driving time to Cody and return, besides getting behind with ranch work. He also harbored a strong dislike for habitual drinkers, drifting vagrants and even itinerant preachers. All of these he considered unproductive and the last two also to be free loaders. His advice to Mrs. Clarke was to 'take an axe handle and give Al a working over.' However, Mrs. Clarke prevailed and Dad took her to Cody."

Apparently, they reconciled and the next we hear about them comes from the October 21, 1936, *Cody Enterprise,* "Word was received last week of the death by his own hand, of Alfred Hyde Clarke, at Cooperstown, New York, where he and Mrs. Clarke had gone early this fall. A revolver was used for the rash act."

Clarke, age 38, had lived on Jim Creek five years. According to folk tale, Marjorie returned to Cody and shortly thereafter committed suicide while staying at the Irma Hotel. According to the *Cody Enterprise* for February 8, 1939, "Mrs. Al Clarke, age 40, was found dead in her room at the Irma Hotel. She was last seen by Mrs. H. T. Newall at 1:30 a.m." Her funeral was from Christ Episcopal church and she was buried in Riverside cemetery.

Probate filed on January 25, 1940, stated Clarke died intestate on October 10, 1936, at Cherry Valley, Oswego County, New York. Former game warden Tex Kennedy picked up the property at the estate sale. Kennedy did not live there long but moved down to a nearby bend in the river and began building the "River Bend Tourist Resort".

Tex sold seven acres of the Jim Creek property, including the cabin and outbuildings to Ray and Audrey McClain Wilde. Audrey felt at home on the North Fork, she had lived at one time on the Stonebridge place and attended the Wapiti school. Ray was foreman at the deMauriac Trout Creek ranch. Later they bought 100 acres more and Ray added two bedrooms, a bathroom and sunporch to the cabin. The Wildes later sold and moved to Cody.

NORDQUIST HOMESTEADS, P Bar P, AND FOUR BEAR RANCH

At the top of foothills of Jim Mountain were the Nordquist homesteads. Pete and Lawrence Nordquist formed a partnership, and briefly John Bloom was involved but the partnership dissolved in 1921. To start their dude ranch they built a modest log lodge and a few summer sleeping quarters of wooden tent frames with floors, canvas tops and sides. Almost all the early dude ranches used this type of sleeping accommodations. During the winter the Nordquists trapped for coyotes and bobcats. Some of the Chicago dudes who came out to the ranch greatly enjoyed the western vacation and helped out financially. When Lawrence Nordquist had an opportunity to buy the remote Dickinson Ranch on the upper Clarks Fork, he sold his share of the P-P, and several of his loyal Chicago "dudes", the Sidleys and the Copelands, continued to spend their summers with him on his L Bar T ranch in that pristine area in the Crandall country.

Vivien Witherbee, from Waukegan, Illinois, a tall, attractive dudine in her twenties, fell in love with 47 year old Pete Nordquist and they were married on December 17, 1923, in Waukegan, followed by a winter honeymoon at the ranch. This is an example of the numerous romances and marriages between dudines and ranch wranglers.

One adventure made a lasting impression on Vivien. Toward the end of January Pete was out riding and four miles from the ranch his horse slipped on a sidehill and fell, breaking Pete's leg. The horse returned to the ranch leaving Pete stranded. The return of the riderless horse alarmed Vivien and she rode down the mountain to the John Yeates ranch for help. Yeates rounded up neighbors for the rescue, and Fred Morris drove his truck up the steep road. By back tracking Pete's horse they found the injured man. They loaded him in the truck and took him to the Whitlock hospital in Powell where he recovered.

In 1926 the Nordquists tried raising silver foxes. In April of that year one pair of foxes produced a litter of five pups. The Nordquists soon learned mother foxes are very nervous and if disturbed or think they are threatened will kill their young. The Nordquists suffered losses and fox farming did not succeed.

As with most property on the North Fork, many loans and mortgages were involved and ownership is difficult to follow. In 1924, Al G. Wilkinson of Detroit, Michigan, bought Lawrence's share. Wilkinson had married Mildred M. Holweg and she took an active role in running the ranch for awhile.

In February 1930, Pete and Vivien sold their share of the P-P and bought the historic Majo Ranch on the upper South Fork. This had been built up by Joe Magill and Joe Jones. Following this change, the P-P was then operated by the A. G. Wilkinsons, William Holloways, and into the picture comes Mr. and Mrs. S. S. Kensel. Kensel went by the name "Dinty Moore" and Mrs. Kensel retained and used her maiden name Olive Fell. In 1930, the dude ranch advertised they had space for 25 guests (in those same frame cabins) hot and cold shower baths provided in a bath house, and of course meals, horses and guides, for $50 per week. Children under twelve years paid half price.

In September 1932 the ranch lodge burned. At about this time the ranch name was changed to Four Bear. The Kensel marriage failed, the dude ranch business languished, and Olive Fell continued to live there year around, trying to make a living from her artistic talents. Olive loved her ranch, the wild game, and her horses, some of which were also wild. She chose a site

Pete Nordquist, Ernest Rueger,Ester Johansson and Carl Johansson around 1922.

at a lower elevation with a spectacular view for a spacious new log house. According to John Yeates she chose the site because she noted on a hot day the horses stood there in the cool updraft from the deep Jim Creek canyon to the west. Yeates recalled the broad concrete walkway to her front door had the converging tracks of several approaching deer imprinted in it.

The complete Olive Fell story falls outside the time frame of this work, but will provide exciting research for future historians.

THE PAT KELLY LOWER RANCH

Patrick Kelly bought the 320 acre Napoleon B. Nuchols homestead one half mile east of Jim Creek and bordering the Shoshone river, and became one of the earliest settlers on the North Fork. Kelly's Jim Creek water right dates from 1897, and in April 1898 he paid Nuchols $1500 for his property. He gave his age as 47 in the 1910 census. Those who remembered him found him very sociable, hospitable, and generous. Kelly also acquired 320 acres on Whit Creek (the upper ranch) from Civil War veteran William Whitworth who had moved up there from his old squatter's cabin above the Canyon where he had formerly lived.

John Yeates explained, "In order to direct the Jim Creek water to the lower ranch, Kelly installed a head gate in Jim Creek, near where Oscar Montgomery later built his cabin, and diverted practically the entire creek. He dug a ditch leading eastward following a south contour around a steep hill and leading to the cultivated area." He mainly grew alfalfa.

In 1902 Pat Kelly and Ed Grinder moved their cattle to the Clarks Fork to winter, and some summers Kelly grazed his cattle as far up as Elk Fork. The Forest Service later prohibited this grazing. In 1907 Pat Kelly fattened hogs to supply meat for the construction crews in the Shoshone Canyon and for the Wallop-Moncrieffe lumber jacks.

Pat and Mary Kelly lived in a log cabin down near the river. Because of poor health Mary returned to Nebraska for treatment. After she left, Pat planned a beautiful spacious home for her to return to. He hired Algot Johnson to build a two story house, modern in every respect with maple hardwood floors, a heating plant and a water system. The house was painted white after it was completed in April of 1909. Sadly, she never returned to enjoy it because she died in Lincoln, Nebraska, in January 1910. The big white house with its sad story became an oft-repeated folk tale on the North Fork.

Following the death of his wife, Pat brought his niece, Nellie Pearl, from Weldon, Illinois, to be his housekeeper. The 1910 census gave her age as 24, and also listed Charlie Sharp, age 26, as his "servant." In 1912, before the numerous tragedies that befell the Kelly place, and before the onset of World War I, Pat Kelly went into the tourist business. In his 1912 brochure he advertised for tourists and summer boarders. His emphasis was not so much on horse back trips, although he would arrange those by "special application," but he used horse drawn coaches. He called his camping equipment "The Outfit" and described it: a cook wagon drawn by four horses, a dining tent with tables, white enamel dishes, and wholesome food. His sleeping tents had canvas floors, beds with springs and mattresses, and "private toilet tent for convenience of lady members of party." Also, a "bath tub was carried along." Kelly emphasized you "can travel on camping trips without having to rough it." 12 day trip cost $60 and 18 days cost $90. His tourist business did not flourish.

Sometime in the 1920's a long frame building was built east of the two story white house and used as a hall for public dances. After it fell into disuse as a dance hall it served as a farm utility building. During his years on the North Fork Pat Kelly gave land for the school, organized dances and entertained neighbors at dinner. He used his camp outfit to take a group to Billings to attend Buffalo Bill's Wild West show in August of 1914. They advertised, "Big Dance at Pat Kelly ranch, good music, $1.00 per couple," and in the late 1920's they called it The Pepper Inn.

During the later years while Kelly still lived on the ranch, he stopped using the Jim Creek water and his water right lapsed. John Yeates applied for the unused water right and it was legally awarded to him. However, the Peppers, later tenants on the Kelly place, in the late 1920's sought to restore the water right by filing a lawsuit against the Yeates. The younger John Yeates said, "In spite of clear evidence to the contrary, the court, out of sympathy for a widow grandmother did grant a 20 acre water right to the Peppers. Even so, there was little change in the unproductive status of the ranch. The water ran nearly continually in the same spot on a small horse pasture and seldom was changed."

To go back and try to explain how Clyde Pepper gets involved in the Pat Kelly ranch, it is necessary to sort out numerous marriages and deaths. Clyde Pepper married Jane Williams in Kansas in 1906, and in 1908 a son is born whom they name Clyde Robert Pepper and the following year Clyde comes alone to Park County, Wyoming. In 1910, twenty six year old Clyde is manager of the H. B. Robertson ranch (later Frost and Richard). In May of 1910, Jane is granted a divorce from Clyde R. Pepper, she is awarded custody of their minor child, and her maiden name is restored. Apparently, from about 1912 Bobbie had been living with his grandparents in Powell, Wyoming. On December 7, 1910, Clyde marries Hazel Scott from Kansas City, at the Pat Kelly ranch, Reverend Wallace B. Dunn, of the Cody Methodist church officiates. The newspaper account stated fifty guests were present, "25 were society people from Cody." To this union is born Clyde Richard (Dick) Pepper on April 18, 1912.

According to Court Records, Jane Williams (the former Mrs. Clyde Pepper) married a man named Allman in Kansas in 1912. Apparently, Bobbie Pepper is living on the Kelly ranch as the *Park County Enterprise* for March 12, 1913, notes that six year old Bobbie falls off a fence and breaks his arm, requiring Dr. Bennett to go to the Kelly ranch to set it. In September Bobbie is sent to his grandparents, George and Sarah Pepper in Powell to attend school. By November Clyde's second wife, Hazel who has been ailing and under the care of Dr. Frances Lane of Cody, travels back to Kansas City for medical treatment. Clyde writes on November 8, to his folks and son Bobbie in Powell on the back of the calender page for October 1913, he says, "am enclosing a $2 bill (sic) for Robert. I should have sent it sooner, but I didn't have any money."

On November 8, 1913, a family member writes a letter for young Bobbie to his mother Jane in Kansas. The writer using Bobbie's "voice" mentions "Mama Hazel has gone to KC to see a specialist and I am going to school in Powell." Apparently Jane is not well either, Bobbie suggests she try the DeMaris or Thermopolis hot springs in Wyoming.

No mention of who is taking care of two year old Dick, perhaps he did go to Kansas with his mother Hazel. Unfortunately, bad luck is coming down hard on the Peppers. The *Northern Wyoming Herald* for January 9, 1914, carried the tragic story: "Clyde Pepper was found dragged to death by a horse at the Pat Kelly upper ranch, one end of the lariat was wrapped tightly around his wrist and the other end around the neck of the horse. He had been dragged in a circle all night and was found by John Yeates at noon on January 9th." Yeates immediately went to town to get the coroner. The paper stated Mrs. Pepper could not attend the funeral because she had gone back to Kansas City for medical attention and her doctor had sent her to Roswell, New Mexico, for treatment of tuberculosis. Pepper had been starting to dispose of his property. He also had taken out a $5000 life insurance policy a few weeks previously, but the policy was ineffective as he had been too busy for the medical examination. He was buried in Powell.

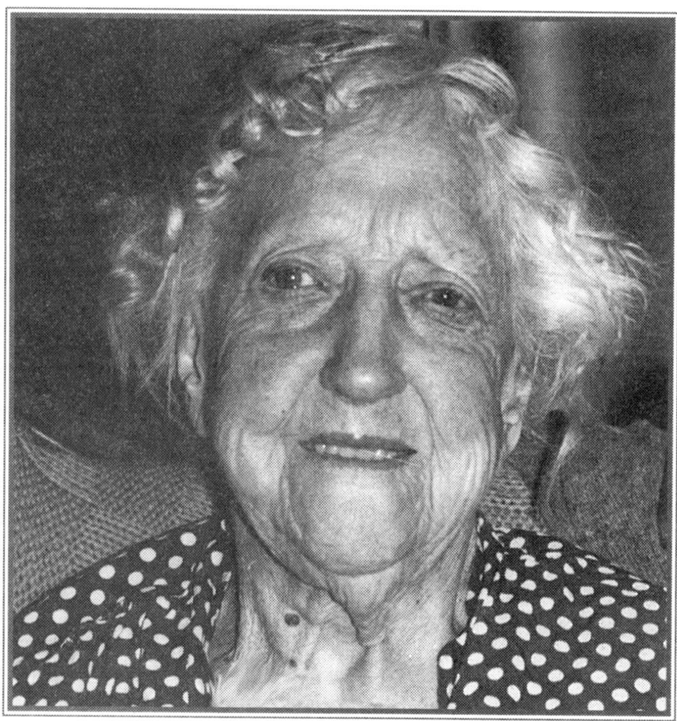

Ethel Montgomery. Photo courtesy of Park County Archives.

On April 19, 1914, three months after her husband's death, Hazel Scott Pepper dies and is buried in Kansas City. It is noted she left a two year old son and 7 year old stepson.

But to add to the confusion, after Clyde Pepper's death, George and Sarah Pepper of Powell, grandparents of seven year old Bobbie, in February 1914, petitioned the court for guardianship of Bobbie. They claimed Jane had sent four year old Bobbie to his father in Wyoming and had "abandoned him and contributed nothing to his support." The paper stated, "one of the hardest fought legal battles ever waged in the courts of Park county," resulted in the court awarding custody to his mother Jane Allman.

Dudines at the Pat Kelly Ranch around 1917. Photo courtesy of Mark Simpers.

During these tragic episodes, Pat Kelly was administrator of the estates and paying up bills. (Clyde's funeral cost $139.25 and Hazel's funeral cost $255.)

Back in Kansas City, Mr. and Mrs. Walter Scott are divorced. Walter Scott held an executive position with the *Kansas City Star* newspaper. In May of 1914, a Cody paper states Patrick Kelly married Mrs. Walter M. Scott, mother of the deceased Hazel Scott Pepper. Also, in that same month, the "new" Mrs. Pat (Maud) Kelly, grandmother of Clyde Richard (Dick) Pepper petitions the court for guardianship of Dick.

For awhile after all these tragedies and legal battles life settled down and news from the Pat Kelly ranch is infrequent. In 1920 Kelly bought an eleven passenger Studebaker automobile. Perhaps it was this same car that is mentioned several years later, in the November 28, 1923, issue of the *Cody Enterprise* which stated Pat Kelly in a snow storm, near the Thurmond/Early place, ran into a road truck and in the accident nearly scalped himself. He drove into Cody where Dr. Trueblood sewed his scalp back together, then he drove back home.

Top, First Green Lantern. Bill Simpers on horse, Talba Simpers on porch. Anhauser-Busch Budweiser advertising near-beer. This was during Prohibition.

Middle, Green Lantern with later additions, gasoline pump, six frame-and-tent cabins west of creek. In front is a Hupmobile with elk antlers on radiator. These tourist friends from Indiana were guided by Ben Simpers and stayed in Robber's Roost Cabin in Trout Creek Basin.

Bottom, new Green Lantern near bridge. Two Conoco pumps one for white gasoline and one for Ethyl.

Photos courtesy Mark Simpers.

Sometime in the mid 1920's Pat Kelly disappeared and to this day is one of the unexplained mysteries of the North Fork.

Several years after the disappearance of Pat, Walter Scott, Mrs. Pat Kelly's ex, comes back to the Kelly ranch from Kansas City but according to Gladys Fenex Andren who lived there at the time, Walter had "no use" for his former wife, Maud, and she returns to live in Kansas City and he continues to live on the ranch.

Dick entered the Wapiti school in 1919 at the age of 7

Kelly House below. Catherine and Clara Bradford. Photo courtesy Park County Archives.

and attended until 1928. While cleaning a gun in 1926 he suffered a shot in his hand, perhaps that is why he did not attend school during the 1926-27 school year, and he stayed in school only three months in 1928, he had turned sixteen, a robust young man, and probably too old for country grade school. He found ready employment as a horse wrangler and guide on dude ranches. He was a likeable young man and remembered for the caring attention he gave his grandfather Scott in later years.

By 1942 Dick Pepper, on legal papers, no longer went by the name Clyde Richard Pepper, he preferred the name Walter R. Pepper. Grandfather Walter J. Scott gave a warranty deed to North Fork property to Walter R. Pepper, October 13, 1942. According to Lonnie Royal, Dick did marry while he still lived on the North Fork. His wife, Alice, was an alcoholic. Later, Dick moved out to California. His good friend and neighbor, Lonnie said, "Dick Pepper died in a logging traffic accident in California."

In the late fall of 1929 Mr. and Mrs. John Fenex and their four children, Jack, Gladys, Lorraine, and Bill moved to the Kelly/Pepper ranch and stayed until the spring of 1930, when Carl Sauerwein acquired the property and did much to restore its productivity.

WHIT CREEK

William Whitworth moved from his location near the mouth of the river up to the creek that bears his name. Apparently he was a squatter on the land. Pat Kelly had the first water right dating back to November 16, 1897. His second water right on the creek dates from May 2, 1904.

The Elmer Dickensen family in 1914, lived in an old cabin alongside Whit Creek, and Elmer worked on road maintenance. When the Stonebridge reservoir went out it flooded their home and they had to seek refuge on the roof of the cabin. Neighbors helped them

Above, Four logs make a load.
Middle, George Mix-Whit Creek Sawmill 1938.
Bottom, John E. Mix on cat pulling a sledge-load of logs.
Photos courtesy of Mabel Mix Durbin.

shovel out the debris after the "flood".

Ben R. and Mary Morris Simpers, and the three oldest children came out from Rockport, Indiana, for health reasons. Their health problem was diagnosed as tuberculosis (or consumption as it was called then) and they slept out-of-door winter and summer for quite a long time and finally were pronounced cured.[7] Mrs. Dahlem was Ben Simper's sister, this probably helped the Simpers decide on Wyoming. The family, eventually included: Morris, William, Charles, and Mark, and girls, Talba, Thelma, Mary, and Norma. The Simpers spent the winter of 1913 working on the Sant Watkins place on upper Sage Creek. In 1914 they moved onto the Stonebridge place and were there two years, in 1916 they moved to Whit Creek and prudently moved the old cabin farther back from the bank of the creek. Simpers and deMauriac bought the Whit Creek property in partnership, but the Simpers soon bought out deMauriac and started the first food service for tourists in Wapiti Valley. They built a house to the south of the old road just before it crossed Whit Creek. Here they cooked fried chicken "to go" and sold to tourists. It went over so well they added a room and put tables in it and started serving chicken dinners. Then they added a larger dining room. They called it the "Green Lantern" lunch station after a place they had known in Indiana, it was a profitable venture but required a lot of work.

In 1931, the Simpers sold their place to

F. O. Sanzenbacker and started building a new tourist facility on the south bank of the river, a little west of the old (second) bridge over the river at that narrow gorge. The new bridge span is much wider and longer than the second bridge. At first they called it Green Lantern Tourist Camp, but when they sold, the new owner soon changed the name to Wapiti Lodge. After Prohibition was repealed the Green Lantern had a license to sell beer, perhaps the first license on the Northfork.

Lora Sanzenbacker was a sister of Retta Westerman and came from Arkansas not too far from where Everett Dickson had lived, although they probably didn't know each other there. Through the Westermans, F. O. "Sox" Sanzenbacker, who after WWI had attended Ohio State University for one year, and Lora, started working for the deMauriacs. The North Fork appealed to them and they bought the Simpers' place, where they farmed and Sox worked on the second bridge and did road maintenance. This was during the Great Depression. Times were tough, even on the North Fork.

Above, Whit Creek Sawmill and logs in 1938.
Below, George Mix and Shorty Bonaue - Whit Creek sawmill.

Photos courtesy Mabel Mix Darrah.

THE WHIT CREEK SAWMILL

Mabel Mix Darrah in 1995 remembered the Depression years she spent at the Whit Creek Sawmill. In 1937 George Mix bought H. N. Black's Green Creek sawmill and moved it to Whit Creek, and Black continued to harvest timber. Mix went into in the sawmill with Burt Stevenson. A number of cabins were built and families started moving in, Stevenson brought his wife Buelah and daughter Joyce. George's brother John M. Mix and his son Ralph drove the delivery truck and another son Elon worked at the mill. The Forest Service marked the trees to be felled and the sawyers went to work.

Timber workers were Glen Fish, who moved his family there; Vic McCoy and wife Leona (George Mix's oldest daughter); Les McCormick; Carl Stalder; John Beales; Gilbert Hunter and wife Margaret (a Mix daughter); Bob Darrah, and Hank Darrah and wife, Mabel (a Mix daughter). George, competent from long years of experience, manned the saw. Sometimes there were as many as 1500 logs waiting to be put through. The younger men rolled logs to the saw, took out the boards from the saw and put them through the edger,and moved them onto a carriage that carried them out to be stacked. These fellows were Don Springs, and Alma Slater nicknamed "Mazoo," who kept the humor light. Paul and Bob Geiger and Shorty Bonaue also worked there. George Mix's son John E. Mix kept logs in place and stacked with the Cat, while Stevenson worked at the mill site.

The women kept busy, Buelah Stevenson did the books and payroll. Emma Mix kept a record of the loads of lumber going out. Mrs. Black cooked for the men who stayed in the bunkhouse, helped by Lorena Mix when she was not attending the Wapiti school.

For recreation the men organized a softball team and played other teams from Cody or North Fork. Picnics up the river or Sunday dinners in each others houses were recreation.

The mill closed down for awhile in winter and gave everyone a rest and vacation. Evenings were spent listening to the radio, including programs like "Amos and Andy", "Ozzie and Harriet", "Fibber McGee and Molly", the ladies liked Oxydol's Own Ma Perkins best, laughing and crying with her every day.

Rent was free and timber slabs from the mill kept their pot bellied stoves going. Kerosene lamps and gas lanterns were not expensive and they had no telephone. Cards, Monopoly, dominos, and "gab fests" rounded out any free time. Sometimes they loaded up a car and drove to Cody for the movies.

In 1938-1939 Morrison-Knudson bought lumber for the Heart Mountain siphon and tunnel. Utah Construction bought lumber for their projects and almost every lodge or home in the river valley had a piece of lumber from the mill, said Mabel. By 1940 war clouds were forming and some of the older men went off to work for the war effort as well as George's three older daughters. All the family scattered except their two youngest daughters, Lorena and Gertrude. Sometime during 1942-1945, Mabel said Japanese internees from the Heart Mountain Relocation Camp were deployed to the Whit Creek sawmill. During their spare time the Japanese set to work to landscape and beautify the grounds, they made many artistic craft objects, including a cedar lamp for George Mix. Mabel treasured many memories from the sawmill and credited her father for his knowledge and long years of experience in sawmill operation.

WEST OF JIM CREEK

Oscar Montgomery took up a homestead on Jim Creek north of John Yeates. Due west was the homestead taken up by Henry Westerman, he relinquished and Robert Holbrook "Brooks" Borron took over this homestead and received his patent in 1926. The Dunn Creek drainage is west of Jim Creek and seldom has water. In early years no one built on Dunn Creek. They built the Borron homestead cabin farther west down near the river. Brooks and Oscar Montgomery fenced their places together according to Huldah Borron, who said, "It was not a place where we could earn a living. Carl Thompson, a sheepman, paid us $100 a year for taking the sheep through the place on their way over to Sunlight. Brooks worked for deMauriacs, and then he rented the Hollister place one year. Then we moved up to what was called the Johnson Place on the south side of the river, Leggs place was south of us and J. F. Kellys on the east. Our first child, Margie, was born when we lived on Brook's homestead,

Ruth, Pat and Bob also were born when we lived on the North Fork, but I went to the Powell hospital when the babies were born."

One of the tragedies of the North Fork was an outbreak of polio in early August of 1930, Huldah Borron recalled, "I believe Dorothy Shull got it first, and Donald Legg came down with it about the same time. Dorothy was staying with the Leggs, and we bought milk from them and Ruth got it. She was about three and one half years old."

In an interview with Jim Montgomery March 25, 1994, he recalled he was visiting the Borrons when they lived on the Johnson Place, Ruth was out in the yard and suddenly lost control of her muscles. Jim said, "Ruth cried, 'I can't walk', so I picked her up and carried her into the house."

Huldah recalled, "Donald got a paralyzed arm and Dorothy had it in her leg and had to wear a brace for a long time. Ruth was paralyzed in both legs. Brooks and I put hot packs on her and massaged her legs."

Brook's father, Bill Borron worked at Holm Lodge during the summers but at this time he was laid up with a sprained ankle and was spending the time with his son and family. Huldah said, "Granddad went to Dr. Howe and the doctor made up such a strong liniment for the ankle that he didn't use it. When Ruth got better Brooks and I talked it over and decided to use it on Ruth's legs. The first few times she didn't even feel it and finally she began to get feeling back in her legs." The Borrons continued to work with Ruth's legs. One would take her under the arms and the other moved her legs until she could walk again, and she had a little cane that she used.

Other complications arose when polio struck the family. Huldah said, "I was nursing Bob at the time and when I heard it was polio Ruth had, I instantly dried up, so we tried to feed him something else and nothing agreed with him."

"Brooks and Sox Sanzenbacker were working on the (second) bridge and Lora Sanzenbacker had just had a baby in Billings and had a formula for her, so Sox got it and gave it to Brooks then we ordered the Pet milk and Karo syrup from town and the baby thrived on it."

Dr. Mills of Powell was the County Health Officer and he visited the North Fork frequently to check on the patients. In Cody there were victims also, including Jess Davis, Beth Wilson, and Glenn Newton, Junior.

Next, on the north side of the river stood the Coy cabin, all alone. This little cabin out on the prairie, north of he river became a landmark. A social worker from Chicago by the name of Geraldine Coy "picked up the mortgage" on the Brooks Borron homestead across the river from the Wapiti Lodge. Here she built a small cabin on the dry, tree-less prairie and spent her summers there for many years. One summer she hired young Elmer Kelly, son of the J.F. Kellys, as horse wrangler and general handyman. One of Elmer's jobs was scrubbing the cabin floor, not a job he thought appropriate for a horse wrangler he told his friend young John Yeates.

Ester Johansson and Ernest Rueger at P—P Dude Ranch.

HOLLISTER PLACE

Across the river from the Coy cabin is Rand Creek. Lee Borron took up land on each side of Rand Creek just west of Pat Kelly on Whit Creek by 1904. Lee Borron married Pauline Nietheimer who was from Austria. In the 1910 census he was listed as age thirty four, Pauline as twenty four, and they had at that time one child, Clara, age four months. Lee sold his land to Elizabeth Hollister, and worked for the Hollisters. Dwight Hollister took up a small piece of land on both sides of the river, north of this parcel. Dwight Hollister graduated from Princeton, class of 1897, and the New York School of Law. The Hollisters married in 1902 according to the 1910 census both Dwight and Elizabeth Hollister gave their ages as thirty-three years old and both had been born in New Jersey. Their eleven month old son Dwight had been born at Elizabeth's sister's home, Mrs. Stanley Christopher, in Kansas City. They had only the one child, sometimes called "Bucky".

During their first years on the Northfork they were gracious hosts, enjoying a bountiful life, Mrs. Hollister enjoyed hunting, and they entertained nicely, and traveled often. Good looking, with an aristocratic bearing, Dwight Hollister was elected to the State Legislature as a Republican from newly established Park County in 1910.

Hollister place east of the Chinese Wall. Photo courtesy of Elmor Jones.

The *Wyoming Stockgrower and Farmer* for August 27, 1909, stated, "Frank Pollack has gone to the Hollister ranch on North Fork to put in the foundation for a large addition to the Hollister mansion which will include a basement for a heating plant and about (sic) five rooms above."

Hollister liked automobiles and had the first car on the North Fork, a Buick which came out on the railroad and arrived in 1910. Hollister tried to run an agency to sell cars and in August of 1911, he advertised in the *Park County Enterprise* a "Model 21, 5 passenger touring car with 'detachable door to be removed in hot weather'", the price was $750 , a high price for those times when Model T Fords sold for $300 to $400. Hollister's dogs often made news; he lost a Great Dane brindle pup in 1910, and in 1914, Joe Magill gave him an Irish Wolfhound named "Kerry."

Through all the years Bill Borron and Dwight Hollister remained friends. Bill worked off and on at the ranch, guided them on hunting trips, and in January of 1916, Bill put up 60 tons of 18 inch ice for them.

The Hollisters had a hook-up on the Forest Service telephone line. Their number was 6F3, three rings on the party line.

The Hollisters hired many people over the years. Olive Watt (Nordquist) was a relative of Art Holman (Art's mother, Annie Hutsonpillar Holman who later married Ed Grinder, was Olive's aunt) she came to the North Fork to work at Hollisters and she helped look after young Dwight.

Lawrence Nordquist of the P Bar P rode down one day to use the telephone and two weeks after that he and Olive were married. Olive recalled, "After I was married, Mrs. Hollister sadly told me, almost with tears in her eyes, she didn't have much to give me for a wedding gift. She put around my neck an old lavaliere on a gold chain. It was set with pearls and light green stones. Of course, I didn't appreciate it because it was out of style, but no doubt the gems were real."

Olive Nordquist also recalled, "Mrs. Hollister told me one time she could have married a rich older man but instead married a poor young man. I think she regretted living poor in her later years. Her sister in Kansas City bought her diamonds as a last fund for her to live on. Mrs. Hollister went to her sister at the end where she died."

All the Hollister employees said they were kind and nice to work for. Huldah Borron said Mrs. Hollister used to have her hair "done" in Cody. When she could no longer afford that she had Brooks cut it off. Emma Kelly said when she came to the North Fork in 1917, Orilla Downing cooked for the Hollisters, Henry Westerman did chores and Retta served as the Hollister's maid.

When the western writer, Hal Evarts and his family were living at Green Creek, their young son, Hal junior, was invited to sleep over with Dwight, junior. In a letter written to Ethel Montgomery October 10, 1978, the younger Evarts wrote, "I spent one night at their son's bedroom and it was more like a toy store than a place to sleep and hang your clothes."

Young Dwight went to the Wapiti school and to Cody High School

Ed Jones the cook at the Frost and Richard Ranch, feeds a black bear from the cook wagon during a Yellowstone Park Tourist trip. Photo courtesy Elmor Jones.

where he unhappily did not 'fit in.' He attended the University of Wyoming for awhile and during the time of the Civilian Conservation Corp camp at Clearwater, he worked there for awhile. Later he went to California and the neighbors lost track of him.

In later years Mrs. Hollister became a recluse. Vayle "Bill" Bosler recalled in an interview in 1990 his mother worked for the Hollisters and Mrs. Hollister stayed in bed all day. Bill's mother would hear a tap, tap, tap at night and couldn't figure out what made it. One night she opened the door a crack to Mrs. Hollister's bedroom and discovered the sound was made by a heavy ring on Mrs. Hollister's finger, tapping the table as she dealt out cards while playing solitaire at night.

During the years deMauriac was expanding his holdings he bought the Hollister land and paid for it in September of 1951, according to county records. Everett and Lillian Dixon moved up there in 1937 and lived in the three room log cabin for fourteen years while Everett was in charge of the farming. Later, Everett and Lillian bought the Hans Nelson place on South Fork, that home having been built by Smith Murray after he sold the Trout Creek Ranch. When the Jack Murrays left Trout Creek they moved into the Smith Murray home on South Fork for awhile, later owned by Hans Nelson.

Orilla Downing was one of the Hollister's last employees. After Mrs. Hollister's death she and Dwight were married. He later took his own life.

The Hollister ranch lay just to the east of the Chinese Wall, and Olive Watt Nordquist remembered taking young Dwight to play on the Wall.

FROST AND RICHARD RANCH

J. W. Arnsberger gave his name to the small stream at Frost and Richard ranch, this creek does not flow far enough to reach the North Fork river. H. B. Robertson took the first water right on the creek on October 10, 1906. Originally it was called the Frank Grinder ranch and H. B. Robertson bought it from Arthur M. Plumb. Plumb shot himself through the heart with a .45-.90 caliber Winchester. According to the *Wyoming Stockgrower and Farmer* for September 6, 1906, Plumb was despondent and went to the bunk house and killed himself. Jack Rollinson describes Plumb as a wife and animal abuser and wrote, "One day he sat down in the bunkhouse with his rifle and blew out what he called his brains."

Fred Richard and Ned Frost formed a partnership and bought the Robertson property with plans for a large dude ranching operation. Frost figured the fur market was very profitable so he spent the winter of 1909-1910 running three long trap lines over in the Clark area and cashed in with a profit of $9,000.

Richard and Frost had started with hunting and pack trips by 1907, and one of their earliest most famous dudes was Malcolm S. Mackey, noted financier from New York City. On a bear hunt in June of 1910, Mackey killed three "fine grizzlies".

In July of 1910 Frost and Richard took out a party for a thirty-one day trip on the upper Greybull. Carl Johansson hired out as one of the guides for this trip. In July of 1911 a party of thirty two traveled to the Park. One of the members of this eighteen day Park trip was Sir Robert Borwick of London, England, a world traveler and hunter. By April of the following year the big main ranch house was completed. Phil Hardifer built the winding staircase in the house that had fifteen rooms and two bathrooms, employing more than a dozen carpenters.

To handle all the dudes Frost and Richard bought twelve dude wagons, freight and cook wagons and buggies. Frost took 114 people with his moveable camp through the Park on one occasion.

In April of 1913, *The Park County Enterprise* stated the Frost and Richard Camping Company had incorporated with stock of $25,000. To upgrade their milk cows they bought a registered Jersey bull from B.C. Rumsey.

Bob Richard note leather vest and brands on horse. Photo Courtesy of Park County Archives.

The year 1913 was memorable for hunting parties, the Buffalo Bill - Prince of Monaco party on the North Fork and Spend-A-Million Gates party in the Thorofare. Both these hunting parties have been extensively written up in many articles and books. Pete Nordquist worked for Frost and Richard on that trip and received one of the fur coats Gates generously gave away.

According to Ted Sherwin's memoirs, "Some of the Frost Ranch guests were movie people, actors, producers, and even the first movie 'censor,' Will Hayes. One of their Hollywood guests, a character actor, used to like to dress up in Indian costumes and sit on the front porch at the Trail Shop when the buses stopped. He allowed the tourists to pose with him and if they offered him money, he took it, usually giving it to us kids after the buses were gone, or buying ice cream for the other Frost Ranch dudes, who had been watching his performance from a distance."

During World War I the dude business declined and Fred Richard tried running a band of sheep in 1915. In 1918 Frost and Richard dissolve their partnership and Richard takes over the ranch but Frost keeps some land and buildings for his pack and hunting business. The Frost family moved to town.

In 1926, Don and Carl Wagoner rented the Richard ranch for two years. Don, newly married to Mary Martin Gipe, lived in a small cabin close to the main house and Carl lived in the other one. Mary recalled in 1993, she put her son, Martin Gipe, age seven, in the second grade in 1927 through 1928 at the Wapiti School. Don and Carl, while living on Whit Creek, experienced the Wapiti tent school by the river. Carl Wagoner later married Clytie Fuson, and Don married Mary Martin Gipe. Both Don and Carl died young. Clytie married Clifford Williams and Mary married Fred Ebert.

Before her marriage Clytie (Fuson) Wagoner had worked for Richards doing dining room work. Clytie came from the Belfry-Clarks Fork valley. Ella Andren worked there also. One time one of the cabin girls got tick fever and had to leave so the dining room girls helped with cabins and laundry. Then the cook got an infected foot and as she was Christian Scientist she sought no medical help but sat on a chair and did what she could to supervise Clytie as she cooked. Clytie recalled in 1994 that they were so short-handed, Fred Richard helped with the dish washing.

Above, Fred Richard center front, Ed Jones, "phonograph Jones", cook with his hand on young Richard boy, along with dudes and dudines. Photo Courtesy Elmor Jones. Below, Frost and Richard camp in Yellowstone.

Fred Richard wanted to build a cabin for his help, so Carl and Don helped the carpenter and they built a nice log house down near the river. The house had a kitchen, living room and two bedrooms, but no interior lining so it proved very cold. They had a water barrel and the usual outside facilities. Not far away, up on the bench above the river were the Bradford Place and the J. F. Kelly Ranch. Elmer Kelly was the same age as Martin Gipe so they walked to and from school together, Martin would have to split off and go down to the river bottom. The Richards later moved this log house up to the main ranch buildings.

In 1930 business had picked up and the Ranch had three 'saddle tours' and thirty guests, but the Great Depression was a difficult time for dude ranchers.

Frost and Richard hired many men and trained them well in the horse packing and dude business. Carl Johansson learned guiding and packing while working for them and E. L. "Phonograph" Jones early gained fame as a camp cook on their wagon trips.

GREEN CREEK

William E. Green took up land at the mouth of the creek that was first called Green's Creek. Then around the beginning of the 1920's it carried the name on some maps as Cabin Creek, to be replaced later with the name Green Creek. Green's water right dated from May 3, 1901. In the 1910 census W. E. Green was from Texas and was age thirty one. His wife Maude McMullen Green was from Nebraska, and age 30. They had one son, Hershel, born in Wyoming in 1904. Will Richard bought William Green's land along Green Creek and later sold to Hal Evarts and J. F. Kelly. Farther up Green Creek in the early days, H. N. Black operated a sawmill before moving his mill over to Whit Creek for George Mix. There is still evidence of the slide where logs were slid off Table Mountain, and an old cabin is still known as the sawmill cabin. Martha Kinkade Todd remembered hearing that Mrs. Tex Thomas, the nurse, lived in the cabin.

In 1904, W. E. Green built a headgate across from the mouth of Big Creek and dug a five mile long ditch to irrigate land north of his ditch. This was called Green's Big Creek Ditch.

Hal G. Evarts of Hutchinson, Kansas, brought his bride to the Frost and Richard ranch in the spring of 1914 for a bear hunt. He bought the Will Richard place on Green Creek. It had a white prefabricated house on it with gambrel roof that became one of the landmarks on the river. The house gained the reputation of being very cold in winter, someone described it as a "thin shell." Even with his feet in the oven and fortified with hot toddies, Evarts couldn't keep warm enough for his hand to hold a pen to write his western stories.

In 1915, Hal Evarts and Will Richard started a "fur farm", they planned to raise skunks first and then black foxes. They built pens and had plans to purchase 75 skunks to start production. *The Northern Wyoming Herald* wrote, "a simple surgical operation on the skunks when they are very young renders the skunks harmless," meaning that the gland containing the skunk's defensive spray was removed. In early days "Alaskan sable and Black martin" were names invented to create a market for skunk pelts. When "truth in advertising" laws required skunk to be called skunk, the long black fur lost its appeal.[8]

Hal Evarts Jr.'s mother recalled "the batches of corn meal mush, flavored with chunks of elk liver she cooked up endlessly to feed the skunks."[9] The younger Evarts wrote his father had to go off to the Army in 1918, and had to leave the care of his animals to Will Richards. He wrote, "Something happened to the skins in the process of curing and Dad received not a penny from his several years of work. Along came the Armistice and he was broke, no job and a family to support. That's what really started him on his writing career. Sheer necessity."

Ethel Busch came out from Missouri to take up a homestead on Ralston bench and in 1911 she went to work for the Hollisters. While there she met Oscar Montgomery whom she married. They homesteaded, worked for deMauriacs eleven years and settled on Green Creek. In 1923, Oscar and Ethel Montgomery bought the Hal Evarts' place on Green Creek, the Sullivans had been living there. The Montgomerys lived on the place for ten years until 1933 when they moved to Mountain View lodge a few miles up river. Later they moved back to the white house on Green Creek and Ethel Montgomery lived there the rest of her life. Upstream from Montgomery on Green Creek lived the Sullivans.

In 1913, Charles Sullivan headed west from Nebraska with his three sons, Walter, Bryan, and Bert, in a wagon. According to the 1920 Census, Charles had been born in Illinois, and son Bryan, 23 had been born in Nebraska as had Bert who was age 20. They came through Yellowstone Park and down the North Fork, found work near Trout Creek and liked the country so well they stayed and took up homesteads on Green Creek. They were log builders and also worked as dude wranglers, but are most famous for their musical ability. Charles played the fiddle, Bryan the banjo and Bert chorded on the piano, and they played for many dances.

During the tragic Blackwater fire, Bert distinguished himself by assisting, in saving the lives of 49 panic stricken boys. Bert Sullivan was in charge of a group of men from the Bureau of Public Roads called in to fight the fire. Post, of Buffalo, Wyoming, urged the Tensleep CCC boys to climb to a small rock ledge and helped by Paul Tyrrell and Sullivan they kept the men prone on the ground while the fire swept the ledge. Sullivan received the American Forest Fire Medal for heroism.

THE KELLY PLACE

Joseph Franklin Kelly sold his saloon in Dubois, Wyoming, and met his future wife, Emma, in a tearoom in Spokane. Emma Gentner Kelly born in Germany on October 21, 1890, came to the United States with a cousin in 1913.

The *Northern Wyoming Herald* noted that "J.F. Kelly, said to be a wealthy westerner, has purchased the Will Richard place on Northfork for $4,000."* When the Kellys drove into Cody in their Ford in August of 1917, they wondered where they could camp, so they inquired of a lady they met on the street and she directed them to the school ground, where travelers with camp outfits were in the habit of camping. Later they learned the lady was Julia Cody Goodman, sister of Buffalo Bill. Unfortunately, while they were camped on the school grounds the family had $175 stolen, so they found it much safer after they moved to Mrs. Kepford's house on Alger Avenue for a short time. On their North Fork ranch, where they settled in 1917, they raised cattle and farmed. Emma raised chickens and turkeys, had a large garden, and sold cream and eggs.

They bought land from Will Richard that had been homesteaded by W. E. Green. The Kelly property depended on irrigation water from the North Fork Valley Ditch, which superceded Green's ditch with a headgate farther upstream inside the Forest Reserve.

"J.F." was rather short, heavy set, and enjoyed smoking his pipe when he came in from the field to rest. Brown-eyed Emma, an energetic five feet two inches tall, is proud of the fact she and the state of Wyoming are the same age and celebrated their centennials in 1990. The Kellys had three children, Joe and Elmer and daughter Barbara.

One time Emma and six year old Barbara caught a ride to town with Wylie Sherwin to consult a doctor for Barbara who was sick. Sherwin's car was forced into the ditch by the erratic driving of bootlegger Jack Morrison which caused the car door to fly open. The child fell out and under the wheel and crushed by the car. Jack Morrison was acquitted of manslaughter after four and a half day's jury trial. Mrs. Kelly remembered, "I tried to reach for the door to close it but I should have hung on to her. I think about it a lot and feel guilty I didn't grab her."

Jim Milstead rented the Graves Place east of Kellys and Mrs. Milstead was the first neighbor woman Emma met. West of Kellys was the Johnson Place, part of the old Vinnie Grinder estate and owned by Elizabeth Hollister. George S. Johnson and wife Melvina worked for Hollisters and lived there at first so it was always called the Johnson Place. When Emma remembered it Hurricane Bill Herrick lived there, and at one time Brooks and Huldah Borron lived there. The Kellys lived on the North Fork forty three years, and it would have been a fitting memorial if road 6CU had been called Kelly Lane.

GRAVES - BRADFORD PLACE

John H. "Jack" Graves, of Buffalo, New York friend of Bronson Rumsey, came west in June of 1902. By 1907 Graves started building up a dude ranch on land he was buying from Elizabeth Hollister. The 1910 census listed ninety seven people on the North Fork. Among those listed were John H. Graves, age thirty four, born in New York as was his wife Ethel, and their two young sons, Davis D. six years, and John D. eight years. Graves planned to build a big log house to run dudes. By 1913 Graves ran an ad in the *Northern Wyoming Herald* that his Three Bar ranch was for sale: "320 acres and could handle 30 dudes". About 1915 the Graves moved to town, and in May of 1917 the Graves family moved to California where Graves went into the garage business. The Hollisters had to take back the Graves property.

In 1915 a very shady character, Dr. W. R. Shore, leased the Graves place from Hollisters, Shore had a bad reputation in Red Lodge, he illegally killed game, he had a $25,000 alienation suit filed against him by a mine bookkeeper in Gardiner, Montana. In 1914 Shore's first wife committed suicide. In the fall of 1915 he picked up $100 that didn't belong to him in the Cody First National Bank. It was no loss to the North Fork when Shore moved on.[10] Then Jim Milsteads rented the place for awhile.

In 1920 the Charles Whiting Bradford family came out to the Richard Ranch (formerly Frost and Richard ranch) as dudes. They were living in California but Bradford had ranched and farmed in Idaho and always wanted another ranch.

The Bradfords spent time on their ranch and daughter Catherine briefly attended the Wapiti school, at times riding her horse to school and putting it up in the barn in back. She remembered classmates Audrey McClain, Bob Richard, and young Dwight "Bucky" Hollister.

Catherine Bradford married Frank McCelland in Hollywood in February of 1932. The Bradford ranch was sold in the 60's.

JAMES A. LEGG PLACE

In 1922 James Legg of Lovell rented a portion of Richard's ranch to farm, and in 1924 he moved to the North Fork. This property goes back to original homesteaders, the Grinders, Vina, (Vinnie) Grinder Stephanson had an original water right dated September 7, 1901 from Canyon Creek.

Maude Legg had been a school teacher over on Crooked Creek, north of Lovell, Wyoming, and knew the Huntingtons and Sherwins there.

James and Maude had eight children, seven of whom graduated from college and five of whom served in World War II. In 1932 Jim planted 3000 trees obtained from the state of Wyoming, and the mature trees are an outstanding shelter-belt landmark of the upper North Fork valley.

Don Legg was one of the polio victims. In 1931 Worth Legg, age fifteen, had to be taken to Cody for treatment for tick fever. The well-liked and industrious Legg family grew strawberries and turkeys in the early 1930's.

ELSWORTH H. JENKINS MOUNTAIN VIEW LODGE

In the early 1920's the Jenkins family settled on Canyon Creek. Nellie Jenkins obtained a patent for the property in 1923. In 1924 Nellie Jenkins sold some property to Wiley Sherwin, and in 1925, Sherwin sold property back to Jenkins. E. H. Jenkins drove the stage for a number of years, probably from 1923 to 1927. Jenkins had ability as a tinkering type of inventor and could take portions of different types of trucks and attach them together. According to Ted Sherwin's memoirs,"Elsworth Jenkins was an eccentric. He lived on Canyon Creek with his three boys and his fat sister, Nellie, who ran the household." He also had a medical problem and goat milk and goat cheese were his preferred diet. They also raised Belgian hares, one night a badger killed thirty nine of their hares.[11]

In 1926 Jenkins opened a store, called the Wapiti Mercantile and also built a large garage under the store, but by 1932 the Keil Company of Montana had to foreclose on the mortgage they held on Mountain View Lodge. This had proved to be a marginal venture and because of the Great Depression, went under.

In 1933 Oscar and Ethel Montgomery moved to Mountain View Lodge. The Keil Company sold to Ethel Montgomery in 1933, and in 1941 the property was sold to Craig Thomas.

When the Montgomerys owned Mountain View they rented a cabin to Captain Watkins and his wife, while Watkins worked at the CCC camp at Clearwater. Jim Montgomery remembered Captain Watkins as a "dapper young military officer and his wife, Marjorie, as a southern belle type." Mrs. Watkins got acquainted with Al Clarke who had bought the old Oscar Montgomery homestead on Jim Creek. Mrs. Watkins and Al had a mutual interest in fishing in the river and soon developed a romance. Little Jimmy Montgomery played spy and learned a lot about life by watching the trysting couple. When Watkins learned of the affair he told his wife they had better get a divorce so she could marry Al. After they married they went back east and Al committed suicide. She returned to Cody and was here but a short time and she committed suicide in the Irma Hotel on February 8, 1939.

The Montgomerys sold to Craig Thomas, principal of Cody High School for many years, and his wife, Marge, who taught at Wapiti School, and the Barney Goffs. Both families lived there, the Goffs lived there a couple years. The Goff girls attended Wapiti school until the family moved back to town in 1939. The Thomas' had a boy and a girl, the boy Lyle, later went by the name Craig and in 1994 was elected to the United States Senate in a Republican landslide.

CIRCLE H - BIG CREEK

Phil Hardifer took up the property up Big Creek and sold it to Manley E. "Budd" Hall in 1926. Bill Leatherman built the original log cabin and Wyoming Hardifer was born in the cabin.

Alice Chauvet came to Cody with her parents, arriving on October 11, 1906, via Toluca, Montana on the train. Alice married Phil Hardifer, a carpenter, and they named their daughter, Wyoming. In 1911 they took up a homestead on Big Creek, living there until 1918. Budd Hall first came to the Cody country when he was fifteen. At the age of twenty two he enlisted in World War I Air Service as an aerial gunner with the 361st Air Service Squadron. Budd Hall was brother of Elmon Hall, husband of Anna Lucylle Hall of Mooncrest Ranch. After Budd and Chella Martin (no relation to B.F. Martin's) were married in 1926, they soon acquired the secluded property on Big Creek and built up a dude ranch. By 1930, a Northern Pacific brochure stated they had tent-house cabins, a separate assembly hall, and shower baths. They specialized in forty day horseback trips for boys through Yellowstone Park and had space for fifteen guests at a cost of $45 per week.

Chella drove the North Fork stage between 1927 and 1930. Chella recalled in an interview, " Most of the people on the river got their mail in canvas sacks. Some like the deMauriacs had a locked sack. I delivered mail from Willard Rhoads on Rattlesnake Creek to Holm Lodge and sometimes to Pahaska in the summer. Sometimes I hauled trunks and passengers. When Miss Shawver and Billy Howell had Holm Lodge I used to bring their money into the bank and deposit it. That would scare me to death. I would take everything out from under the seat and put the money in the bottom and put the tools and stuff on top of the money."

Chella continued, "I never hauled any whiskey to town. Sometimes we had the law officers in the back seat, covered up so they could sneak into the area where there was a still, during Prohibition." One time Chella took them up to the Circle H and the law officers slept out and went out early up Hardifer Draw to make a raid. When they got there they found the note, "Just a little too damn late".

Chella recalled that cloudbursts were common where they lived. She said, "There were no roads into Big Creek when we bought the place. We built the road. Cloudbursts along the creek would take out hunks of the road. The cloudbursts were wicked. There are two forks to Big Creek, East Fork and West Fork. We used to time the cloudbursts. It would take an hour for the flood water to come down the East Fork and two hours for West Fork. When the storm ran the ridges we could see the lightning strikes and the roar was terrible."

In 1932 Mr. and Mrs. Bart Lewis bought property on Big Creek below the Halls. Bart Lewis' leg was burned when lightning struck a tent he was working in and it killed his dog.

In an interview in 1984, Budd said he had worked for Hal Evarts, and Jim Milstead when he rented the Graves (Bradford) place. Budd said, "Back on Grinder mountain is the Grinder Rock. When high water is over the snow covering it is gone and you can see the Grinder Rock." Mark Simpers stated when a big rock in the middle of the snow-covered saddle on Grinder mountain was exposed it meant the high water had peaked.

Budd was personally involved in the Blackwater Fire. He had a pack outfit and crew of men and went in to retrieve the bodies of the victims. "There was a spring and they were all kneeling down with their heads in the water. I packed those men out of there. Rigor mortis had set in and we had to break them down to get them on the pack horses."

Other early residents of Big Creek were L. Chester Freeman who planned to build a seven-room house with bath on Big Creek in 1917. For a short time Claude Shull and L. C. Freeman were going into the dude business and called their place the Rim Rock Ranch Company. At the end of January 1917, the the Cody newspaper stated "L. C. Freeman of the Rim Rock Ranch went into business in Cody in the Western Auto and Garage Company."

This short-lived Claude Shull and Freeman association should not be confused with the later Rim Rock Ranch on Canyon Creek.

When Chris Pike was first married he brought his bride, Winifred, to the L. C. Freeman Ranch where he worked. Chet moved to town and went into the trucking business, and in the lumber business with his brother Sox Freeman who bought him out in 1926.

HARDY SHULL PLACE

William "Dad" Edwards homesteaded the place on Half Mile Creek, receiving his patents in 1908 and 1911. He sold to Hardy Shull in 1915. According to the 1920 census, Hardy Shull was forty one years old and had been born in Missouri, but his father was from Watuga County, North Carolina. Hardy's younger brother Claude followed a few years later.

Hardy came west in 1900, or even earlier and worked on various ranches, and counted George Marquette as a friend. He worked for Charles Marston when he ranched on the land later covered by the reservoir. Hardy worked felling trees for logs for four winters and on the log drives and suffered from arthritis in later years from working in the icy river water for long periods of time.

Hardy met his future wife, Delia Cody, at the Morris Ranch, she was a sister of Mary Cody Morris and both girls came from Dublin, Ireland. Both ladies vehemently denied any relationship to the William F. Cody family. Hardy proposed to her on horseback and after their marriage he proved up on his homestead below Signal Peak, later adding to his property by buying land from Chet Freeman. The Hardy Shulls had three daughters, Josephine, Frances and Rita. When Frances was about ten years old she was stricken with tick fever, as were so many other rural dwellers, including her cousin Dick Shull. Their neighbor across the river, Jimmy Osborne, provided a home remedy, he dug up some Oregon grape roots, brewed a bitter tea from the roots and Frances drank the tea and recovered. Her cousin Dick was taken to the doctor and he also recovered. The river had to be forded or crossed in a cable car until they built a bridge.

CANYON CREEK

The last four places on the south side of the river just outside the Forest Reserve were on Canyon Creek. The Mountain View Lodge has been described. The upper place on Canyon Creek was originally a Ranger Station. In 1923 a torrential cloudburst washed out the buildings of the Ranger Station where Clifford Spencer was stationed. The U.S.F.S. abandoned the place and established the ranger headquarters at Wapiti.

Farther down Canyon Creek is the homestead taken up by Jimmy Osborne. The original 16'x 16' homestead cabin sturdily constructed of massive twenty inch fir logs, neatly and evenly hewn is part of the present house. Osborne had been a dentist, one time he tried to make the molds for some false teeth for himself. Somehow, he didn't get the mold out of his mouth in time and luckily Brooks Borron came along and helped him remove the hardened plaster from his mouth. The predicament embarrassed Osborne and he never spoke to Brooks after that.

In October of 1923, Jack Spicer bought the Jimmy Osborne ranch and planned to do a little farming. In 1925 both Jack and his nephew Lonnie Royal had spotted tick fever.

A complete story of Jack Spicer and moonshining and bootlegging on the North Fork is found in a separate chapter.

THE TRAIL SHOP

In 1909, the George Sherwin family, with son Wylie G., moved from Brown's Valley, Minnesota, via Oklahoma, to Lovell, Wyoming. Wylie and his father built a sixteen by twenty foot log cabin on Crooked Creek, north of Lovell. Here Wylie and his first wife, Mildred Huntington Sherwin, and baby Virginia lived, and where sons Ted and Clifford were born. A second daughter, Betty, was born in Lovell in 1920.

A neighbor family, Jim and Maude Legg, had moved over to the North Fork and after talking with them, Wylie felt confident there was a good tourist business opportunity just at the entrance of the Forest Reserve. This convenient spot lay halfway between Cody and Yellowstone Park.

In the spring of 1922 the family set out on the three day trip with team of Barney and Chub, wagon-load of belongings and a milk cow tied alongside the wagon. The family lived in a tent until a two room log cabin with front porch was built. The following year the Trail Shop opened for business selling cold drinks, candy, souvenirs, gasoline and oil. They stored gasoline in large metal barrels and poured it from a spigot into measuring cans, then into the gas tank. In 1924, they added a spacious lodge building and three double overnight cabins. It was a sad blow to the family when Mildred Sherwin died of tuberculosis. Later Wylie married Nina Russell on January 18, 1930. Budd and Chella Hall rode over from the Circle H to stay with the Sherwin children when Wylie and Nina went to Denver on a honeymoon. A cold spell at this time froze the chickens' feet and they had to be killed.

When the Sherwins first went into business they sold waffles and honey, and homemade doughnuts and coffee. Those good doughnuts made them famous. One time a Yellow Bus had motor trouble and stopped to get some water and Wiley asked them if they would make it a regular stop. In an interview Nina Sherwin said, "The driver carried the message to the Yellowstone Park Transportation Company and they wrote and said if he could provide an adequate rest room the buses would stop. This we did and the buses stopped there for years on their trips to and from the Park to Cody." This went on probably from about 1924 until into the 1950's.

Besides Wylie's four children, Wylie and Nina had one son, Russell. The Sherwin children gathered petrified wood, especially from Flag Peak, and animal horns which they sold to the tourists. The Trail Shop was named for the "Yellowstone Trail." one of the early tourist routes.

Soon after the Sherwins moved to the North Fork, Ted Sherwin recalled, "Dad decided it would be a neat idea to put an American flag on each peak. (Signal and Flag Peaks rise 1000 feet above the river on each side at the entrance to the Forest Reserve.) He and Don Huntington put up the first flags, provided by the Forest Service, about 1925. . . Later we got the Rimrock Ranch to take care of the flag raising on the south, Flag Peak, and we continued to put up the other one...It got more and more difficult because the rocks were tumbled off by hikers and poles were harder to find."

Nina Sherwin recalled, "Tex Wisdom was the ranger at the East Gate and he would call down and tell us when there was an extra big bunch of buses. We had a pop cooler that would hold nine bottles in each row of choices, but when we needed extra we would get a tin tub and put ice and pop in it. Pop was delivered by truck and we bought the assorted flavors. We also sold ice cream cones from our own homemade ice cream. We made it in five gallon cans, about twice a day. We had power driven freezers in the garage. We bought our cream and eggs from our neighbors the J. F. Kellys."

Winter jobs consisted of getting out wood and sawing it up. Getting a supply of ice was another job. Nina recalled, "We cut ice in various places, down here on the river, or from the reservoir, and sometimes from the pond near Blackwater. The men got together to cut ice and the women got together to prepare the dinner. The chunks of ice were probably about 100 pounds, and were buried in sawdust until needed the next summer."

Nina told about their busy summer season starting when the Park opened up. "We had six cabins," she said, "They were furnished with bed, springs and mattresses, a little wood stove, a table and two chairs. Some of the tables pulled down from the wall with cupboard space behind them. The little stoves were oval shaped and the tourists could do some cooking although we also served meals." Feeding the tourists was an unpredictable task. Sometimes all the cabins would be filled and no one wanted a meal. On other occasions perhaps half the cabins would be filled and everyone wanted a meal. "We phased out the meals and increased the souvenirs in the store," Nina said.

NOTES

1. Boyer came to the Cody area in 1892 and retired at age 75. He died in Fromberg, Mt. at the age of 93 he had married for the second time at the age of 92 to 71 year old Dollie Trotter of Red Lodge. They honeymooned at the G.A.R. reunion in Gettysburg.

2. This is based on a quotation from Homer, "He was a friend to man, and lived in a house by the side of the road."

3. An excellent description of the Murray's life on Trout Creek has been included in Gladys Andren's book, *Life Among the Ladies of the Lake,* pp. 82 to 87.

4. Alice deMauriac Hammond related this on page 114 of the Park County Story, compiled by Lucille Patrick.

5. *Dr. Chase's Recipes,* published c. 1884, the author stated, "Climate is the physician's only dependence for the cure of his consumptive patients." This book was loaned by Evelyn Lawson, great granddaughter of William T. Borron.

6. Had previous experience with the plumbs and writes about them in his book, *Pony Trails in Wyoming.*

7. According to Dick Frost in *Tracks, Trails, and Tales.*

8. From Wyoming Wildlife for October 1986.

9. Written to Ethel Montgomery October 10, 1978.

10. When Dr. Shore lived in Gardiner he was called to attend an old bear trapper, John Graham sixty-three, who was mauled by a trapped bear on May 4,1912, on Crevice Mountain near Jardine, Montana. The trapped bear got out of thes sixty pound bear trap leaving three bloody toes and hence forth was called "Old Two Toes." Dr. Shore was unable to save Graham and he died. (From Lee H. Whittlesey, *Death in Yellowstone (1995) p. 56.*)

11. Which was duly noted in the *Park County Enterprise* of September 14, 1921.

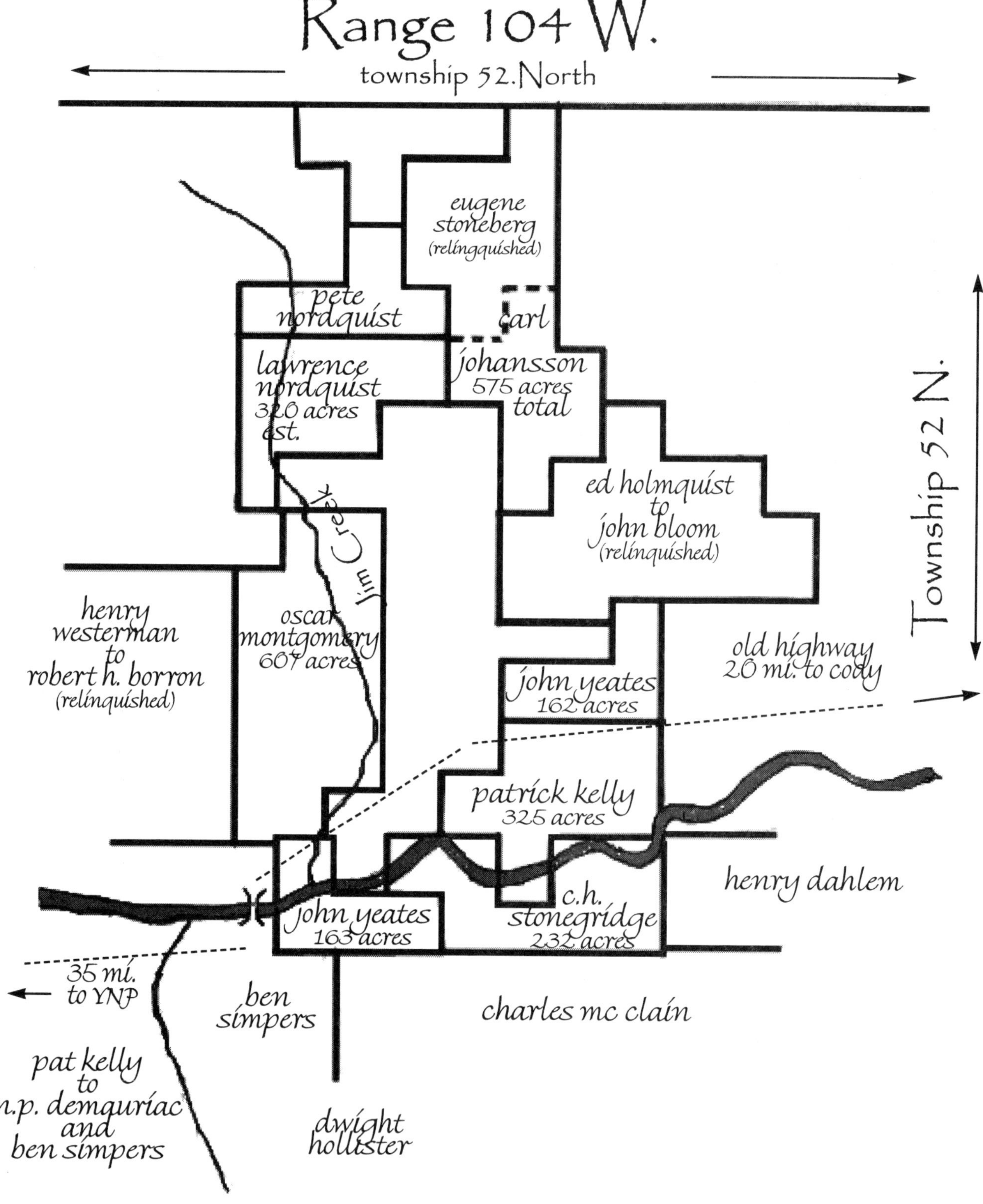

Property Location of Early Land Ownership on Jim Creek and Vicinity

North Fork Lodges

Mildred Martin. Photo courtesy of Park County Archives.

Rimrock Dude Ranch

The first dude ranch near the east entrance of the Shoshone Forest Reserve is the Rimrock. It superceded the old ranger station that washed out with the devastating storm of 1923. At that time, they closed the station and moved the ranger and his office to the present location at Wapiti. In 1930, the Earl Martins moved from Absorka Lodge to Canyon Creek and improved the road up to the place. Their Forest Service permit for three acres, dates from March 25, 1930. In 1931, John S. Dubois, a dude from Plainfield, New Jersey, reportedly bought one-half interest in the Rimrock Ranch. Through Mildred's cousin, Vinnie Johnson, the Western artist Frank Tenny Johnson visited Rimrock Ranch and liked it well enough to build a log studio there. He painted many famous Western scenes, specializing in night scenes. Most lodges operated seasonally but Rimrock became the home for the popular and well-liked Martin family and their two boys went to the Wapiti school. The older, Earl Junior, followed his father into ranching, while the younger, Paul, became an artist.

The Trail Shop

Started in 1922,the Trail Shop was owned by Wylie Sherwin for forty years, longer than any other lodge owner on the North Fork. Although Wylie thought he had built just outside the Forest boundary, the Trail Shop is actually in the Forest Reserve. A later government survey confirmed that most of the property was inside the forest reserve. But Nina Sherwin noted, "We had ten acres just east of the Trail Shop outside the Forest Reserve."[1] The Trail Shop is covered more completely under the section on Earliest Settlers.

Nameit Creek Lodge

Leonard C. Morris received his permit for a resort on Nameit Creek on October 18, 1927. Morris, son of the Fred Morris family of the lower valley, married Dorothy "Dottie" Nauss in February of 1927, in Philadelphia. Charles Sullivan with his sons, Bert and Bryan built the lodge for Morris. This lodge, known as the Lazy Bar H ranch, was the first lodge on the North Fork to have private baths in every cabin. Their advertisement in a 1930 Northern Pacific brochure, mentioned the private baths and electric lighted cabins. They could accommodate 15 guests.[2]

Leonard and Dottie Morris bought the Fred Morris ranch around 1935 and moved down river to run it. The Leonard Morris' sold Nameit Creek Lodge to William Waller in 1945.

Wapiti Inn

Colonel Cody received a permit to build a hotel on not more than five acres of land at the mouth of Elk Fork on October 31, 1904. The contractors were Buckstraw, Plumb and others. In 1906 John Thompson and his wife were "conducting" Wapiti Inn, and in 1910 the John Goffs were running it. At that time the rates were $2.50 per day or $16 weekly. Then the Louis Deckers took over management. In July 1911 Mrs. Elizabeth Eberle, the mother of Mrs. Harry Miller, wife of the Ranger stationed at Wapiti, took charge for the summer.

In 1908 a traveler described a lunch menu: fried trout, cold boiled ham, new potatoes, vegetable, hot biscuits, corn bread, wild current jam, cake and ice cream. The traveler said there were about thirty saddle horses available.

Dahlem sawmill. Photo courtesy Mark Simpers.

Sweetwater Resort

The first public mention of Sweetwater is from a newspaper item in the *Wyoming Stockgrower and Farmer* for March 26, 1908. The item stated that John B. Goff, William Wilson and associates had "located oil land 25 miles up North Fork. A sample of the oil was sent to State Geologist Becker." The oil was dipped off the top of a spring.

In May 1913 there was talk about trying to start a sulphur mine up at Sweetwater, and the May 12, issue of the *Northern Wyoming Herald* carried a notice of Incorporation of Wapiti Mining Company, with capital stock of $100,000. The men starting this project were Dwight E. Hollister, William T. Borron, and F. J. Hiscock.

The *Northern Wyoming Herald* of April 18, 1913, stated that "W. T. Borron was in from

Wapiti Sulphur Mine on the North Fork. He said five men have been at work there all winter. The owners plan to sell stock."

Sometime in the 1920s Edgar D. "Kid" Wilson (no relation to William Wilson) began spending some time at Sweetwater. Since early days a primitive cabin had been used and in 1927 Kid Wilson built a log house. He began to bottle and sell the mineral water from the Sweetwater Spring. An August 7, 1929, advertisement in the *Cody Enterprise* stated the water sold for $2.40 a case.

In March 1935, the Sweetwater Mineral Springs Company applied for a permit from the Forest Service to build a resort. In the spring of 1935, Bob and Laura Williams and two children came from California and spent the summer at Sweetwater. A contract was drawn up between Kid Wilson and the Williams to build and operate a tourist lodge, featuring the mineral waters, for a percentage of the profits. Laura and her son Bob Williams stated that

Cable bridge built by Bob Williams across North Fork to Sweetwater in 1936. Konrad and Carl Johansson on far end. Johansson photo.

they planned to capitalize on the medicinal qualities of the spring water and build the most modern lodge in the region, with electricity, water and sewer facilities in all the cabins. Log siding came from Black's sawmill on Green Creek and granite for the fireplaces came from the canyon. Before the family returned to California, one double cabin and five single cabins had been completed, and the dining room and spring house were nearly finished and furnished.

Soofoo, the Chinese cook, former employee of the Fred Morris dude ranch, cooked for the crew of workmen. Early in the spring of 1936, Williams had a crew building a cable bridge across the North Fork. The bridge was built entirely of oil field surplus materials, including well casings and cables. (This bridge washed out in 1981). In the spring of 1936, flash floods washed out three bridges across Sweetwater. Financially and emotionally this disaster broke the Williams and they did not pursue the resort project.[3]

B.C. Rumsey - June Creek

In 1927, Bronson Case "Bob" Rumsey, divorced his first wife, Anna Rumsey. She stayed on at the Blackwater Lodge which she and Bob had operated since 1914 when Bob Rumsey and George T. Beck had first started it. After Rumsey married Elizabeth Lynah in 1928 he established a new lodge. Rumsey's application for a lodge at June Creek was issued on February 13, 1929.

Bridge, over the North Fork at Sweetwater, in 1985.

Rumsey felt seclusion and privacy were commendable qualities, so he built only foot bridges suspended by cables across the North Fork for access between the highway and the lodge. During low water wagons could cross the river, also occasionally on the ice. But during the summer tourist season everything had to be carried across the undulating foot bridge. Cars had to be parked on the north side of the river and everyone walked across the foot bridge and up the hill to the cabins. After his marriage to Elizabeth Lynah, Rumsey continued to take his family to Islamorada, Florida, for the winter months, where he ran a small fishing resort. The Rumseys had two sons, Bronson Case Rumsey and James Lynah Rumsey. Later, Elizabeth divorced Bob and married Dr. John Daniel of Savannah, Georgia. Bob Rumsey's last home was on the old Thurmond Place, on a piece of land Bob bought from N. P. de Mauriac, east of Trout Creek. Log builder Hans Snortland built the log home. Lightning struck it in the early

Rumsey dudes ready to leave in the Rumsey's Pierce Arrow. Betty Rumsey in Leather riding skirt, around 1924. Note canvas mail pouch. Below, Rumsey cabins at Blackwater around 1924.

sixties and it burned to the ground. Bob lost a lifetime of memorabilia.

B.C. Rumsey - Blackwater Camp

During the late summer of 1900, Frank Hammitt, William T. Borron, and M. O. Newton, all of whom were working for the Forest Service built a bridge over the bridge at Blackwater Creek, the first bridge built by the government on the Forest Reserve.[4] They also built the first ranger cabin, called the Blackwater Ranger Cabin. Both the cabin and the bridge were destroyed by fire in 1905 and not rebuilt.

George T. Beck and B.C. Rumsey were issued a permit for a tourist resort on Blackwater on August 24, 1915. The Blackwater permit for twenty acres in

the Forest Reserve, is one of the largest on the North Fork. Most resorts varied in size from three and a half to four acres. From a rock cliff jutting out over the river, Rumsey thrust his cable suspension foot bridge across the North Fork just upstream from the mouth of Blackwater Creek, keeping automobiles at a distance from the resort.

During the early years, dude lodges kept milk cows if they wished and could graze the cows and their dude horses on the forest land in the vicinity of their lodge, but they could not exceed 250 animals. Bob Rumsey herded some of his Guernsey and Jersey cows left over from his days of running a dairy near Beck Lake, south of Cody, up the river each spring. These cows gave rich, creamy milk, but for a month or so each spring the milk and cream carried a very strong taste of wild onion, a favorite of the grazing cows. When feed was short both the cows and horses tended to wander, usually heading down river. This gave the horse wrangler plenty of riding to chase them down. In the fall the cows went into pasture down country and usually they trailed the horse herds over to the Crow Reservation, where they spent the winter. Over on the South Fork, the Valley Ranch also trailed their very large "remuda" over to the Crow Reservation.

Swinging foot bridge over North Fork to reach Blackwater Camp.

Below, "pet" bear on end of chain at Blackwater Lodge. Note circular path worn by bears pacing.

Top, Elizabeth, Dan, Sox (Jr.) Freeman and Ester Johansson, around 1924.

Middle, Betty Rumsey with hand on horse and two "dudines" around 1924.

Below, main lodge at Blackwater Camp.

In September 1920 Bob Rumsey took his father Bronson Rumsey and H. M. Gerrans, both of Buffalo, New York, on a hunting trip. The two elder men were associated with Colonel Cody and George T. Beck in the founding of the town of Cody, residential streets were named for them. Also in 1920, Bob Rumsey ran for Senator to the State Legislature but did not win. He was keenly interested in politics and vocally against Prohibition. After many tries, he was elected to the state senate in 1935.

W. T. "Bill" Borron worked for Rumseys in 1920. Always versatile and helpful, he washed 73 blankets for the lodge.[5] From Blackwater, Bill went up to Holm Lodge where he was a dependable summer employee for some seventeen years. In June 1924 the S. B. Freeman children, Sox Jr., Elizabeth, and Danny, spent vacation time at Blackwater, while the Freemans got settled in Cody. Margaret Hoglund (Coe) from Upper Sage Creek worked at Blackwater helping to take care of the children. Huldah Johansson was doing the cooking.

For a few years, Mr. and Mrs. Johnny Goff worked for Bob Rumsey and were winter caretakers around 1925 and 1926. Probably 1924 to 1926 were the peak years for their dude business, which had an upswing after a low point in 1923, when Blackwater Camp had been offered for sale. Rumsey outfitted a pack trip in late June of 1926, for eighteen boys and girls. Bryan and Bert Sullivan, Carl Johansson, John Fowler, and Carl Hammitt, all worked at times for the Bob Rumseys; along with Elin Larson a Swedish friend of Hulda Johansson.

Bob Rumsey lived an interesting and colorful life. He graduated from Yale University and in 1902 taught at St. Mark's School.[6] During the summer and fall of 1903 he brought a group of boys to the McLaughlin ranch, later Valley Ranch, and tutored them. This could have been what inspired the Valley Ranch Boys School that ran for a number of years. Bob tried having a school at Blackwater for eastern boys. This ran during the winter of 1922, and possibly other years.

After Bob Rumsey divorced Anna Rumsey, she continued operating Blackwater Camp as a dude operation, with the help of her daughter, Betty Perkins, Bob's stepdaughter. There were accommodations for forty guests. Ill health forced Anna to sell, and the May 14, 1930, issue of the *Cody Enterprise*, stated Blackwater Camp had been sold to Tex Wisdom. Tex came to the area as an enlisted soldier when Yellowstone Park was under military control, and he was a ranger at the East Gate for ten years. In 1937, Blackwater's rates were $35 a week.

Absaroka Lodge

A few miles up the river from Blackwater is Gunbarrel Creek, where on February 13, 1917, Earl Crouch applied for permit from the Forest Service to build a camp and he was allotted three acres on the east bank of Gunbarrel Creek.

Earl Crouch, born in 1881 in Kansas, drifted west to Laramie, Wyoming and then to Cody, where he got work guiding for the Frost and Richard's Yellowstone Park trips. After he married the widow Neva Hill, they settled in at Absaroka. In 1925 Earl went with the writer Hal Evarts to Alaska. Earl is best known for his "gold mine" up Eagle Creek, and like most prospectors he had boundless optimism that the gold quartz would pan out richly, but it did not.

In 1924, Earl Martin and Tracy Hill, the latter a stepson of Crouch, bought Absaroka Lodge, and in 1927 Earl Hayner bought an interest in the lodge. As newly marrieds, Earl and Mildred, settled in at Absaroka. Mildred described their experiences in her book, *The Martins of Gunbarrel.*[7] The Earl Martins moved down to Canyon Creek in 1930. In 1950s Peg and Fred Garlow owned Absaroka Lodge, and the allotment had increased to nearly seven acres. Fred, a grandson of Colonel Cody, was a competent and personable dude wrangler.

In a Union Pacific brochure of 1930, the lodge was called the LV Bar ranch, with accommodations for twenty guests. One 1930 tourist advertisement stated, "Hot water brought to the cabin each morning and free use of the bathhouse. Rates, $45 per week."[8] A later feature of the ranch was the six weeks boys' camp, three weeks of which were spent in the mountains on a pack trip. As with most of the tourist lodges, pack trips were a drawing card.

Elephant Head Lodge

A few miles above Absaroka Lodge is Elephant Head Lodge, which took its name from an eroded rock formation. Mrs. Josephine Thurston, wife of early Ranger, Harry Thurston, applied for permit for a summer home on September 13, 1920, and for a resort December 28, 1926, for slightly less than one acre. In the Union Pacific brochure it states, "It is a small place—accommodations limited to the requirements of eighteen or twenty guests—and should not be confused with a hotel or a tourist resort." It also mentioned there were many "mementoes of the late Col. W. F. Cody, interesting to the visitor and cherished by the owner of the lodge, his niece."

The lodge also boasted of one of the few hook-ups on the Forest Service telephone line. Because the region had been settled for only a few years, family reunions were rare. However, the W. J. Kissick family of Gillette, Wyoming, held a family reunion at Elephant Head Lodge for eleven children and their families in August 1931.

Goff Creek Lodge

On June 1, 1906, Johnny Goff and family, with almost 100 pack horses and a pack of hunting dogs, came down from Gardiner, Montana, after being employed to exterminate mountain lions in the Lamar Valley area. The stream came to be called Goff Creek. For awhile, the Goffs ran the Wapiti Inn near Elk Fork for Colonel Cody.

According to Ray Prante, "Mrs. Palm, an osteopath or chiropractor, here in town, started a summer home there. She already had the logs there and hired Dolph Thomas and Clarence Williams to build the cabin, so they built the cabin where the logs were piled. But the permit was for farther back, the cabin wasn't on the permit at all." Eventually, Mrs. Palm sold to Tex Kennedy and he lived there for several years when he was game warden. On June 3, 1929, I. E. Kennedy received a permit for 3.5 acres. His place was to be called Kennedy's Game Lodge. In May of 1936, Kennedy sold to Irene and Ray Prante. Irene Prante received her permit for 3.5 acres May 1, 1936.

Ray Prante recalled, "We traded our house in town for the place on Goff Creek. He (Kennedy) had a main lodge and one double cabin outside. He had built onto it and when we got it there were a couple of rooms on the side." The Prantes owned the lodge until December 1947.

Holm Lodge

The Crossed Sabres Ranch, another name for Holm Lodge, is the second oldest dude resort on the North Fork. It was built in 1907, on Libby Creek by Aron "Tex" Holm of Holm Transportation Company. Tex Holm, a bright, cheerful, and genial promoter, who, as the years went by, attained a weight of over 250 pounds. Original stock holders were Tex Holm, J. W. "Billy" Howell, Bill Hogg, R. L. Donley, Bill Simpson, Jakie Schwoob, Ted Hogg, George Taylor, Billy Diggen (sic) and a Mr. Lowell. This lodge was first called Holm Lodge Number 1, Numbers 2 and 3 were in Yellowstone Park. Aron,"Tex" Holm applied for permission for a storehouse on March 29, 1909, from the Forest Service, and received it the same day.

Below, Mrs. Tex Holm and Tex Holm of Holm Lodge. Photo from the Park County Archive collection.

Summer business kept all employees occupied and wild animals proved no problem. However, an occasional bear broke into the lodges and sometimes a bear attacked someone. A human/bear encounter occurred in August of 1911 that made the Cody newspaper. Charles Clark, aka Louis Gokal, aka Charles Clark Gokal, one of Tex Holm's "partners" was attacked and injured by a "cinnamon" bear. It took fifty stitches to close the wound in the right thigh and left leg. The victim got between the sow and her cub, so the sow attacked and knocked him twenty feet. They captured the mother bear and sent her to the U. S. Zoological Gardens in Washington, D. C. but they kept the cub at the lodge as a pet, a common custom in early days. Almost every lodge had to have a "pet" cub bear as an attraction.

The Holm Transportation Company took dudes and tourists from Cody to Holm Lodge via Stanley Steamer. In February 19ll, the *Cody Enterprise* stated that "Tex Holm has purchased a forty-five horsepower Avery Traction eighteen passenger automobile to use between Cody and Holm Lodge." Holm's park tours cost $50 round trip from Cody. The trip from the lodge through the Park was made by horse and wagon.

The largest touring party was in 1912, when 84 traveled through the Park, including the

Holm Lodge cabins. Photo courtesy of Park County Archives.

Tex Holm and Grace Miller at Holm Lodge. Grace was the wife of Ranger Miller. When he divorced her she married Carl Buckingham. Grace died of influenza in 1918 in Worland.Photos courtesy of Park County Archives.

president of the Stetson Hat Company, J. Howell Cummings. In 1912, Wallop-Moncrieffe Lumber Company constructed six new frame sleeping cottages. In further expansion twelve four-room tents and twelve single room tents on Libby Creek provided room for 200 tourists. The plans for a three-story Alpine-type Inn did not materialize. The original lodge burned in 1914 but they soon rebuilt.

Holm Transportation Company went into bankruptcy in 1914. In 1916, three 12-passenger Stanley Steamers sold at public auction in a mortgage foreclosure. With reorganization, J.W. Howell, Bill Hogg, L. R. Ewart, and Ted Hogg were investors and in 1916 Miss Mary Shawver bought into the business and soon the other investors sold their shares to Howell and Shawver. Between World War I and the Great Depression, times were prosperous for the dude business, and the combination of Miss Shawver's capable supervision and Billy Howell's genial guidance made Holm Lodge a first class resort. Billy always wore a necktie and rode a picturesque pinto horse called Navajo. Through the years there were many harrowing accidents at the various dude ranches. An early one involved Billy Howell, who apparently was out getting firewood. According to the *Park County Enterprise* for October 30, 1912, "Billy Howell cut his right leg below the knee with an axe, a terrible gash to the bone. He was hauled to the lodge in a lumber wagon. Kid Wilson was at the Lodge with his automobile and took Billy to town as fast as the car could be made to speed up."

Hans Snortland handcrafted furniture at Shoshone Lodge.

Mary Shawver told about another accident Billy Howell suffered. "Mr. Howell was far from home and cut his ankle with an axe. . . He and Earl Hayner sewed the wound with a common needle and white thread which Howell carried in a little bag with a few cartridges and small tools. . . Later when an interested surgeon examined the ankle and scar he unhesitatingly gave the two men Grade A."[9]

In 1926 Billy Howell had to go to a Billings hospital for surgery. The *Cody Enterprise* duly reported that after the surgery he developed hiccups which they treated by placing a silver tube in his throat. Billy swallowed the tube, and the paper reported, that in due time "it passed naturally."

The July 27, 1927, The *Cody Enterprise* reported there had been a very bad cloudburst storm at Holm Lodge. Children playing near Libby Creek reported it was rising rapidly but could not get any adults to pay attention to them. When everyone heard the roar and saw the seven-foot wall of water they were convinced. Luckily, only the bathhouse was demolished.

In 1930, many of the sleeping accommodations were still "tent cottages" according to the Union Pacific brochure. The brochure further stated that the cabins were heated (wood stoves) and "centrally located bathrooms afford plenty of hot soft water day and night. The dairy herd and ranch garden contribute largely to the excellent meals. Telephone and daily mail service keep guests in touch with home.

Shoshone Lodge dining room furniture crafted by Hans Snortland. Typical of "lodge style".

Shoshone Lodge

This resort was first named Star Mercantile Mill and Lumber Company. A Forest Service permit was issued on May 6, 1928.[10]

The Cody Enterprise of June 13, 1928, reported that Henry Dahlem had bought out John Vogel. It was later called the Red Star Camp, but when World War II came, they changed the name to Shoshone Lodge. This permit was for 35 acres on both sides of Grinnel Creek, the largest allotment issued.

Betty Woodruff stated there once had been an old historic trapper's cabin on the main fork of Grinnell. The cabin had a trap door to a storage area under the floor. Water flowed close by keeping the storage area above freezing. Later the Forest Service burned the old cabin.[11]

Master log builder Norwegian Hans Snortland and Jim Wilson built the new main lodge and the one of a kind designed pine and rawhide chairs and other furniture in 1935 and 1936.

Pahaska Tepee

The first, and by far the most famous, lodge on the North Fork received the first permit for a hotel to Colonel W. F. Cody, on December 14, 1903.[12] The *Wyoming Stockgrower and Farmer* of August ll, 1903, tells about the new road to the Park and the establishment of the Walter Braten and Sam Berry road ranch. The *Park County Enterprise* of June 11, 1910, stated that electric lights and bathhouses had been installed at Pahaska, and credited Buffalo Bill as "always abreast or a little bit ahead of the times." Cody wanted to string electric lines up the North Fork Valley as early as 1904. He ordered two cars, 60 h.p. White Steamers, to run between the Irma Hotel and Pahaska. Jack Winter, who arrived in Cody to deliver one of the Steamers, drove it for several years.

In the early days, many of Colonel Cody's relatives were employed at Pahaska. Among them were Mr. and Mrs. Roy Myers, the Louis Deckers, Cody Boal, Mrs. Fred Garlow, mother of Fred and Bill Garlow, George Walliker whose wife was Fred Garlow's sister.

Other permits were issued for North Fork resorts which never materialized. Jim McLaughlin, who later owned Valley Ranch, applied for a permit on June 7, 1916, for three acres at the junction of Elk Creek (Fork) and the North Fork river. B. G. Neeland applied for a permit January 1, 1919, for a resort 400 yards north of the Government Road on Grinnell Creek. This permit was revoked. It probably superceded the Fenton-Neeland resort permit January 16, 1917. Neeland had several run-ins with the law, poaching game and bootlegging.

There were ten lodges within the Forest Reserve in 1937 and there are still only ten in the 1990s. The main difference is that the rates charged have increased. In the early days, charges ranged from $30 to $45 per week. In the 1990s that is the average charge per day, and weekly charges range from $700 to $900.

Braten Cabin in 1903. Photo by J.E. Stimson, courtesy of the Wyoming State Archives and Museum and Historical Department.

NOTES

1. Nina Sherwin interview July 1985.
2. Leonard Morris had tick fever in June of 1934. Probably the use of the newly discovered tick serum had not been available. The first tick serum was available in March of 1934.
3. According to an interview by Retha Miller in the *Cody Enterprise* for July 8, 1985.
4. Some sources credit Carl Sorenson and Frank James for building the cabin in 1899.
5. Duly recorded in the Cody Enterprise for June 16, 1920, by Bill's good friend, editor, Caroline Lockhart.
6. St. Mark's school founded 1865, near Boston, Massachusetts, a boarding and college preparatory school.
7. Mildred Martin, *The Martins of Gunbarrel,* The Caxton Printers Ltd., Caldwell, Idaho, 1959, describes their early married life at Absaroka Lodge. It tells about "Dad and Ma Crouch," moonshiner Jack Spicer, dance caller Hurricane Bill Herrick, and other colorfully described characters on the North Fork.
8. 1930 Union Pacific brochure.
9. Mary Shawver,in her book of Memoirs, page 89,After Holm Lodge was sold in 1947, Miss Shawver wrote a 93 page book entitled Sincerely, Mary S. containing anecdotes and vignettes of the thirty five years she and Billy Howell ran Holm Lodge. Pictures of pet bear cubs and other vintage pictures are included.
10. However, some reports place the date of starting the sawmill, store and tourist resorts as early as 1924.
11. Betty Dahlem interview, May 25, 1985.
12. This brief summary will not duplicate the excellent historical coverage in W. Hudson Kensel's book *Pahaska Tepee, Buffalo Bill's old hunting lodge and hotel, a history, 1901-1946,* published by Buffalo Bill Historical Center, 1987.

Summer Homes

Besides the resorts and lodges, from at least 1914 on the Forest Service allowed a few summer homes to be built. Early ones were built on Pagoda Creek, the first permit granted in 1925. Dr. Frances Lane had the first summer cabin on Pagoda Creek, from around 1925. Laundry man John Cook had a cabin on Pagoda, which he sold to the Fred Worsts. At that time they paid $50 a year for the permit. In the mid-1990s, Betty Jean Worst Rogers said the fees have mounted to nearly $800, with very strict regulations.

On Aspen Creek, Henry Coe built a home and lived there year- around for a short time. Later the Chris Pikes lived on Aspen Creek. E. E. "Ted" Ogsten and wife Helen for twenty-six years owned a cabin built by Jim Wilson on Aspen Creek. Ogsten was one of the original thirty one Park rangers sworn in after the U. S. Army left Fort Yellowstone.

On January 1, 1932 Carl Bloom of Powell and his brother, John,(no relation to Wesley Bloom) had a permit for the cabin which they built south of the highway on an unnamed spring up-river from Aspen Creek and across from June Creek. John married Mary Somes, a dudine from Absoraka Lodge and they made their home there until John died on September 29, 1943, at the age of 48. (Another Absaroka "dudine," named Charlotte, married Earl Hayner. Charlotte was petite and went by the nickname "Jumbo.")

There were summer homes on Moss Creek and Eagle Creek. In 1921 Dr. Trueblood had a cabin on Newton Creek. One of the earliest groups of summer homes were built near Kitty Creek, and called the "Cody Colony" or "Home Colony." In 1919, L. R. Ewart, F.F. McGee, J. W. Rousseau, H. A. Luce, F. R. Pearson, Mrs. Liddiard, J. D. Buchanan, J. H. Vogel each leased one half acre of land. C. E. Sullivan and Sons were building the Home Colony cabins in May of 1919 with the Rousseau cabin one of the first finished. Whether all these eventually were built is not certain. Some like J. H. Vogel did not build until 1924, and F. F. McGee built in 1931. Judge Percy Metz during 1930s through 1950s had a cabin on Kitty

Summer cabin, John Bloom.

Creek named "Metz Aerie" by the Judge's mother Jennie. [1]

Across the river from Eagle Creek a number of summer homes were built. In November of 1932 the fire that destroyed the Greever cabin started from smoldering logs in the foundation under the fireplace. They rebuilt.

In 1931 Earl Crouch built a bridge at Eagle Creek which would help him get materials in and out, to and from his mine. Earl also built a cabin on the south side of the river. According to Eda Forgey Williams, Carl Hammitt had a trapper's cabin on the south side of the river. R. N. Wilson bought the cabin from Hammitt in 1915 for $10. Irene Wilson replaced the old cabin in 1935, Carl Forgey was long-time caretaker of the cabin and when the Wilsons died they willed the cabin to him.[2]

Permits for cabins date from 1917 to 1923 on Eagle Creek. The Boy Scouts of Powell had a camp east side of Eagle Creek and around 1927, they purchased the summer home of Mable Veitch for their use.

In 1928-29 the Cody Schools sponsored a Boy Scout troop. In 1934 Frank Kraus started Troop number 50, sponsored by the Elks Club. Glenn Nielson, Paul Stock, and Lloyd Taggart were major doners in obtaining and developing the Buffalo Bill Scout Camp between Kitty Creek and Fishhawk Creek on the south side of the river. Reverend R. N. Buswell started the yearly roadside cleanup on the North Fork with Troop 54.

The group of cabins on Mormon Creek was called the "Powell Colony". In 1920 seven Powell men planned to build summer homes there. Not all were Powell people, because Dave Jones, a Cody merchant, built an 18 x 32 foot summer cottage on Mormon Creek near Holm Lodge in May of 1914. He called his place "Brigham Lodge." The Tom Trimmer family enjoyed their summer cabin on Mormon Creek.

Walt Owens and Roy Holm in partnership bought the Holm cabin,built around 1922 by Scotty Clark, a Cody blacksmith. In August of 1924, the G. A. Holm family held their family reunion there for 32 members of the family. This was one of the very earliest family reunions celebrated on the North Fork.

Major Hoopes, early deputy sheriff, and later Dwight King, a game warden, had at times, cabins in, or near, the Powell Colony.

The A. F. Chapoton Cabin near Pahaska dates back to December 31, 1921 when Chapoton applied for permit for a resort on 1.75 acres. J. C. "Kid" Nichols and family spent some summers there from 1927 on for a few years. In 1925, J. D. "Denny" Start had a cabin across the river below Grinnell Creek. The *Park County Enterprise* May 19, 1926, stated he was building a bridge across the river. According to his obituary, Denny was born December 8, 1859 and died in February of 1956, but this age does not agree with the 1910 census, in which he was listed as 45 years of age and from Texas. His father and mother had been born in Tennessee. His mother, Margaret Hamilton Start, was third cousin of Alexander Hamilton. Denny's cabin was headquarters for his fur trapping. As far back as 1905, Denny, a tall, ramrod straight thin man, advertised his services as guide and outfitter in Cody.

NOTES

1. *He Wore A Stetson; the story of Judge Percy Metz*, by Vera Saban. Big Horn Book Co. Basin, WY 1980. p.117
2. Interview with Eda Forgey Williams, April,1995

North Fork Schools

Marquette Schools

From 1897 through 1910,few children lived on the lower North Fork. In the early years most children lived in the farming area of Poverty Flat and Marquette. In 1887, twenty-nine enrolled in the Marquette Schools of District No. 23, and the last count showed 10 in 1910, the year before, 1909, the count peaked at forty-four. In 1888 the Clerks Enrollment Report listed forty children and three schools. In 1889, thirty enrolled with only one school counted. The statistics for the 1890 era are missing.

In 1901 there are thirty-six children enrolled with two schools listed, but by 1902 the enrollment dropped to sixteen in District No. 23. A South Fork school started as Ishawooa District No. 27. Their enrollment stayed between twenty-seven and forty-four. School District No. 23 of Big Horn County included the Marquette community and the North Fork of the Shoshone River, and the South Fork until 1902. They conducted school in various buildings and homes.

Marquette School 1898, Dolly Martin teacher.

Pioneer of the Clarks Fork, Quincy "Quince" Chance, stated that about 1890, he and his sister Lily, and some of the Yost children, possibly Claude and Albert, also from the Clarks Fork attended the Marquette School, fifty miles from their home, one winter because there were no schools in their area. Daisy Sorenson taught the school, she later married George T. Beck. Quince remembered attending school in a cottonwood log building "above the canyon."[1] These children boarded with a local resident, and it is quite possible they boarded with the Ed Hutsonpillar family or Anna Hutsonpillar Holman, because the Chance, Yost, and Hutsonpillar families had all come north from New Mexico around 1888 or 1890.

Tent school, March through May of 1911, Wapiti. June Hale teacher, students Vera Wagoner, William Leabold,Don Wagoner, Hershel Green, Leonard Morris. Photo courtesy of Park County Archives.

Two school houses were built. One on the Brundage property, catered to lower the South Fork and Irma Flat, and probably built in 1904 at a cost of $650. The other school on Poverty Flat may have been nearer new Marquette. A 1898 photograph of a school taught by Dorothy (Dolly) Martin shows a 16´ x 30´ building of large, squared cottonwood logs, eight logs high, with a pitched roof. The report of School District Clerk states the school building cost $200 when it was constructed. Posed by the side of the school are teacher Martin and 20 pupils. Two women sit on the doorstep, dressed in traveling clothes. One may be Belle T. Howell, County Superintendent. One man is on horseback, possibly a school trustee, and the other man leaning against the building could be W. T. Borron, who might have driven the ladies to the school in a buggy. In 1897 Grace McMullan taught the twenty-nine pupils for 180 days for $50 a month. She married William T. Borron and taughtlater in Mexico. The trustees that year were T. E. Jackson, L. H. Rand and J. W. Arnsberger. The last two had interests on the North Fork and streams were named after them.

In 1898, Anna Thurmond (Sweney) taught School No.l and Dorothy Martin (Trimmer) taught School No. 2 and 3. Andrew J. Martin and W. T. Borron were Marquette Trustees; M.S. Jones represented Ishawooa pupils. Mrs. Belle T. Howell, County School Superintendent was replaced in 1899 by W. O. Lester. In 1899 Dorothy Martin taught the school, followed by Nellie Edick who taught two years and married Ranger Jesse Nelson. In 1902 Harry Thurston taught and Ed Grinder, C. A. Marston, and A. J. Martin were on the School Board. In l903 Anna Howe taught followed by three teachers in 1904, Leota Cook, Danneta Hicky and J. M. Snyder. In 1905 and 1906 J. M. Snyder taught and in 1906 James Dickson is listed as teaching three months. T. S. Riddle was added to the School Board. In 1907 James Dickson taught six months and C. P. MacGlashan joined the School Trustees. W. F. Brown replaced E. C. Hoover as School Superintendent of No. 23, but he served only two years. In 1909 Alice Newman taught six months and Myrtle Thompson two months, each earning $70 per month. In the final year for the original Marquette school, 1910, Myrtle Thompson taught for 137 days for $70 per month.

The school term varied from forty to 180 days with an average of 120 days. The teacher's monthly salary was $40 in 1898 and increased to $70 in 1910. The assessed valuation of District No. 23 in 1904, was $131,615 and in 1905, $135,000. Thereafter it decreased annually to $45,000 in 1910, due to reduced farm production and value pending the forthcoming flooding by the Shoshone Reservoir. The next ycar Park County was established from the western section of Big Horn county, and the North Fork became School District No. 9.[2]

First School at Logan Creek

During the years 1909 and 1910,while the Shoshone (Buffalo Bill) reservoir starting to fill, buildings were being vacated or moved. This event coincided with the division of Bighorn County and the formation of Park County. At the same time they formed a new school district, No. 9, for the increasing number of settlers on the North Fork.

To establish a school district, it required a minimum of eight school age (six to twenty-one years) resident children. In 1912 they began an annual census of such children to qualify for county funds.[3] To establish a functioning school for the year 1911, they formed a temporary board of trustees with Eugene Wilder, Jack Murray, H. K. Barbee, and clerk Lee Borron. Miss Jessie Hitchcock still served as County Superintendent of Schools. This school board hired June Hale (Brundage) of Mt. Carol, Illinois as the first teacher and the first school opened at Logan Creek on March 6, 1911 in a 10′x 12′old log cabin with a low dirt roof and a small peep hole window. The nailed a three-and-a-half by five foot chipped blackboard to the front wall and an old chair, a table with a drawer, and two badly scarred desks with brands carved by Holman, Brundage and Snyder boys. The double seat desks had been used and abused at the previous Marquette school. A pile of books in a corner were so dilapidated Miss Hale decided to use blank composition books and make her lessons from her own old text books. Pupils consisted of two primary and two third graders. During the first three weeks the pupils were Don and Vera Wagoner, who lived at the Logan place, and Leonard Morris and Billy Leabold, both from the Fred Morris ranch three and one-half miles up the river. The Leabolds came from Philadelphia and worked at the Morris ranch.

After three weeks, the Wagoners moved up to the Pat Kelly place on Whit Creek and the school moved with them. It was then held in a tent down by the river at Wapiti.[4]

A brief description of the first three month North Fork school at Breteche Creek possibly in 1906 is rightfully placed first in this chronological account. There is no written record of this school but a transcribed interview of Mrs. Huldah Borron, widow of Robert Holbrook (Brooks) Borron, said they had school there. Brooks, age 7 and Glen age 6 in the May 22, 1905 census, were the older sons of Grace and W. T. Borron. Mary Helen Daley also remembered hearing about an early school there. The three month school was reportedly conducted during he summer of 1905, and other students were Johnny, 8, and Wanetta, 7, McClure; Marland, 7, and Lovina 6, Murray and their teacher was James Dickson. Following this summer session the Borron boys attended the Marquette school. The McClure family moved to the South Fork.

Wapiti School

Three weeks later, the Wagoner family moved up the river six miles to the Pat Kelly upper ranch on Whit Creek and the school moved with them. This time temporary quarters were prepared over a weekend when Fred Morris donated a tent frame and floor and a 8′ x 10′tent. They hauled it across the original iron truss river bridge and placed it twenty-five yards up stream from the bridge, near the river edge. They moved and installed the same furnishings, plus a box cupboard nailed to the wooden tent frame. A round heater stove and a pile of cedar chunks complete with axe constituted the heating system. A ten pound lard bucket filled from the river supplied drinking water. A loud ticking Ingersoll watch told the time. Miss Hale relocated her living quarters from Trout Creek to the Wagoner home on Whit Creek. A new student, Hershel Green, joined the school and a few others attended part time. A bench with boxes for desks accommodated extra pupils.[5]

Attendance was good considering the distance some pupils traveled. Billy Leabold age thirteen, and Leonard Morris, age six, rode double on horse-back, a distance of three and a fifth miles, with Billy in the saddle and Leonard behind. Leonard's mother pinned a pillow inside Leonard's overalls in the morning and Miss Hale replaced it for the ride home in the afternoon. The boys faced a strong cold west wind on those March mornings. Wet April snows nearly caved in the top and walls of the tent school on several mornings. At noon the pupils placed their dinner pails in the center of the table sharing their lunches buffet style. Occasionally Don age eight and six year Vera's younger brother, Carl walked down from their home with a pail of hot chocolate for lunch and stayed on to take part in the classes.[6]

Wapiti School yard 1922-1923 school year. Beth Sharp, teacher, in front of horse stalls and outhouses. Boys to west, girls to east, Jim Mountain to north.

The Hollister Ranch sported the only automobile (a Buick) on the North Fork so most residents on their infrequent trips to town traveled by team and wagon or buggy, or horse-back with pack horse when necessary. Frequently these returning travelers brought special treats for the occupants of the tent school. Toward the end of May the tent became very warm and the river was rising with spring run-off, creating a playground hazard. They celebrated the end of school May 26 with a school program and picnic at Elk Fork, attended by parents and friends.

SCHOOL YEAR 1911 - 1912

From the year 1911 records were kept concerning the Wapiti school. John Yeates compiled the statistics.[5] Total number of days taught, Sixty. Number of pupils taught, five. Condition of School buildings and furniture: Tent house 10 x 12, furniture very poor and two small black boards.

Prior to the closing of the tent school on May 26, 1911, and in anticipation of the need to build a permanent school house and engage a teacher for the coming year, the First Annual Meeting of School District No. 9 was held May l, 1911. Parents and concerned residents met at the Wapiti Post Office located at the Dwight E. Hollister Ranch to elect trustees and initiate necessary action.

The following accounts of annual meetings and significant school events are given by years for 1911 through 1932. This information is taken from three sources: minutes of school district meetings, the school board clerk's warrant register of expenses, (beginning 1921), plus miscellaneous interviews and newspaper items. Detailed reports compiled by John A. Yeates are available at the Park County Archives and his research has been used in this section on schools. Only the first three meetings are presented here, the remainder appear later in the chapter.

Parents called the First Annual Meeting, District No. 9, May 1, 1911, 2:00 p.m.

Teacher's Report of School District No. 9
For Term Commencing March 6, 1911
Ending May 26, 1911
Park County, Wyoming

Names of Pupils	Age	Days	Residence
William Leabold	13	50	Morris Ranch
Don Wagoner	8	60	Whit Creek
Herschel Green	8	23	Green Creek
Leonard Morris	6	49.5	Morris Ranch
Davis Graves	7	0	(These children
John Graves	9	0	were included in the
Samuel Miller	6	0	census but never
			were enrolled in 1911.)
Vera Wagoner	6	60	Whit Creek

I hereby certify that, under the provisions of an Act of the State Legislature, approved February 6th, 1901, I have given instructions in the humane treatment of animals of not less than two lessons of ten minutes each per week.

Miss Myrtle Conklin taught school during the 1919-1920 school year. She roomed with the Simpers. Photo Courtesy Mark Simpers.

Wapiti School, second grade with John Yeates, Cliff Sherwin, Jim Shull, Elmer Kelly, Frances Shull and Dorothy Shull. Photo courtesy John Yeates.

Wapiti School in 1925-1926 school year with newly awarded plaque above the door. Teacher Miss Vera Schultz. Photo courtesy John Yeates.

Dated, June 21, 1911

Signed, June M. Hale

LOCATION; Wapiti Post Office at Hollister ranch. Business; Dwight E. Hollister was chosen chairman of the meeting and J. H. Graves chosen as clerk. Trustees: Those elected were: Lawrence Wagoner for a one year term, Lee Borron for a two year term, and D. E. Hollister for a three year term.
RESOLUTIONS PASSED: That; Whereas no reports as to the financial condition of the district are available it is resolved that the determination of the period of the school term and the location and building of a suitable school house be left to the discretion of the trustees with full authority to take such action in these matters as may seem best to them.
SUMMER ACTIVITIES: Pat Kelly donated over two acres of land adjoining the road and east of Whit Creek for a school site "for as long as it might be needed". The legal description read "within the west 1/2 of NE Qtr., Sec. 24, Township 52, Range 105 West." Fred Gail built the frame school house with one main room and two cloak rooms on either side of the front entrance. Oscar Montgomery hauled the necessary lumber and later Pat Kelly donated a large heating stove.[6] Although no record of school can be located,on January 6, 1912 funds were raised for furnishings with a dance held in the school house attended by fifty people. Donations were accepted to help furnish the new building. The Cornstalk Fiddlers, Fay Hiscock and W. T. (Bill) Borron provided the music. On May 4, 1912, they organized a Leap Year dance in the new school with Grace Miller (Mrs. Harry, wife of the Wapiti Ranger) as floor manager.

Sketchy records suggest Annie Sweney taught for about three months sometime during 1912 -1913. Hershel Green, Leonard Morris, John and Davis Graves are listed as students, as are Roy and Vera Lehman. Ethel Montgomery (Mrs. Oscar) recalled a teacher rode up from Trout Creek and Hershel Green rode down from Green Creek and many times they were the only two in attendance.

SCHOOL YEAR 1912-1913

Second Annual Meeting, District No. 9, May 6, 1912
LOCATION; Wapiti School House, all subsequent Annual meetings were held at the Wapiti school house.
TRUSTEES: Borron and Hollister, and Mrs. C. P. Thurmond was elected, replacing

Lawrence Wagoner.
RESOLUTIONS PASSED; That: a special tax of two mills be levied for teacher's funds. That: the number of months of school term be left to discretion of school board. That: the matter of assisting in the maintaining of a school near Mr. Reese's (Rattlesnake Creek) be left to the board to look up the legal aspect and act in best way possible.

J. H. Graves, Clerk

Classes were begun September 30, with Mrs. Annie Thurmond Sweny as teacher and six students. It is estimated school was held for 90 days, starting September 30, 1912. Park County Treasurer dispensed $194.12 to Wapiti, and the District was assessed at value of $120,047.

SCHOOL YEAR 1913-1914

Third Annual Meering, District No. 9, May 5, 1913, 2:00 p.m.
TRUSTEES: Director, Lee H. Borron; Secretary, Mrs. Anna Sweny. J. E. Lehman was elected as incoming trustee.
BUSINESS: moved, seconded, carried that a special tax of two mills be levied for the teacher's fund and other expenses.
RESOLUTIONS: That: The school board be authorized to transfer teacher's fund to general fund and vice versa. That: The length of school term and the matter of assisting Mr. Reese with a school (at Rattlesnake Creek) be left to the discretion of the school board. That: The building of a coal house and a shed for horses be left to the discretion of the trustees.

Annie L. Sweney, Clerk, Pro Tem

On December 19, 1913, a special meeting was called to solve the problem of horse shed and coalhouse, fencing, dictionary, and water fountain. Mr. Hollister stated if $150 county funds could be obtained for shed, school could be held an additional month. Mr. Hollister offered to haul one 4-horse load of lumber; Mr. Richard to haul other supplies; Fred Morris to supply large posts for uprights. The school board to erect and frame using one carpenter, rest of work to be donated. Ladies offered to give a hot dinner one day for the workers.

Note:

County Treasurer dispersed $184.63 to Wapiti.

Number of students, six, another was taught at home by a tutor. Annie Sweney taught 1913 through 1914.

Students probably were: Leonard Morris, Davis Graves, Roy and Vera Lehman, Lester Marlow and Lisle Dickenson.

OTHER ACTIVITIES: A basket dinner, Fourth of July celebration was held at the school house and speeches were given by Lee Upton, Clyde Pepper, and John Yeates. At 6:00 p.m. Mr. Pat Kelly drove up with his commodious four-horse carriages and extended an invitation to all to visit the Pat Kelly Ranch. This invitation was promptly accepted and the entire group spent the evening dancing and socializing.

On Thanksgiving Day 1913, a community dinner was given at the school house.

The School At Rattlesnake

Arthur Reese and family were early homesteaders on Rattlesnake Creek and in 1909 Reese constructed a log building for a school. Three teachers who taught there at various times were Miss Rana Brown, Miss Nye, and Miss Virginia St. Denis (Cleas).

The annual school census for school district No. 9 of Park County lists the following for the years 1912 and 1915 (the first and last years they were counted in school census) only as follows:

Names of Pupils	Residence	1912 Age	1915 Age
Leona Reece	Rattlesnake Creek	12	15
Lucille Reece	" "	10	13
Willard Reece	" "	6	9
Howard Rhoads	" "	-	15
Helen Rhoads	" "	-	10
Willard Rhoads	" "	-	6
Samuel Miller	Trout Creek	7	10

(never attended a rural school as he was taught by a tutor at home)

The trustees of District No. 9 agreed "that we give school No. 2 a school of five months term provided that it didn't raise the taxes this year or put the District in debt, and that the patrons of school No. 2 pay for one month's school, making a six month term credit to district No. 9."

"Mrs. Rhoads said that they would furnish a school house, fuel, desks and everything. The district, to see that they have books like the state provides." "We decided to pay the teacher $50 per month holding as she didn't have to pay for keep of horse or such a long walk she could teach for less." There are no more statistics on Rattlesnake School and records for Wapiti School are resumed.

School Year 1914-15

The fourth annual meeting of District No. 9 was held May 4, 1914 at the school house. There was discussion but no action concerning the length of school year, school in the summer, and need for classroom equipment. A definite date was set for work on the shed and E. M. Thurmond would furnish cedar posts and fence the yard for $30. Miss Effie Abramson (later Mrs.Ernest Shaw) taught the two girls and eight boys for a six month term. School District assessed at $147,684.

School Year 1915-16

The fith annual meeting held May 3, 1915. Joe Lehman, president. Fred Richard to become director.

In the Business Session Mr. Hollister resolved: "that it is the sense of this meeting that the best interests of District #9 would be served by a division of said district and that the clerk is hereby directed to send a copy of this resolution to the County Superintendent with a request that she make such division and recommend same to the County Commissioners." This was carried by one vote. Harriet E. Thurmond, Clerk

The teacher, Miss Ruth Clark, taught 153 days, one girl and five boys,an eight month school term. Probably Hugh and James Thurmond found the distance too great, they attended only seventeen days.

Dist. assessed at $141,621.

Miss Clark had to close the school once during January due to cold weather. Henceforth, Dist. 9 would no longer list students residing at Rattlesnake Creek.

School Year 1916-1917

The sixth annual meeting held May 2, 1916

Ben Simpers elected three year term as trustee. A special tax of five mills was levied to cover expenses for coming year because if the average attendance is not six pupils or more, the general county fund of $300 is withheld. It was voted the next school term be nine months.

Miss Ruth Clark taught two girls and four boys for 179 days or 1,033 student days or 96 percent. This high percentage could be because the students lived close to the school, Simpers on Whit Creek, Nedward Frost and Jack Richard and Dwight Hollister close by. The assessed valuation was $127,047 for the school district.

School Year 1917-1918

The seventh annual meeting was held May 7, 1917, and Mr. Hollister was re-elected trustee. It was determined the school term would be nine months and teacher's salary be $75. School schedule 9 to noon and 12:30 to 2:30 and started Sept.l0th. School Dist. was assessed a valuation, $107,688.

Teacher, Miss Delia L. Scanlan taught four girls and six boys for 176 days.

School Year 1918-1919

The eighth annual meeting was held May 6, 1918, Ben Simpers presided and Fred Richard was reelected. It was voted a special tax of two mills be levied for the ensuing year.

Miss Anna McDaniel taught four girls and ten boys for 165 days. Assessed valuation $123,067, finally the assessed valuation begins to rebound after several years of decline. From 1915 to 1919 enrollment grew from ten to eighteen, and continued to grow steadily until 1931. Anna Mc Daniel, a cousin of Mrs. Simpers, lived at Simpers on Whit Creek and later married Nicholas Hevron and returned to Indiana.

School Year 1919-1920

The ninth annual meeting was held May 5, 1919, Ben Simpers chairman, Dwight Hollister moved Ben Simpers be elected clerk. A one mill levy was approved.

Miss Myrtle Conklin taught eighteen students for 173 days at an annual cost of $71.82 per student or a daily cost of forty two cents per student. Again, the assessed valuation goes up, to $144,915. During the year the school suffered vandalism. Myrtle, tall dark haired and good natured, also lived with the Simpers family.

School Year 1920-1921

The tenth annual meeting was held as usual in the Wapiti School house on May 3, 1920, without any special celebration of the first ten years. The daily cost per student was forty cents, the lowest of the first twenty-one years.

Miss Evea Hoisington taught five girls and ten boys for 180 days. Her salary was $100 per month. The assessed valuation rose to $153,543.

The School at Logan Creek Reopened

The log cabin school at Logan Creek had brief use as the initial location of the first Wapiti School in 1911. Again, in 1920, it was used for the same purpose.[7] The Henry Dahlem family with seven-year-old Mary Helen and two preschool sons, Clarence and Harry, had moved to Breteche Creek in 1919. Mary Helen entered first grade at Wapiti that year and the next school year she attended only four days and the family moved to Trout Creek where Henry was employed as foreman.

The Cecil Huntington family with sons, James, Carl, Don and preschool daughter Dorothy were living at the Logan Creek place. The Floyd Early family lived on the Thurmond place just east of Trout Creek and had seven year old son Vincent and preschool daughter, Marjorie.

The three families hired Miss Eva Taylor, sister of Roxielettie Yeates at a salary of $100 per month. Eva made the six-mile-trip daily in a two wheeled, spring mounted sulky cart drawn by one horse. Mary Helen and Vincent joined her on horseback to and from school, Mary Helen rode"Dickie" and both youngsters carried their lunch.

About the middle of the school year the Huntingtons moved away. The winter weather made the school cabin difficult to heat in the morning so the Earlys offered the front room of their log home as a class room, and they used it for the rest of the term, for Mary Helen Dahlem and Vincent Early. The Logan School closed permanently the spring of 1921.

The following year, nine-year-old Mary Helen rode Mr. de Mauriac's horse "Rocket" from Trout Creek to the Wapiti school. On one occasion while enroute to school the saddle cinch was loose and when about half way to school the saddle turned spilling Mary Helen on the ground. She then removed the saddle, left it by the side of the road and began leading the horse back towards home. While driving down the road with team and wagon, John Yeates came upon the saddle and put it in the wagon. A short distance farther he caught up with Mary Helen, saddled the horse, Mary remounted and proceeded to school.

A year later the Dahlems moved back to Breteche Creek and Mary Helen and her brothers all attended the Wapiti school until the winter of 1922 when the family moved to Sage Creek, south east of Cody. Thus ended the Logan School and records for Wapiti School are resumed.

School Year 1921-1922

The eleventh annual meeting was held May 2, 1921, chaired by John Yeates, and this year Hollister suggested a special levy of 4 mills, and the patrons agreed to paint the school house. We have a record that the District expenses amounted to $1,173.32 which included teacher's salary, $925 and text books, $76.74. Evea Hoisington taught five girls and ten boys for 180 days or 1826 student days, 67.6%. Her salary was $100 per month. Assessed valuation rose to $153,543.

The School Year 1922-1923

The annual meetings continued to be held each spring in the Wapiti school house. Most teachers taught but one year although Evea Hoisington stayed two years. The twelfth annual meeting showed the district went in arrears $189.67. Miss Elizabeth Sharp was teaching thirteen boys and six girls in all grade levels except third and seventh. During the school year 1922-23 there is a detailed tabulation of Dist. 9 income (only one of two from the district).[8]

The School Year 1923-1924

The School Year 1923-24 saw teacher Miss Eileen Redmond teaching grades 1-9, nine girls and twelve boys for a salary of $120 month. But the Receipts dropped to $1,191.81. This is the first year a "school wagon" operated for students west of the school.

The School Year 1924-25

The first of two different teachers, Miss Gladys Dowling taught the first two terms, then resigned to be married. Miss Grace Holthues finished out the spring term with eight girls and eleven boys. The assessed valuation of the district dropped to $113,825. Claude Shull had the bus contract for $650. Total expenses were $2,357.44 less $120 high school tuition. This is the year the school bought a piano for $100 from L. C. Freeman, a miscellaneous expense.

School Year 1925-1926

The school year 1925-26 had Miss Vera Schultz for teacher with a heavy load of nine girls and eleven boys, for which she received $100 per month. The total expenses were $2,279.46, reduced by $180 High School tuition. Claude Shull bused 14 children to school for $60. a month.

The School Year 1926-1927

The school year 1926-27, the fifteenth year of the school, saw a record enrollment of eight girls and fifteen boys, taught by Miss Lucile Beaty at $100 per month. The assessed valuation increased and Claude Shull received $75 a month for his bus service. In the Warrant Register of expenses are noted items, library $67.73 and new equipment, $74.70, probably *The Book of Knowledge* encyclopedia and playground equipment.

In the fall of 1926 the Wapiti school board thought they had a contract with a lady from out-of-state to teach the term starting in a few days. At the last minute this person cancelled her agreement.

Up at the Simon Snyder dude ranch in Sunlight, Miss Lucile Beaty, a junior at the University of Iowa in Ames, was finishing her summer job. Lucile recalled, "Vaun (Mrs. Stanley Landgren of Cody) phoned me one day and said, "Sis, come in on Saturday because the school board up at Wapiti are in need of a teacher." " A teacher! I had never taught a day in my life."

Lucile came to town, the school board interviewed and hired her and she began teaching the following Monday. Lucile said, "There were six great big boys, taller than I was and they were ready to give me trouble, the same as they had the previous teacher, and I had no teacher training, was just young and willing."

"One morning during the first week of school I found the door off its hinges when I arrived. Pretty soon the kids began coming in, looking anxious for some reaction on my part. After the big ones got there I said, 'Well, I can see we are going to have a manual training class today. I have to find out just how a door is put on because I found it leaning against the wall. I can't put it on so you kids are going to have to show me.'"

The kids looked guilty but they knew she wasn't angry and wasn't accusing them so the prank just fell flat. As the days went on she joined them in playing games at recess. Lucile admitted, "I don't think I taught them half of what they should have learned, I felt more like a kid with them. We took our dinner pails and hiked out and did our spelling lessons on the rimrocks. I loved it at Wapiti, I enjoyed the children and the people were so wonderful."

A major acquisition for the school was a twelve volume set of the *Book of Knowledge* in the 1926-27 year. Poems were read aloud with emphasis on memorization and recitation. Longfellow's poem *The Village Blacksmith* epitomized the noble and spiritual attributes of the highest caliber man, a meaningful beacon to guide the attitudes of students.[9]

The School Year 1927-1928

The school year 1927-28, enrollment reached twenty-nine - eleven girls and eighteen boys with only one teacher, Miss Elsie Mailander who taught this roomful for $125 per month. Claude Shull received $75 a month for bus contract. This term, Wapiti School qualified as a Wyoming Standard School, meeting qualifications set forth by the state and certified by visitation of Mrs. Mildred Anderson, Park County Superintendent of Schools. The school received an enameled steel shield with the identifying words and they promptly mounted it above the front door of the school house.

The School Year 1928-1929

The eighteenth annual meeting showed new names appearing on the board, J. F. Kelly, Bill Borron, Oscar Montgomery. Elsie Mailander and Miss Mayabeth Brosman took on the task of teaching twenty-nine students, this time twelve girls and seventeen boys .Elsie handled the big kids including two highschool ninth graders and Mayabeth had the lower grades. Neither teacher returned. During the year 1928-29 the grades were divided, a folding partition was placed in the school room and two teachers were employed. One group included grades one through five and the other grades six, seven, and eight. This year Budd Hall had the bus contract, $100 per month. James and Herman Jenkins were taking the 9th grade class.

School Year 1929-1930

The nineteenth year (1929-30) is memorable for an enrollment of thirty-four students, fourteen girls and twenty boys, taught by Miss Vera Schultz, $125,for the upper grades and Mrs. Flossie Wood, the lower grades, $110 per month. Charles Wood had the bus contract for $100. Teachers' salaries were the major expense of the budget of $3,599.72 reduced by $225 high school tuition for Bill Simpers and Worth Legg.

John Yeates recalled "Mrs. Woods maintained strict discipline and was fiercely determined to produce academic results. Winning the annual county spelling contest in the spring of the year was a challenge she accepted. In preparation for this contest we began early in the year with daily practice of spelling sections of the official book. Mrs. Woods chose a group of us in the upper classes she thought to be worthy contestants and in addition to daily drill we also traveled to someone's home on Friday evenings where we might spell through the entire book. This intense drilling did produce results. In 1931 Ted Sherwin won first place in this contest. The following year 1932, his younger sister, Betty won first place for the girls, and Jack Yeates took second place, and winner for the boys. Lucille Legg took third place. Betty received a trip to the state contest at Douglas, Wyoming, in the fall of the year."

The School Year 1930-1931

1930-31, and the twentieth annual meeting of School District No. 9, at Wapiti School. Flossie Woods taught the upper grades for $125 and Fern Ashley the lower grades for $110. There were eight girls and fourteen boys with two boy in high school (ninth grade).

The School Year 1931-1932

Mrs. Flossie Wood taught for $125 per month and Miss Mary L. Johnson for $110. Mary Johnson enhanced the curriculum with instruction in Spanish songs and words. There were nine girls and eight boys, the girls for the first time outnumbering the boys, and there was one boy and one girl in high school class, Charles Simpers and Dorothy Legg. Charles Wood had bus contract for $95 and N. P. de Mauriac received $25, monthly for furnishing transportation for Huetta Newton, daughter of Wesley Newtons, who lived on the the Thrumond Place. School ran for 172 days. Of the expenses, Teachers' salaries and Transportation were highest, but fuel and janitor supplies had reached $122. Total expenses were $3,839.15, less high school tuition of $225, left final expenses of $3,614.15.[10] This was the twentieth anniversary of the Wapiti School but was not celebrated. The Great Depression had hit the West. Enrollment had dropped to around seventeen. Assessed valuation had dropped but teachers' salaries remained the same.

John Yeates contributed the following personal memories from his eight years at Wapiti.

School Yard Games

Until 1926 there was no playground equipment. The children played games dependent on weather conditions. Popular games were hide and seek, hoop rolling, marbles, top spinning, steal sticks and duck on the rock. Wet snow meant snow ball fights and forts. Bean shooters and sling shots were fun until Miss Mailander considered them hazardous and confiscated the equipment. Another short-lived game was one-on-one whipping contests. The boys made whips with eighteen inch handles attached to a three foot leather strap. Only the sides of the legs were to be hit, the fellow who could whip the most furiously and also withstand the most pain won, according to John Yeates, a student at the time.

Rolling old tires around the school yard and from high off the hill south of the school yard progressed to Jimmie Shull fitting himself inside the tire and riding it down the hill across the road until stopped by the board wall in front of the girls' outhouse. The teacher soon ended this hazardous school yard escapade, but Jimmie won hero status among his classmates.

During the 1926-27 school year, homemade swings and teeter-totters and commercial model "Giant Stride" were added to the equipment.

Bringing the "milk bucket" of drinking water from Whit Creek or the river for its place on a table in the girl's cloak room was a highly sought assignment for fifth grade boys. Prior to 1913 a bucket of water and dipper sufficed, but then the state law required individual tin cups, which were hung on the wall. An enamel wash basin was available for the occasional hand washing. The walk to the river was a special adventure for two boys who shared holding the bail of the full bucket on the walk back to the school house. The boys usually found time to skip a few flat rocks across the river while there."

Other Contest Achievements

"In 1930 a Rural Day Program for country schools was started and held in the spring at the Cody High School and its athletic field. In preparation for these contests we at Wapiti set up some homemade high -jump equipment, dug a soft dirt pit for broad jump, and competed with each other in running a 50 yard dash. Virginia Sherwin worked hard on a piano solo and I was coached on how to recite a poem with proper expression. On the day of the contest Ted Sherwin and Bill Simpers tied for third place in track and field with ten points each. Virginia won first place in music playing Mendelssohn's "Spring Song " With very little competition I received first place with my recitation. Wapiti students continued to place in the various categories in subsequent years," according to John Yeates.

Hardships and Hazards Enroute to School

Hardy Shull and Claude Shull settled on the north side of the river near the eastern boundary of the National Forest. Hardy Shull's family had three daughters, Josephine, Frances, and Rita, and lived one-half mile north of the river. Claude Shull's family were Mary, Dorothy, Jimmie (Tuffy), Dick, and Minnie Bell. They lived a mile farther north of the river.

At that time there was no bridge over the river; it had to be forded with team and wagon. Later, in 1923, when the older children were school age, Claude contracted at $100 per month to provide bus transportation for students living in the west end of the valley, upstream from the school. He drove a Dodge panel truck with roll-down curtains and benches for seats. With no bridge available he kept it on the south side of the river. The Shull children of both families crossed the river via team and wagon, then rode to school as the bus picked up other students along the route. This was the first use of automotive transport of school children on the North Fork. Former students had traveled via horseback or horse and buggy and those living east of the school continued to do so. Around 1922-23 the Bradfords spent part of the school year at their ranch and Catherine rode her brown mare "Midget" to school, treating him to a little exercise and a nose bag of oats at noon. Later, the Yeates family acquired the mare providing John Yeates transportation. The Shull's river crossing worked well most of the school year, except during spring run-off when the river was not safe. Then the crossing could be made only by use of a hand-operated cable car, suspended downstream from the normal crossing. One child at a time rode the cable car operated by Claude or Hardy each morning and afternoon.

Josephine Shull related to John Yeates some memorable winters, "cold, miserable walks across a hayfield to the cable car". Her mother would supply her with two hot potatoes to carry in her pockets as hand warmers. Her mother also dressed her warmly in long underwear under her cotton stockings. Josephine believed the lapped-over legs of the underwear under her stockings gave her legs a lumpy and unstylish appearance, so she would stop on the far side of a haystack, out of sight of the house, and roll down her stockings, roll up the underwear legs and redo her stockings for a smoother appearance. This procedure had to be reversed on the homeward trip.

Two years later they built a pole bridge over the river and Claude could drive his bus the full route most of the time. One winter, for a few days deep snow prevented use of the bus and Claude hitched his team of horses to a wagon chassis equipped with sled runners as a means of transport. Thus the children on the bus route arrived at school, although quite late. Ted Sherwin, also a student, living at the Trail Shop told John Yeates he remembers well those winter sled rides.

In spite of these transportation handicaps, Frances Shull completed her eight year enrollment at Wapiti school with perfect attendance. Jimmy Montgomery claimed perfect attendance also.

Summary of Attendance Data 1911 through 1932

Of the original 1911 group of pupils, Billy Leabold returned to Philadelphia, Don and Vera Wagoner moved to the South Fork, Hershel Green's family moved away. Only Leonard Morris, whose family was most active in establishing the school, continued to attend until 1916 when he attended eastern schools. Roy and Vera Lehman, children of Wapiti Ranger Joe E. Lehman, attended only until 1915, although their father is listed as Wapiti District ranger until 1922, but he was probably in the Cody office. Dwight Hollister, Jr., whose lawyer father was a great help on the school board for many years, attended from 1916-1921, is not listed 1921-22, and returned 1922-23, briefly when he was twelve. Catherine Bradford is listed as a student during years 1922-1925. All the Simpers children starting with Talba in 1913, Morris, Thelma, William, Charles, Mark, Mary and Norma completed their elementary education at Wapiti School. Virginia, Ted, Clifford and Betty and Russell Sherwin went to Wapiti as did Worth, Dorothy, Lucille, Cecil, Beulah, Joan,Gordon and Don Legg. Josephine, Frances, and Rita Shull attended all grades, but their cousins, Mary, Dorothy, Jimmie ("Tuffy"), Minnie Bell, and Dick moved away in 1929.

Orilla Downing's (Hollister) daughters, Georgia and Doris, briefly attended in 1918-19. The McClain children, Ed, Cecil, Billie and Audrey, came in 1918 and attended until 1927 with Billie the last enrolled. Fred Richard's boys attended, Jack until 1924, and Bob until 1925. Young Nedward Frost attended from 1916-1919. In 1921-22 Charles Sullivan's grandchildren, Charles, Lillie and Neta Fay stayed a school year. Dick Pepper apparently dropped out in the 1925-26 year, attended for 90 days in 1927-28, and drops out at the age of 16. Carl, Don and Dorothy Huntington went to Wapiti for a few years, but their parents moved around frequently, and Carl and Don, soon left school to join the work force. Gilbert and Clyde Dugger, whose parents were working at Mountain View Lodge, attended for a few years, until 1931. Seven year old Martin Gipe, step-son of Don Wagoner, one of the original Wapiti enrollees, attended briefly in 1927- 28, when Don was renting the Fred Richard Ranch.

Elmer Kelly and John Yeates, Jr. entered school in 1924 and Jimmy Montgomery started in 1928, all completing the eight grades. Second generation Montgomerys attended Wapiti.

The Jenkins boys, Herman, Jim and Robert, began attending Wapiti school in 1923, and by 1928, James and Herman were taking ninth grade classes. The old-time Thurmond family from Marquette settled east of Trout Creek and were represented by Hugh and James in 1915-16. The Dickinson children attended off and on, Lisle briefly in 1914, and Lisle and Murl in 1918-19.

The enrollment shot up just before the Wall Street Crash of the Great Depression during the school year 1929-30. Two teachers handled the 34 students, a record high enrollment for many years. Three families caused this peak enrollment: an Adams family with four children moved into the house Fred Richard had built down near the river; the Fenex family moved onto the Kelly/Pepper Place with four children; and a Bauer family entered five children in school and stayed less than four weeks. However, by the 1931-32 school year, three families with a total of thirteen children moved out of the district and the enrollment dropped to 17, including Charles Simpers and Dorothy Legg enrolled as ninth graders. Sherwin, Simpers, Legg, Shull, Yeates, Kelly, Montgomery, were the permanent valley residents.

NOTES:

1. Interview with Quince Chance, April 10, 1969.
2. Detailed statistics of the School District 23 from 1897 to 1910 are available at the Park County Archives as compiled by John Yeates.
3. It will be noted that in taking the school census it was necessary to list all young people between ages 6 and (usually) 21 years of age in hopes of getting enough to qualify for a school. A folk tale circulated that one year Mrs. Dave Corder, not yet 21, was counted to boost the number needed. The Corders lived on the Stonebridge place.
4. June Hale's memoirs furnish this school information.
5. The listings of this census for the ensuing years is the basis for tables of attendance provided in this chapter.
6. John Yeates said no sources of information have been found regarding the cost of the school building or the source of the funds, although Park County probably provided them. It would appear there was no school during the winter of 1911-1912 and that the building may have been completed late in 1911. Park County records show $30 dispensed to Wapiti.
7. The following account is not substantiated by any administrative records of attendance of financial support because none can be found. The account is based entirely on an interview with Mrs. Roy (Mary Helen Dahlem) Daly, from her recollections and on John Yeates' information as related to him by his Aunt Eva Taylor who taught there in 1920.
8.

Date	Source of Receipts	Amount
Aug. 2, 1922	District No. 24 Bank Account	$451.32
	Charles McClain, Treasurer	60.36
Sept. 7, 1922	Special Tax	41.90
Oct. 11, 1922	Special Tax and Poll Tax	149.63
Nov. 10, 1922	Oil Royalty (Oregon Basin field)	298.17
Nov. 10, 1922	Forest Service	5.00
Nov. 10, 1922	State Land Income	182.52
Feb. 15, 1923	Special Tax	474.76
Feb. 15, 1923	Poll Tax	98.00
Mar. 15, 1923	General School Fund	258.38
April 18, 1923	State Land Income	222.45
May 17, 1923	Special Tax	101.87
May 17, 1923	Poll Tax	2.00
Total Receipts		2,346.35

9. John Yeates memoirs.
10. These statistics are condensed from complete reports compiled by John A. Yeates and can be found in the Park County Archives.

Below the Federal highway signs annoucing the current roads to Yellowstone, and right the way the road looked when Stimson took his photograph on the way to Yellowstone through the Cody Gateway. Photo courtesy of Wyoming State Archives, Museums and Historical Department.

Roads and Tourism

The earliest marks of travel on the North Fork were the game trails used by the 18th- and 19th-century Indians who sometimes transformed a single path into a set of parallel paths when they traveled with lodge poles fastened on each side of their ponies. The earliest such set of parallel tracks appears on the first government survey map of 1883. The map shows a road coming west around the south side of Cedar Mountain, crossing Carter Creek, then crossing the South Fork of the Stinking Water two miles above the confluence of the North and South Forks. The ford across the North Fork was one-half mile above the mouth of Rattlesnake Creek. The road was so little used in the upper valley that it soon petered out into a trail.

Below, the site of Stimson's Yellowstone road photo near Newton Creek in the 1990s.

Colonel William F. Cody proposed a road connecting the east side of Yellowstone Park with the Big Horn Basin. The first step was taken by the Forest Service when they blazed forty miles of trail on the North Fork in 1899. Before bridges were built, the water level in the lower reaches of the rivers greatly affected how easily and safely the rivers could be forded. During high water they could be impassable from late June until the middle of July.

By 1902 Felix Alston had a government contract to build the first road to Yellowstone Park for $1000. Walter Braten hauled several tons of materials and supplies on the new road and built a road house where Pahaska now is. Braten was a colorful pioneer, who had lived from age ten to fifteen with the Oglala Sioux. Later he became a

scout with Custer, but he fell ill with typhoid and was unable to travel to the Battle of the Little Big Horn. His road house was sometimes referred to as the Berry and Braten camp because Sam Berry was associated with him in their hunting and guiding business. The Sam Berry Meadows north of Pahaska are named for him. Colonel Cody promised that if a road from Cody to the Park were built, he would see that accommodations for travelers were available. The short-lived Braten road house, was a forerunner of the Pahaska Hotel and tourist complex. Well-known Anton Gerharz came to Cody from Wisconsin in March of 1903 to work as a timekeeper for the road crew. One newspaper credited Henry Gerharz of "being in charge of the 1903 road building." He was in the first wagon to go into the Park on the new road. The Gerharz family was still active in the accounting business in Billings, Montana, in the 1990s.

Above: Yellow buses wait outside the Trail Shop.Hiscock postcard.
Below: Frost and Richard wagon on corkscrew bridge. Ed Jones driving and dudine riding alongside. Photo courtesy of Elmor Jones.

During the horse and buggy days the trip from Cody to Pahaska was too long for one day's travel, so Colonel Cody built the Wapiti Inn, east of Elk Fork, a central A-frame facing south with long wings extending east and west on each side. Five rooms in each wing opened off the long porch that ran the entire length. Rates were $2.50 a day or $15 a week.

Wapiti Inn was situated east of Elk Fork, north of the present highway. A name first suggested for it was "Shopski Wickiup," or Home of White Beaver.[1] , but Wapiti Inn was chosen. Application for permit to build was granted from the Forest Service on July 23, 1904. The Wapiti Inn had a telephone and the number was six rings. Possibly Dr. Frank Powell,

"White Beaver," [2] was in charge of construction. The inn, built in 1905 operated until 1913, when automobiles supplanted horse travel. Then Wapiti Inn was torn down, and the salvageable materials were taken to Pahaska to be used for cabins there. Many Mormons from the new settlements in the Big Horn Basin found work building the road. Mormon Creek, one of the tributaries of the North Fork bears their name. One time in 1902, a Cody dentist, Dr. Chamberlain, went up to the Mormon camp to do dental work on the men building the government road. The road officially opened on July 10, 1903. That same year, Cheyenne photographer, J. E. Stimson, made a trip by horse and buggy, camping along the way and doing a little fishing, from Cody up over Sylvan Pass. His guide, Fred Chase, furnished the horse and buggy. Stimson took many photographs of this first road. Also in 1903, Mrs. Chamberlain[3] traveled over the new road and publicly announced it was "safe." No longer would Park visitors from the Big Horn Basin have to travel the longer Dead Indian-Clarks Fork route.

The early road inside the Forest Reserve, where the road enters a narrow canyon, had so many dugways (roads cut on a sidehill) and blind curves it was necessary to put up "walk ahead" signs for the safety of travelers. The signs advised the horse drawn vehicle to stop while someone walked ahead to peer around the curve to see if the "coast was clear." It was not easy to back a team if one met an oncoming conveyance. Some of the first automobiles used loud horns to warn oncoming traffic to pull into a "turnout," a place wide enough for two vehicles to pass. Road building quickly moved forward. By 1907, because of the building of the Shoshone Dam, a scenic road paid for by the government had been built through the previously impassible canyon. Federal money paid for a new road to the Wapiti bridge, referred to at that time as the Kelly bridge, and for a new steel bridge. This came about because the rising water of the reservoir flooded the old road, closer to the reservoir.

A lady dude stands by while her pipe smoking husband roles up the bedding on a Frost and Richard Camping trip. Below, the husband gives his wife a boost aboard her horse. Photos courtesy Elmor Jones.

For a few years, Park County was responsible for maintaining the road between the bridge and the Forest Reserve and a contract was awarded to David Lewis of Cowley for $3,475 to do this.

By 1908, the first horseless carriage traveled on the upper North Fork to Pahaska, bringing distinguished guests, Secretary of the Interior Garfield and Mr. F. H. Newall, Director of the U. S. Reclamation Department, from Pahaska to the Wallop-Moncrieffe boom near the Trimmer ranch. By 1909, Gus Holm was driving his Studebaker on the road and by 1910 Colonel Cody bought Palace White Steamers to carry passengers between the Irma Hotel and Pahaska. The fare was $5. Kid Wilson drove the early horse stage (four-horse mountain coaches) from Cody to Holm Lodge but in 1916, he easily made the transition to driving seven-passenger Buicks and 30 hp., twelve passenger Stanley Steamers. Later Wilson drove a 1924 seven passenger Buick with the first four wheel brakes.

Helen Spencer (Mrs. Clifford), wife of Ranger Spencer, was one of the first women to drive a car, a Model T Ford, on the North Fork. Other early model cars traveling the North Fork road were Oaklands, Thirty Buick, Palmer-Singer 6 cylinder, Hudson "33"runabout, Pierce Arrow, and E.M.F. Machine. The Studebaker E.M.F. "30" Touring car sold for $1,250 in 1910, and $1,100 in 1912 through the Cody Trading Company. The Studebaker Flanders sold for $740. Tex Holm used an Avery Traction 45 hp. eighteen-passenger to haul passengers. By 1920, the most numerous were Model T Fords, selling at that time in Cody for under $400, Will Richard had the first Ford agency in Cody.

Sylvan Pass "snowcut" showing dirty snow and levels of removal. Photograph courtesy of Park County Archives.

John Murray and pile of rocks left from 1916 through 1919 rock clearing efforts.

Below(bottom): A pile of rocks gathered from 1916 through 1919, when citizens turned out to clear the roads.

H. B. Robertson traveled by motorcycle between his ranch and Cody, probably the first one to travel by that means, perhaps around 1910.

A real boost came from Wyoming Congressman Walter Mondell, who introduced a bill on January 26, 1910, into Congress for $20,000 for repairing and maintaining the road from the Forest Reserve on North Fork to outlet of Yellowstone Lake.

Also, in 1910, the government "replacement" road was finished and three automobile-loads of people

visited the government dam in the canyon and drove on to the Pat Kelly ranch for a "sumptuous dinner" of roast chicken.[4] Pat Kelly had been uncooperative in granting right-of-way across his land, requesting an injunction to have the road follow the original C. E. Hayden survey. Reclamation Engineer Cole said his crew would quit work unless they could build the road the way the government wanted it. This stubborn standoff between Cole and Kelly was finally resolved when the county paid Kelly $1,500 for the disputed right-of-way. Kelly preferred to say

Above, the abandoned corkscrew bridge and below how it looked when it was the only way into the east entrance of Yellowstone. The bottom photo was taken around 1910, the corkscrew bridge was near Sylvan Pass.

these payments were "for damages." Pat Kelly had already been paid $543 and his wife Mary Kelly received $123 in 1910 (hence it was said he was paid twice for the road). Also, rancher C. P. Thurmond was paid $100 for the road to cross his land east of Trout Creek. The new steel bridge crossing the narrow gorge at Wapiti was put in by Des Moines Construction Co. it was finally ready in July 1910.

In 1909 Milton Benedict and a gang of workmen were repairing the road and in 1911 Ed Hutsonpillar had a gang of twelve men working on the government road above Pahaska. One time Hutsonpillar's crew got sick from eating "tainted" meat, but luckily all survived. Over the years other road crews pitched camp on the North Fork. In 1926 and 1927, Joe Freeborg kept his teams busy grading the roads, while his wife Elsie cooked in a tent for the crew. Sometimes Freeborg's job was to blast out the Sylvan Pass snow drifts in the spring. Black powder did a dirtier but better job than the dynamite once used. The men shoveled the snow part way up the bank and the men on the higher level shoveled it clear, according to Eileen Freeborg Thomas. Sometimes the dynamite charges were set in place in the fall.

In the early 1900s roads were proliferating all over the country. Before they were given federal highway numbers, the highways had names. The North Fork was part of the Black and Yellow Highway from the Black Hills to Yellowstone Park and was marked by rocks painted yellow, usually with a black "H" painted on them. Then there was the "Park to Park" road link, in which the Yellowstone Trail Association included the North Fork road. The Trail Shop at the entrance to the Forest Reserve took its name from it. By 1932 the Atlantic-

Prince of Monaco (behind driver) and entourage at Frost and Richard Ranch September 28 th, 1913. Chinese Wall and Jim Mountain in background. Photo courtesy of Elmor Jones.

Valley Ranch Boys Party at Holy City near their 1st camp at Horse Creek. Carl Johansson head guide right forefront in photo.

Yellowstone-Pacific Highway was routed via the East Gate of Yellowstone. In 1923 the state highways were first marked by a numbering system, replacing the multitude of names formerly used. Federal highways, numbered 14, 16, and 20 funneled east to west travel on the highway along the North Fork river.

In May of 1913, Senator Francis E. Warren of Wyoming got a bill passed allocating $75,000 to improve the East and West entrance roads to Yellowstone, and an additional $15,000 for improving the Cody road within the Forest Reserve. Senator Warren early on favored allowing automobile traffic in the Park.

Felix Alston again had something to do with the North Fork road in 1913. At this time he was Superintendent of the Penitentiary at Rawlins and brought nine prisoners to work on the road under one supervisor. George Saban was one of these road workers. Twenty-four years later his son, James Saban, lost his life in the Blackwater Fire.

Many notables traveled the North Fork road in 1913, among them Secretary of Interior Lane and wife, and in September the Prince of Monaco and entourage traveled to Pahaska. By November 1914, eight miles of park road from Moss Creek to Chimney Rock had been completed using the money Warren helped to get. At a width of 18 feet, the road "approaches a boulevard." But money was slow to come in for roads. Private donations were solicited. In 1915, Childs, the Yellowstone Park concessionaire, gave $400 for the road and in 1916 the Burlington Railroad pledged $600 for it.

From 1916 to 1919 local residents, Cody businessmen and anyone and everyone pitched in to clear the North Fork road of rocks. To this day the rocks they cleared and piled up still can be seen. In 1917, on "Good Roads Day," Ben Simpers was "Captain"

Valley Ranch Boys party coming over Table Mountain from Southfork.

for the volunteer road work on the North Fork.[5] In 1918, 25 cars "full of workers were clearing the North Fork road." In June of 1919, the public "enrolled" to work on twenty miles to the Wapiti bridge. Lee Upton said, "We slid a few rocks off the road." Lee with two helpers figured they donated $17.50 worth of work.[6]

Besides Colonel Cody, Harry Thurston of the Forest Service, Walter Mondell and Senator Warren , other great promoters of the highway included Jakie Schwoob of the Cody Trading Company, Mrs. Chamberlain of the Cody Club, Gus Holm and L.L. Newton, of the Good Roads Club.

Tourists were first counted in 1903 when the road was opened. Only 310 entered the East Gate of the 13,165 total Park visitors that year. See footnote for other significant years and numbers of persons entering Yellowstone Park through the East Gate.[7]

In 1923 the East Gate counted 459 persons riding or walking into the Park, according to the *Cody Enterprise*.[8]

The magazine *Wyoming Wildlife* for September 1993 stated that the North Fork highway was an historic treasure.The article cited the average number of cars per day on the North Fork for June, July, and August 1989 (1,490) and 1992 (1,615). The magazine projected that in the year 2010, 2,300 cars per day would travel this road. In 1920, for the whole year, 4,276 autos entered the East Gate.

On August 1, 1915, cars were finally admitted to the Park. On that day 3,050 cars entered, through all entrances.

Colonel Cody sank a lot of money into building up Pahaska. His application for the hotel dates from December 14, 1903. His friend, A. A. Anderson, designed the lodge and probably Dr. Powell, another friend,supervised the construction. Many of his relatives were employed from time to time in both Wapiti Inn, Pahaska, and the Irma Hotel. But by 1916, Colonel Cody, always overly generous, had hit hard times and Pahaska, with all its equipment was listed in Bankruptcy, Court Case #385. The sale listed everything from the hotel, barely twelve years old, to linens, dishes, pots and pans, furnishings, right down to the twenty eight slop jars.

Two years before, in 1914, nearby Holm Transportation Company was bankrupt. The original owners bowed out and after reorganization, Holm Lodge started to become a successful dude facility. Incidentally. On the South Fork, at this same time, The Valley Ranch, started to become a world class dude ranch.

Rustic Bridge, Cody Gateway, 1903. Stimson Photo courtesy Wyoming State Archives, Museums and Historical Department.

In 1918, Raymond W. Allen of the Forest Service headed a project to build a rest area for tourists at Elk Fork Campground. This pleasant grove of cottonwood and aspen trees had become a popular place to stop for horse back riders and wagon travelers, a halfway point to the Park. The area consisted of a log building with shower bath and lavatory. Water from Elk Fork was piped to a boiler, and if the tourists wanted to go to the trouble of chopping wood and starting a fire, they could have hot water. At this time all the camps along the North Fork "are being enlarged and improved with toilet rooms and good trails to the streams for water." [9] Allen encouraged campers to keep a clean camp by burying refuse at least 200 feet from the road. After World War I, tourism again flourished. Money from Federal Road funds became available. The first major amount of $85,000 was allocated for the Cody-Yellowstone Park road in the Shoshone Forest Reserve. [10]

The devastating Canyon Creek "flood" tore out the ranger station in 1923. This cloudburst storm swept eastward from Yellowstone Park, damaging almost every North Fork tributary as water, boulders, debris, sand and gravel came rushing down. Debris closed the road and 135 cars were stranded.

The road was closed in the canyon for ten days in October 1924 for "blasting." [11]

Another road closure came when a rock slide filled the canyon in December 1926. It took workers until the end of February 1927 to open the road again. W. K. Everingham and Co. had the contract. Rerouted travel followed the road built by the Bureau of Reclamation in 1910 around the south side of the reservoir. Local residents sometimes took the gamble to make an ice crossing between Bartlett Lane on the east side of the reservoir and Logan Creek area on the other side, with varying degrees of safety and trepidation. Strong west winds easily sailed the cars off course and sent them dangerously close to holes of open water.

In 1928 Taggart Construction Company was low bidder [12] on North Fork road improvement and in October started construction from Rattlesnake Creek to Jim Creek. In 1929 the road was straightened from Green Creek to the Trail Shop. Federal Funds in the amount of $65,000 paid for this improvement. In 1930 the twenty-year-old-bridge at Wapiti was replaced by a new $64,000 steel bridge.

Also in 1931, the famous corkscrew bridge built in 1907 near the summit of Sylvan Pass was abandoned by the new two-lane highway. This corkscrew had been improved from the original wooden trestle to a cement-walled underpass and rock-filled abutments.

One of the most important improvements came in October 1931 when $160,000 of Federal Road money was appropriated for oiling 23 miles of road from the canyon to the Forest Reserve. In 1933 another big chunk of Federal Road money, $525,000, was allocated for the Cody to Park road. Two years later the final improvement of the highway from the Ranger Station to the Park Entrance was awarded to Tomlinson-Arkwright Construction Company in a contract for $243,711.

When Joe Freeborg had the job of crowning, planing,and dragging the roads, he camped at Hanging Rock. When the Taggarts were building roads, they had camps near Morris Ranch and at Hanging Rock. A lot of cribbing work was done on the river in the early days to keep the river from washing out the road. Water often flowed over the old road at Hanging Rock during high water. "Cribbing" and "riprapping" described methods to control and hold the river where the road builders wanted the river to flow. Boulders, logs, and sometimes junked cars were fastened with cables to divert the water. One troublesome spot was the Thousand Foot Cliff, also called Hanging Rock, where riprapping failed to keep the water off the road. By raising the road the "cave" under Hanging Rock was filled.

During the Depression, road work and bridge construction gave local residents employment when times were hard and work was scarce. No longer did community volunteers have to rally round to clear the roads. Tourists soon flowed through the North Fork on oiled highways 14, 16, 20 that converged in Cody, funneling record-breaking numbers of tourists along the Park road. This scenic route was unmarred by advertising signs because in 1925 the Cody Club promoted a "signless road" to Yellowstone.

In 1937 former President and Mrs. Hoover drove the North Fork. Ted Sherwin tells that the Hoovers saw a stranded tourist and stopped to offer assistance. The tourist was out of gas, so he asked Mr. Hoover to stop at the next gas station and request someone to bring some gasoline, which Mr. Hoover did when he came to the Trail Shop, thus giving the Sherwins a chance to see an ex-president. Ten years before, in August 1927, the youngsters on the North Fork lined the road to see President Coolidge and family drive by. J.F.Kelly and

Above: Bridge over Clocktower around 1913.

John Yeates took their sons Elmer and John Jr. to town to see the President in his private railroad car. John Yeates remembered, " the President spoke not a word."

NOTES

1. "'White Beaver' Powell and "Buffalo Bill" Cody were business partners in several enterprises that either failed or never got off the ground." *Doctor, Lawyer, Indian Chief, the life of Frank Powell, Medicine Man,* p.47. by Eric V. Sorg, Wyoming History Journal, Vol. 67, No. 1.

2. Sorg; pp.37-38.

3. Agnes B. Chamberlain, *The Story of the Cody Club*, Cody Wy. 1940 and wife of Dr. Chamberlain.

4. *Park County Enterprise,* March 9th, 1910.

5. Chamberlain, chapter on roads pp.34-49.

6. *Northern Wyoming Herald*, June 1919

7. 1903 (310 visitors), 1911(1,524), 1912 (1,430),1920 (16,193), 1923 (43,354), 1926 (45,037),1928 (47,577), 1929 (60,749),1930 (51,718), 1932 (45,130), 1933 (49,892),1934 (79,028), 1935 (94,652). These figures were taken from late August issues of the *Cody Enterprise* for various years and then in subsequent years the totals were larger, perhaps because the September numbers were included. For instance, 60,247 in 1928 and 75,856 in 1929. The Park archives at Mammoth did not have the figures broken down for each specific gate, and without archival figures, these newspaper figures cannot be considered accurate.

8. *Cody Enterprise*, August 1923

9. *Northern Wyoming Herald* , June 12, 1918

10. *Cody Enterprise*, July 25, 1923

11. *Cody Enterprise* for October 10, 1924

12. $75,000, (another newspaper account stated $80,035.)

Hunting and Trapping on the North Fork

Native Americans hunted and fished the North Fork of the Shoshone and its tributaries from time immemorial. Hides and bones in Mummy Cave dating back 1,300 years prove this. By the early 1830s the trappers infiltrated this area. The best record comes from Osborne Russell's *Journal of a Trapper.* Russell explored, trapped and hunted in the Greater Yellowstone Ecosystem all through the 1830s. While the north branch of the Shoshone River did not provide the marshy habitat for beaver that was found on the upper South Fork swamps and meadows, an interesting history of hunting and trapping on the North Fork emerges.

Osborne Russell's *Journal* provides a record of his travel in the river valley from July 24, 1835, to July 28, 1835. He and companions came down the South Fork and camped near the confluence of the two forks. Osborne wrote, "Here some of the Trappers knew the country. This stream is called the Stinking Water." [1] This would indicate other trappers had been in the area, but no written record of them survives. However, Walter Kepford had found a tree up Belknap Creek, a branch of the South Fork of the Shoshone river, on which was inscribed the date 1821. He had this section of the tree at the Belknap Ranch house when the building and tree section burned to the ground in 1928.

Joe Meek briefly mentions the Smith-Sublette 1829 trip down the North Fork under harsh December conditions. John Colter is credited with naming the river in 1807, from his olfactory experience, probably a translation from the Crow language. George Drouillard, a French Canadian/Shawnee, also from the Lewis and Clark Expedition, recalled camping near the forks of the rivers in 1807. There is no record of his going up either fork, but he passed on information about the country told to him by the Indian tribes.

Though the wiry, agile mountain bison no longer inhabited these mountains, they had left their mark by gauging out wallows on the high mountain plateaus such as Table Mountain. "All over this table land are evidences, in the way of wallows, showing the former presence of a vast herd of mountain buffalo." [2]

After 1875 the bison were gone, but mountain sheep inhabited the cliffs on Rattlesnake Mountain, Sheep Mountain and all the lower ranges. Before many years passed, the sheep that were not killed were driven from the bluffs and cliffs to find new habitat much higher than in

John Goff with three hunting dogs before 1910. Park County Archives.

pre-historical times. In 1889, William Hornaday writes of killing mountain sheep on the south end of Rattlesnake Mountain.[3] By 1910, early North Fork settler John Yeates had to go high into Trout Creek basin to kill a mountain sheep ram.

Elk and grizzly bear were also animals of prairie and lower elevations and they, too, were forced to move into higher elevations. By 1925, the last grizzlies lived on Table Mountain and the head waters of the river systems, moving ever higher. Mahlon Frost, father of Ned Frost said he had killed 566 bear during the time the family lived on Upper Sage Creek.

The presence of game animals lured hunters, and many of the hunters came from the East or Europe. Charles A. Marston could claim fame as one of the earliest guides on the North Fork. He guided Dr. William T. Hornaday, a brilliant and well-trained early naturalist, on a hunt in 1880. Marston guided widely on both sides of the Montana-Wyoming border. In 1892 he guided Thomas Moran, artist, Elwood Mead, surveyor, and William T. Jackson, photographer, each famous in his own field.

A hunt hosted by Colonel Cody in the fall of 1901 can boast of having the first church services on the North Fork above Marquette. Walter Kepford of the South Fork was outfitter and guide. He had 17 saddle horses and 10 pack horses. The trip took eleven days from the Carter Ranch, five in camp situated a mile below the junction of Middle Fork and North Fork, near what is now known as Three Mile Camp Ground. Members of this party were Colonel Geary of Oklahoma City, Reverend Beecher of North Platte, Curtis Henckle, Secretary of State of Wyoming,, Billy Sweeney, two Sioux, Black Fox and Iron Tail, and the Colonel's good friend, Mike Russell. As on the later Monaco Hunt, the Colonel did not hunt but played the part of the good host. Frank Hammitt, Sam Berry, Pat Kelly and 12-year-old Art Braten came by to partake of the Colonel's hospitality. Perhaps they added their voices to Reverend Beecher's Sunday service. It was reported the men enjoyed the singing.

Some animals moved farther afield into wilderness areas, the mountain lion was targeted for extinction. The events leading to the extermination of the few lions in Yellowstone National Park go back to President Theodore Roosevelt's lion hunts in Colorado.

In 1905, John Goff guided Roosevelt so successfully near Newcastle, Colorado, that the President asked Goff to go to Gardiner, Montana, to destroy the lions "infesting" the Park, for which he would be paid $75. a month, plus $5. for each lion. He would be the first government trapper in the area since he was hired by A.A. Anderson of the Forest Reserve. With nearly a hundred head of horses and a partner, his pack of cougar dogs and his family belongings, Goff traveled north. His pack of dogs consisted of two groups, those trained as trackers and those trained as fighters. Bloodhounds, foxhounds and airedales were kept for treeing lions, bobcats, lynx and sometimes bear.

When Goff had cleaned out the few lions found in the Lamar Valley, he and his family rode down into the North Fork of the Shoshone in 1906. They pitched their camp eight miles downstream from the east entrance of the Park on a creek that came to be called Goff Creek. Roosevelt and Goff corresponded and Roosevelt hoped to hunt on the North Fork, but he never did. Besides Goff, Frost and Richard outfitters, and Aaron "Tex" Holm used hunting dogs extensively until they were outlawed on Forest Reserves in 1910. After that date, they could be used on private lands only. However, government trappers still could use dogs on the Forest Reserve. Goff's two most famous dogs, "Meeker" and "Tige," were sold to outfitter Joe Jones of the Majo Ranch of the South Fork in 1913. The peak of hunting frenzy fell in late fall from 1900 to 1916 and the hunters were hell-bent on exterminating predators and bagging big game. In fact, 1913, could be called "The Year of the Hunter," topped by the Prince of Monaco's hunt, hosted by Buffalo Bill, north of Pahaska near Torrent Creek on the upper North Fork. Fred Richard was the head guide and they used 70 horses to pack in the hunting party and their camp. Ned Frost was guiding "Spend A Million" Gates on a trip up the South Fork into the Thorofare the same fall.

Less prestigious was J. A. McGuire's hunt on Table Mountain that same year. McGuire, editor of *Outdoor Life*, was outfitted by Joe Jones of the Majo Ranch at the head of the South Fork, and guided by Lawrence Nordquist. His prize was "Old Eph," a big grizzly which is displayed to this day in the Colorado Museum of Natural History in Denver, Colorado.

Another hunt started out in an unusual way. Outfitter John Reckless Davis met his hunters at Pahaska in May, 1913. These European dudes had traveled by railroad across the United States to Gardiner, Montana, then by horse-drawn coach to Mammoth. From there they traveled by skis through the Park, over Sylvan Pass and down to Pahaska. The group came from several European countries. "Mr. O. Toaks, was a lecturer from London; Sir Henry Kent, a Colonel in the British Army; Count Fritz Kieberlein, a German botanist; Sir Patrick English, an author from Dublin, Ireland." [4] The party was on a spring bear hunt. In May, 1911, Ned Frost guided financier Malcolm S. MacKay for a month-long spring bear hunt.

Besides the notables from far away, local North Forkers hunted. Mr. and Mrs. Dwight Hollister, with William T. "Bill" Borron as guide, hunted in the Thorofare. The R. G. Millers from Trout Creek hunted with Frost and Richard. In March 1913, Mrs. Miller "captured" a lion measuring eight feet from nose to tip of tail. When the Millers subsequently sold Trout Creek to N. P. deMauriac, the main residence came replete with stuffed animals and birds, horns, antlers, elk hides and bear skins. The bear skin rugs in the living room had life-like heads, large glassy eyes, gaping mouths with red tongues and polished fangs.

Less affluent local ranchers hunted for winter meat, mostly legally in season, but poaching was a problem for the fledgling Game and Fish Department.

The following year, 1914, Joe Jones of the Majo Ranch again outfitted a party consisting of four New York hunters for a 29-day spring bear hunt in and around Table Mountain. They bagged six brown bears, one black, and six grizzlies (four full grown and two cubs). One great old sow was 8'4" long.[5]

Some of the earliest guides included Charles Marston from 1880 on; Sam Berry, when he wasn't serving time in the penitentiary; Walter Braten who started a camp at the site later called Pahaska ,John Goff, Wesley Bloom, John McLaughlin, W. E. Green, Benjamin Franklin Neland, aka "Porcupine Pete" ,who got in trouble frequently with the law; Bill Borron, Ned Frost and Will Richard, whose expertise was passed on to the next generation of guides such as Carl Johansson, Pete and Lawrence Nordquist, Ed Holmquist, Ed "Phonograph" Jones, and many others, many of whom worked for Ned Frost and Will Richard.

In an newspaper interview in 1972, outfitter and hunter Ned Frost, said, "At that time one never went over the high passes into the back country as we have done with our hunting parties, but would hunt around Carter Mountain, Greybull (river) or up the North Fork, usually around the mouth of Elk Fork."[6]

Two major themes evident in hunting from the early 1890s to the 1930s. The first is the hunter's constant intent to eradicate and exterminate predators which preyed on game animals the hunters wanted to keep for themselves. In this the sheepmen, and to some extent the cattlemen, joined forces with the game protectionists against wolves and coyotes. These hunters and stockgrowers were aided and abetted to the full extent of the law by the government trappers hired by the United States Biological Survey. From 1905 to 1907, the Shoshone Division of the Forest Reserve hired hunters to reduce the population of mountain lions.[7] It is interesting the United States Bureau of Biological Survey is credited as doing a good deed for conservation as late as the 1940s by trapping, shooting, and poisoning predatory animals.[8] A column of "Wapiti News" in the *Park County Enterprise* May 18, 1921, exhorted readers to keep up the fight against the predatory animals. The article stated, "The bear are out but the bear hunters have not the luck they are supposed to get. Predatory animals are not as numerous as they were last winter and the deer did not suffer as much as usual. If there was a bounty placed on coyotes and mountain lions, it would help in exterminating these animals and the people of this county need all the protection for game they can get." Little was then understood about the slow reproductive rate of grizzly bears, which don't mature until they are ten years old and do not produce cubs every year.

Bolstered by scientific research contemporary attitudes are completely different. In the July 1992 issue of the *National Geographic*, Maurice G. Hornocker, states that his ten-year research proved lions will not overrun an area, only so many cats can live in a given area. He said, "Second, our research debunked the idea that lions are a danger to big-game herds. The lions will kill very young or very old, non-breeding animals. In fact, during our study, deer and elk populations actually increased, while the number of lions remained stable." [9]

Perhaps in those early days the settlers bringing out wagon loads of game shared in decimating the wild animals. The newspapers were quick to lay blame on outsiders, too, stating the Mormons from Otto and Lovell brought four big wagon loads of game out of Fishhawk in November of 1911.[10] These were part of the 500 elk killed on the North Fork out of 669 game licenses issued. At that time, resident hunting licenses were $2.50, good for two elk, two deer, one male mountain sheep and game birds. Nonresident licenses cost $50.

Harry E. Miller, an early Ranger stationed on the North Fork recalled, "When I was at the Ranger Station at Wapiti, Phonograph Jones and Pete Nordquist trapped up Elk Fork. The pair of them—about 1913—would come to the station about daylight, wake me up, build a fire, get breakfast, then Jonsey would bake seven or eight loaves of bread, some pies and a couple of cakes. They would leave me stocked up and take the rest with them." [11]

Those were the golden years of trapping and hunting on the North Fork of the Shoshone River. If the first theme was extermination of predators, the second theme was conservation of game animals. There were voices crying for protection of the animals in the wilderness. William F. Cody, went on record favoring a reduction of the hunting season. *Outdoor Life* editor, J. A. McGuire, wanted all the North Fork to be a game preserve. Earlier the Lambs Club of New York in 1897 proposed a plan to enclose 50,000 acres of the North Fork with an eight-foot-high woven-wire fence. There also was the lone voice of William L. Simpson in the Wyoming State

Legislature, who proposed bills to protect sage grouse and mountain sheep. The Wyoming legislature voted against these important conservation bills. Some positive action did come about. The legislature did designate some game preserves. On a 1916 Park County map there appear three "State Game Preserves." The smallest, the "Boulder State Game Preserve," lay between the South Fork and Greybull River drainages at a very high elevation. The largest, the Shoshone State Game Preserve, stretched twenty miles from Table Mountain to Yellowstone National Park and from Ishawooa Creek, some fifteen miles to the North Fork River. The third, the Hoodoo State Game Preserve, covered a ten-mile wide strip east from Yellowstone Park between the north curve of the North Fork River to the Montana boundary. The Shoshone reservoir is listed as Wild Bird Sanctuary on another 1916 map. These game preserves were phased out in less than a decade.

The wisest and most knowledgeable voice to speak out for balanced game management was Dr. William T. Hornaday, the eminent naturalist of his time, teaching themes of conservation, ecology, and preservation of bio-diversity over half a century before these ideas became common among biologists. In 1935 he sounded an alarm: "The people devoted to the exploitation of wildlife for pleasure and profit have fought to retain all their man-made rights to kill wild creatures—even while those helpless ones disappear! Meanwhile the defenders of the wild species of birds, beasts, and fishes have battled to avert the great catastrophe of species extermination that long has been looming up as a probability."

Hornaday was not anti-hunting. Among his many hunts all over the country, he writes of his successful Big Horn sheep hunt of the south end of Rattlesnake Mountain when on November 16, 1889, he killed a fat ram weighing about 300 pounds. Although he does not give the horn measurements, he said the tail was three inches long.

By 1917, when Hornaday wrote and advocated conservation, he spoke out that Wyoming was not passing protective game laws. Hornaday said, "Wyoming's greatest crime was annihilating all big game in the Big Horn Mountains."

Hornaday presented a list of rules for hunting and wild life preservation. He corresponded with local residents, getting extensive coverage in the *Northern Wyoming Herald* from February through July 1917. His comments were adversely received by the local hunters.[12]

To counteract Hornaday's accusations, the Wyoming Game Protective Association was formed. The main emphasis of the organization encouraged law officers to crack down hard on poachers, but they also planted fish. They planted 500,000 Mackinaw trout in the Shoshone Reservoir (now the Buffalo Bill Reservoir). This was not a new idea; there had been fish stocking of some streams since 1912.

The Northern Wyoming Game Protective Association had been started in the late 1880s by William Pickett and Otto Franc. They had hired Warden J. W. Sharrock to patrol, and Hornaday had encountered him on his hunt with officers from Fort Custer in November of 1889. Hornaday quoted Sharrock as saying "Things have changed a whole lot in Wyoming during the last few years. The game is a-goin' mighty fast." Sharrock attributed it to market hunters from Montana, Indians, settlers, and "officers and soldiers at Fort Custer." [13]

The First World War diverted attention from game protection, so Hornaday had little luck in getting his ideas accepted. The U. S. Biological Survey trappers, "take" continued to be published as success stories.

In 1921 a report was released in the first part of April with a tally for a nine-month period describing the success of the government trappers in Park County:

Bears (sheep killers) 7
Bobcats 82
Coyotes. 2,698
Mountain lion 1
Canada lynx 1
Grey wolves. 108
Badgers 21
Mink (weasel family). 2
Skunks 7
Porcupines. 109
Total . . . . 3,036 trapped

In addition, 1,700 wolves and coyotes were poisoned. What the report meant by "1,766 strayed from traps" is not clear.

As recently as 1933, for the fiscal year ending in June, the Biological Survey reported 101,727 predators killed state-wide.

The Biological Survey has been supplanted by the Animal Damage Control (ADC), a federal agency devoted to killing predators. Besides aiding ranchers by destroying predators, the government aids and supports the stock-growers with highly subsidized grazing fees and wool supports. It is the consensus of many that the ADC is an antiquated government subsidy program which should

Ed Holmquist and Carl Johansson at mess house at Trout Creek Ranch ready for a hunt around 1912.

Hides and antlers from successful hunts. The buffalo skull was picked up in the vicinity. John Yeates outside homestead cabin. (Yeates photo, c.1910)

be stopped.

The government trappers were not the only ones out for predators. As far back as 1903, sheepmen were paying bounties of $2. each for wolf, coyote, and bobcats. After 1914, the bears retreated far back into the mountains. The mountain lions were doomed. An article in a 1920 Cody newspaper is typical of the then-current attitude. "Tex Kennedy and Pete Nordquist killed a mountain lion on the rim rocks north of Blackwater. It was three years old, eight feet long. They killed it just after it had 'snuffed' out the life of a young deer." By 1922 mountain lions were nearly wiped out. Ranger Clifford Spencer had a horse killed far up the North Fork by a lion, and Spencer figured the lion had come over from the Sunlight area. Bob Rumsey reported he had seen the carcass of a mountain sheep killed by a lion near Aspen Creek.[14] This was the last sighting.

Why did the North Fork continue to supply elk, deer, and bear despite incredibly heavy hunting? Why did the big game animals not vanish as they did in the Big Horn Mountains and the Black Hills? Fortunately, the North Fork is part of the Greater Yellowstone Ecosystem, its core being Yellowstone National Park,, where game is protected. The Park's abundance spilled over into the Thorofare, making it a hunter's paradise, and also replenished the North Fork and South Fork. During the winter of 1928, the husband of the late Margaret Hoglund Coe, Pierson "Stace" Coe worked for Freeman Lumber Company at Blackwater. They lived in a cabin at Blackwater that winter. Margaret remembered standing in their cabin doorway one late fall day and watching the elk migrate down from the mountains, having come from the Thorofare over Rampart Pass. She counted thousands as they filed past all day.[15]

Osborne Russell mentions his beaver trapping expeditions, which took him back and forth into the headwaters of the North Fork from August 7, 1837, to August 12, 1837. [16] Frost recalled Uncle Billy Whitworth's tales of Jim Baker and Whitworth trapping during a winter in the 1850s on Whit Creek and Jim Creek. Then, in the late 1800s, Wesley Bloom, Charles Marston and Jim McLaughlin were trapping the same streams. Later, almost every rancher or lodge owner engaged in winter trapping. Rancher John Yeates trapped the mouth of Jim Creek for beaver, and ran a winter trap line for coyotes. Henry Westerman in the late 1930s set traps for beaver in Trout Creek.

In 1912, Denny Start trapped a two-year-old silver tip near Pahaska in May.[17]During the First World War, some of the men went off to war so trapping declined.

Then, in January 1919, Billy Howell of Holm Lodge, while getting on crutches with a broken leg, killed a lion on Kitty Creek. He set three coyote traps around a partly eaten

Game Warden Dwight King with hunting dogs and lion. Park County Archives photo.

elk carcass. Three days later Billy followed the trail of a missing trap and shot the lion through the head. By December 1924, Howell reported a $1,500 fur catch.

In March of 1920, the Cody Trading Company displayed in their windows "Fur catch, winter of 1919-1920, Value $10,000, Fox, Marten, Coyote, Mink, Weasel" from the fur packs of E. L. Jones "Jonsey", Ed Holmquist, and Max Wilde.[18]

In 1926 Benny Reif and Vern Spencer brought in a fine catch of 74 martin, 14 fox and "many other pelts." Also in 1926, Chet Freeman and Hurricane Bill Herrick got a radio installed at their trapping camp up Elk Fork.. Art Capron trapped on Elk Fork in 1926 and Jimmy Osborne trapped on Clearwater, while Hardy Shull trapped close to home on Big Creek. In 1927 Roy Glasgow and Denny Start trapped near Pahaska and got 38 martin. The next year Roy Glasgow had a trap line far up the North Fork on Red Creek. In February 1928 he "sprung his traps and came to town with twenty-five martin, one cross and one red fox and ten weasels." [19] Red Powell was trapping in January of 1928 on Elk Fork. Don Wagoner and Fred Roland ran a trapline on Fishhawk in December of 1928. In 1933 Roy Glasgow came out of the upper North Fork with a good "fur pack.". [20]

After 1935 or so the trapping declined as a popular and/or profitable winter venture. Maybe the men were away during the Second World War, or the animals were trapped out.

In the 1990s Clytie Williams still had a photograph of the furs Carl and Don Wagoner had trapped one winter on the North Fork.

In the late 1930s Judge Owens of Cody tried planting chucker partridges, for which he had paid $1 per egg, in various areas in Park County. Some were planted on the Charles Bradford ranch but they did not survive.

John A. Yeates remembered hearing coyotes near their ranch on winter nights. Sometimes the ranch watchdog would answer their yelps and howls. Since coyotes have a keen sense of smell, the slightest human odor warns them of danger regardless of the desirability of the bait. So John's father boiled his steel traps and chains in a mixture of water and wood ashes and never touched them with bare hands but always used clean cotton gloves. Baited traps were set so they were most easily reached as the coyote approached from the downwind side. Usually two traps were set eighteen inches apart by digging a shallow hole for each and attaching the chains to a driven steel rod. After the traps were cocked, or set, a wad of wool was placed under the trip pan. This prevented dirt or pebbles from interfering with the downward motion when it was stepped on. Dry dirt scattered over the traps in their shallow holes helped conceal them and a branch of leafy sagebrush was brushed over traps and human tracks in order to mask any telltale odors. The traps were checked weekly; sometimes a magpie or a crow would spring them and sometimes they were mysteriously sprung by some unknown visitor. During a winter twelve or fourteen coyotes would be caught. They were skinned, the hides stretched, scraped, and the fur brushed. Most hides brought $7. to $9. Although a thickly furred pelt might bring up to $12.

John Yeates' father obtained a trapping permit for beaver when a few animals decided to settle in at the mouth of Jim Creek and soon were working on the few cottonwood trees there. Beaver were not so wary of the traps, but also escaped fairly easily. They were strong enough to pull out the stakes holding the trap, and if this were not possible they bit off their own foot held by the trap. A better way was to attach a run-wire from a tree or stake to a heavy rock anchored in deep water. The trap was attached to freely slide down the wire but was prevented from coming back out of the water. Thus, when a beaver stepped in a trap he could make a run for the safety of deep water and was held there and drowned.

Beaver pelts brought only $3 or $4, and buyers preferred the long guard hairs to be removed. This was done by placing a stretched hide over a full tub of water outside in freezing weather. When the tips of the guard hairs were submerged and became frozen in the ice, pulling the hide free would remove them. It was more trouble than it was worth.[21]

Clytie and Carl Wagoner and winter fur catch at Pahaska around 1932. Their catch included 50 martin, five coyotes, two red fox and one badger. Clytie Williams photo.

NOTES

1 Osborne Russell, *Journal of a Trapper,* edited by Aubrey L. Haines, Second Bison Books printing 1965, p.25

2 McAlleenan, J. *Diary of the Wyoming Bear Hunt* press of J.J. Collinson and Co. New York. New York (1914) p.5

3. William T. Hornaday, "Diversions in Picturesque Game-Lauds, Golden Days in the Shoshone Mountains," *Scribners Magazine*, Vol. XLIV no. 5, Nov. 1908 p. 577

4. *Northern Wyoming Herald,* May 22, 1913

5. McAlleenan, J. *Diary of the Wyoming Bear Hunt* p.50

6. The *Cody Enterprise*, July 1, 1972, p.18

7. *Shoshone National Forest History* p.5.

8. *Wyoming—A Guide to its History, Highways, and People* WPA 1941, p.48. "Classified as predatory mammals are Bobcat, lynx, wolf, mountain lion, coyote, skunk, badger, civet cat, weasel, porcupine, jackrabbit, raccoon, and stray domestic cat."

9. Author's note: Unfortunately scientific research came seventy years too late.

10. *Park County Enterprise*, November 25, 1911.

11. According to *Diary of a Wyoming Bearhunt*, Jonsey trapped 10 coyotes, three lynx and 10 bobcats that year.

12. Correspondance between Hornaday and local residents *Northern Wyoming Herald,* July 25, Feb. 16, and Mar. 21, 1917. *Wyoming Wildlife* June 1992 p. 9, "Late-coming pioneers pursued big game for sale to urban markets and their own use as well...The combination of unregulated shooting, competition from domestic livestock, and the introduction of new diseases spelled the end for the native sheep of the Big Horn Mountains." The big game were exterminated from over-kill, plus the fact the Big Horn mountains and the Black Hills, for example, had no corridors for game to return and repopulate after the original elk, bear, and mountain sheep had been killed off."

13. Hornaday, p. 577.

14. *Cody Enterprise,* December 3, 1922

15. Letter from Joan Coe Dunrud, September 14, 1983

16. Osborne Russell, *Journal of a Trapper,* edited by Aubrey L. Haines, Second Bison Book printing, 1965, p.25.

17. *Park County Enterprise*, May 25, 1912

18. F.J. Hiscock photo postcard.

19. Park County Herald, winter 1926.

20. Park County Herald, spring 1926.

21. John Yeates memoirs.

Freeman Sawmill

Although not the first or only sawmill on the North Fork, the Freeman sawmill was, perhaps, the most visible. Early on there had been a saw mill on Green Creek. Around 1935, George Mix and Stevenson started a sawmill about three miles up Whit Creek. Both the sawmills on Green Creek and Whit Creek were steam-powered. At the time of World War II and the building of the Heart Mountain Japanese Internment Camp, the Federal Government bought the Whit Creek sawmill, hired George Mix to manage it and employed Japanese internees to run it.

John Vogel and Henry Dahlem ran a sawmill on Grinnell Creek from 1924 on for a few years. They moved the old Wallop-Montcrieffe steam-powered tractor up to their sawmill to provide power.

Stockpiling logs from the winter harvesting on Blackwater Creek around 1925.

L. C. "Chet" Freeman came to the Cody area about the time of the first World War. He took up a homestead on Big Creek around 1919, and later sold it to Bart and Missy Lewis. Chet Freeman learned about the lumbering business from his association with early lumberman H. B. Robertson, who had a sawmill on Green Creek.

The S. B. Freeman family were dudes at Rumsey's Blackwater Camp during the summer of 1924. Chet Freeman started a trucking business in Cody, and S. B. "Sox" Freeman was in partnership with him for about a year,. Then Sox bought out Chet and in late 1927 or early 1928 sold the trucking business to Scotty Edmonds. Chet and Sox struck oil in Oregon Basin

Margaret and Pierson Coe at Blackwater Creek on homemade skiis, winter of 1928.

and decided to put their money together and start the Freeman Lumber Company here in Cody and supply the lumber from timber on the North Fork. The sawmill was established on a flat, close to the river just below the sharp bend of the North Fork river at Mummy Joe Cave. L. C. "Chet" Freeman applied for a permit for a Sawmill with the Forest Reserve on May 27, 1927, and it was granted the same day for 3 -1/2 acres. Sox Freeman, Jr. said that the mill was in operation for only five years, from 1925 to 1930. [1] Some of the employees were O. E. Knight, Nick Knight, Pierson Coe, Ed Tuttle, Clint Jones, Jimmy Allen, Hollis Mees. W. H. Klitz was foreman and Elsa Perkins did the cooking. Wages for most of the men was 50 cents an hour, although some received up to 60 cents an hour. Nick Knight had one team and Pierson Coe had two teams. At first they were paid $1. a day for the teams, but later they received $1.50 per day.

The logging was done up Blackwater Creek during the winter. The logs were skidded to the top of the ridge across the river from the camp. This was called the skid pile. In the spring there would be a big stack of logs near the top of the ridge. The men strung a cable from the east side of the river to the top of the ridge on the west side of the river, and one by one the logs rode down and across the river. They closed the logging camp in the summer time and did nothing but saw in the mill. Come winter and snow, they shut down the saw-mill and then a small crew went back up on Blackwater and cut designated trees. There was no indiscriminate and destructive clearcutting. In the winter a small crew brought out the logs with horse-operated equipment.

On May 1, 1930, they were employing 15 men at the sawmill and by June 1, there were only eight men. They operated with a steam engine to run the sawmill and burned slabs for fuel. Sox recalled, "When my father shut down the mill he said he left a million board feet still up there. They didn't bother to bring them down because he couldn't make any money cutting them. The Forest Service took a lot of the logs to make railings in camp grounds."

Sox continued, "Besides the mill, there was a cookhouse, a bunkhouse, and a storage house for food. We built a cabin near the sawmill but it had to be removed because the new road went right where the cabin had been. The last payroll was June 1, 1930. At that time there were eight employees, Renfroe, Jim Allen, Bob Despain, Ed Tuttle, A. Anderson, Stewart, and Perkins, the cook and Klitz, the foreman."

Sox said they hauled the lumber that was left and put it on a lot near the lumber yard. "My dad would sell it for native lumber, a little cheaper than the rest. When they put in the Heart Mountain ditch and were tunneling through Cedar Mountain, the Utah Construction Company ran into the limestone caves and needed lumber to shore up the tunnel and they bought up all they could and the lumber from the Freeman Sawmill on North Fork is inside of Cedar Mountain."[2]

The February 16, 1927, issue of the *Cody Enterprise* stated there were plans to get out 2,500,000 feet of railroad ties and mine props. J. N. Langworthy was Shoshone Forest Supervisor at the time and he thought it was the first step in a lumbering industry of great magnitude. Timber would also be cut on June Creek where there was heavy infestation of bud bark beetle, so it would be "good to lumber it." The Forest Reserve claimed they made a "very attractive price to Freeman" and "gave him a very liberal margin of profit." "25 cents on every $1.00 goes to Park County and 10 cents to forest road and trail fund."

As far as can be determined, no railroad ties ever came out of the North Fork. According to Sox Freeman, "In 1930, they shut down the sawmill because they lost a lot of money in one year, and then he (the elder S. B. Freeman) devoted all his time to his lumber yard in Cody." According to Forest Service Regulations, all evidence of the Freeman sawmill was painstakingly removed.

NOTES

1. From an interview with Sox Freeman Jr. about 1984.
2. Sox Freeman Jr. interview.

Top, a horse-drawn sledge for hauling logs at June Creek during the days of the Freeman Sawmill. Below, the remnants of another horse-drawn sledge at June Creek .

Forest Service on the North Fork

The North Fork figures prominently in the history of the Forest Service, because the Shoshone National Forest was set aside by proclamation of President Benjamin Harrison as the Yellowstone Park Timberland Reserve on March 30, 1891, the first one so designated.

The interconnection and networking between early pioneers of the North Fork is interesting. Ranger Jesse Nelson, a short, wiry man, recalled in his memoirs, that his family and Elwood Mead's were well acquainted in southern Indiana, and through Mead, Nelson met Colonel Cody and subsequently became a Forest Guard on the Shoshone Division of the Yellowstone National Park Timberland Reserve. This later became the Shoshone Forest. The first supervisor was A. D. Chamberlain, who, according to Nelson, was a "political appointee who spent practically all his time playing solo in the saloons of Cody."[1]

Chamberlain wrote from his office in Evanston, Wyoming, to Congressman Frank W. Mondell in Washington, D. C. on January 8, 1899, in regard "to making forest rangers game wardens."[2] When Chamberlain had been in Cody he said he had talked with "all the most prominent settlers and law abiding citizens living adjacent to the timber reserve." All agreed "it is high time that something was done to protect and preserve the game in that country, as they are becoming scarce."

Chamberlain further wrote of the deplorable situation; "I know of the instance in Stinkingwater where the game warden has been taking out several hunting parties this fall and he killed a large number of elk and deer and saves only the hides, horns and teeth, leaving all the four quarters in the hills to rot. The hotel I boarded at all summer has had almost all of the time elk meat at the table, sold to the landlord for beef"

Chamberlain wrote on the same subject to Governor DeForest Richards in Cheyenne. He must have been one of the first whistle blowers. Although he does not name names, it is quite possible he was referring to Sam Berry, who was appointed a game warden by A. A. Anderson, the New York artist who built the Palette Ranch over on the Greybull. In this letter, Chamberlain said, "There was one artist reported to me who traveled very close to the East line of the National Park, in the timber reserve, whom, I am informed, you can trace his course through the mountains by the dead carcasses."[3] Forest Supervisor A. D. Chamberlain suggested that it be a misdemeanor to hunt without a license, and that only male animals be shot.

Many of letters refer to the lack of funds to run the new Timberland Reserve. In two letters, he recommended Frank Hammitt, from Cody, Wyoming, for "any position on the Paris Exposition." "You can say to the Senator that Mr. Hammitt is a thorough linguist; he speaks French, Italian, Spanish, and Russian fluently; also reads Latin and Greek. He is thoroughly acquainted in Paris. . . if he can secure an appointment it will be a valuable acquisition to our exposition."

According to a 1940 Shoshone National Forest brochure, Frank Hammitt "met his death July 25,1903, plunging over the precipitous walls of Russell Creek Canyon in Sunlight . . . " " Hammitt was trained for the priesthood, but gave it up for the life of a cowboy. For seven years he was chief of cowboys with Colonel William F. Cody's Wild West Show before he became a forest ranger."

One wonders if Hammitt ever got to Paris, because during the summer of 1900, he, John Wilks, Jesse Nelson, William T. Borron, Leonard Carey, Frank James, M.O. Newton, and George L. Berry were appointed rangers. Chamberlain had divided the Shoshone Forest into ranger districts.

In 1900 Hammitt, Borron, and Newton built a wagon bridge over the North Fork at Blackwater Creek, the first bridge built by the government on the Forest Reserve. They had helped build, perhaps earlier, a ranger cabin at Blackwater. In 1905 a fire destroyed both the bridge and the ranger cabin.

From 1898 to 1910, Gifford Pinchot was Forest Service Chief. He was a trained forester who believed in sustained yield by marking mature trees for cutting, and replanting. He believed in careful long-term use. Cameron W. Garbutt becomes superintendent of the National Forest Reserve until 1902, when A. A. Anderson was appointed special superintendent of forest reserves. E. D. Blakesly is from 1902 to 1903 supervisor of Shoshone division. From 1903 to 1907, W. H. Pierce, a portly, Southern gentleman, was Shoshone Forest Supervisor. Harry Thurston and Milton Benedict build the

First ranger's cabin at Blackwater, built in 1899 by Carl Sorenson and Frank James and/or Frank Hammitt and W. T. Borron. The cabin burned in 1905. J.E. Stimson photo from 1903. Used by permission of the Wyoming State Archives.

Wapiti Ranger station 1903 using logs from Fishhawk Creek. [4] In 1904, Pierce strung the first telephone line from Cody to Wapiti. In 1905 the administration of the Forest Service transferred from the Department of Interior to the Department of Agriculture. In 1906, the controversial A. A. Anderson left the Forest Service. Pierce was followed by Harry W. Thurston, who held the post from 1907 to 1911, riding the perimeters of his domain on his faithful horse "Old Doc." He was followed by Raymond W. Allen, who served from 1911 to 1919.

During his tenure, W. H. Pierce,was responsible for getting the Forest Service telephone line built "up the river." The Rocky Mountain Bell Telephone Company opened the line to Wapiti in January of 1907, and probably at first it was inexpensively strung. Later, from 1912 through 1913 new poles were set and the line extended to Pahaska and the East Gate.

W. H. Pierce and family lived part of the time at the then-new Wapiti ranger station, and hated it when the headquarters were moved to the Pioneer Building in Cody for the next twenty years. William Henry Pierce died February 5, 1925, at the age of 74, in Santa Rosa, California. Ranger Jesse W. Nelson carried out Pierce's request that his ashes be flown out over the ocean and scattered. This could have been the first aerial funeral.

When Harry Thurston died, on May 9, 1952, it was his wish to be buried near the Wapiti Ranger Station. A pine tree in a small enclosure, south of the highway at the foot of the ridge and west of the Station, marks his grave. Besides his ashes, the ashes of his wife Josephine and daughter Elizabeth are also buried there, by special dispensation.

To mark the entrance to this oldest of Forest Reserves, near the Trail Shop the CCC boys erected two rock pillars, eight- feet high at the entrance of the Shoshone Forest. These were later removed.

In 1932, Lawrence Tenny Stevens had planned to sculpt three tablets, naming three mountain peaks, all near the newly enlarged eastern boundary of Yellowstone Park. The peaks were Cody Peak, just west of Pahaska; Plenty Coup Peak, at the head of Crouch Creek; and Chester A. Arthur Peak, on the divide between Middle and Canfield Creeks. Time and vandalism have destroyed the William F. Cody plaque, once situated one mile east of Pahaska, near a turnout below Grinnell Creek. Three markers were planned, but probably only the one tablet was completed. By the mid 1990s only crumbles of the remaining masonry have been piled in the sagebrush. The plaque has vanished.[5]

It was in the early thirties that the Forest Service began waging war against the pine bark beetle, aided by the Civilian Conservation Corp enrollees. The CCCs built four more campgrounds on the North Fork and built 40 miles of horse trails. In 1939 the CCCs had cleared a path through the timber for a 600-foot- long tow for the newly planned ski run across from Grinnell Creek. The 80-member Shoshone Alpine Club spearheaded the project. The CCCs improved seventeen campgrounds and facilities which gave good service for sixty years.

In an interview, Helen Spencer, widow of Ranger Clifford Spencer, discussed the life of the early rangers and their wives. "We lived at Canyon Creek ranger station from 1922 until July 22, 1923. The disastrous cloudburst storm tore out the station. They just abandoned that place and we moved up to the Wapiti Ranger station."[6] They found that old 1903 log house a mess, and it had to be renovated. Helen lived in the old building for about ten years without a bathroom. The CCCs put in the bathroom and fireplace around 1934. "It was such a treat to have a bathroom and bath tub," Helen recalled.

"The Forest Service did not get any money in those days to hire a trail crew so I went along to help. I didn't get paid for it." She was Clifford's trail crew, and his dogs, Buster and Keno, followed along.[7]

In the interview, Helen said, "In my early days of riding I wore a divided skirt made of tan cotton cloth, not denim, and either sturdy shoes or lace boots. In cold weather I wore wooly chaps, a warm coat and cap."[8] The ranger's job was to clear all the trails every spring. He owned his own string of horses and when they camped, they hobbled one horse and belled the rest. Sometimes they were gone two or three weeks. They took along a Dutch oven, potatoes, eggs, bacon, canned milk and fruit and whatever baked goods Helen could bring. They also fished for food.

Helen was injured in 1924 while helping Clifford with the plowing of the meadow pasture. While leading the horse, it spooked, knocking her down and the plow struck her leg.

Another time Helen became deathly ill with a ruptured tubular pregnancy. Dr. Llewellen told Clifford via telephone to get her to town as quickly as possible. It was winter, the Canyon road was closed, and they had to travel the road south of the reservoir. They ran out of gas on the way. Finally, they reached the doctor, but they still had to travel to the Powell hospital. She was given a shot for pain and four hours to live. She recovered and was out of danger the next morning.

In 1935 J. N. Langworthy retired after thirteen years as supervisor of the Shoshone National Forest. In 1941 they celebrated the 50th anniversary of the Forest Service. According to Raymond W. Allen, who was Supervisor in 1913 A. A. Anderson had invited the Prince of Monaco to come to the Cody area in 1913 to hunt. "Anderson called me to the Irma, Buffalo Bill's Hotel, for a conference. Upon meeting him, he, in his staccato fashion of speech, asked me to his room. After peering up and down the hallway in a secretive manner he carefully locked the door and requested that I immediately call in the entire ranger force, then consisting of eight men, to serve as a guard for the Prince." Allen said one ranger did spend some time with the party, but the remainder of the force continued their regular duties and "no incident befell the Prince."

Carl Johansson started the Horse Creek picnic area in the late 1920s when he was head guide for the Valley Ranch Boys Party. This group had been in the habit of camping at Hanging Rock, but the area proved too small for pitching the boys' tepees, so Johansson grubbed out sagebrush from an area just west of Devil's Elbow. This provided plenty of space for the tents and an open field for evening softball games, so the site evolved into the easily accessible Horse Creek picnic area.

The entire Wapiti Valley in the 1990's has eleven campgrounds, three picnic areas, twelve resorts and lodges, a Boy Scout camp, a ski run and resort, and 68 summer cabins.

There are also thirteen trailheads, two information sites, one documentary site and three national historic sites: Pahaska Tepee, Wapiti Ranger Station, and Mummy Cave. The Blackwater Trail is a national recreation trail.

CIVILIAN CONSERVATION CORP CAMP AT CLEARWATER

The Civilian Conservation Corp established a camp at Clearwater in 1934. It was designated Forest Camp F-24 W, Company 1852, and the purpose was to give work to unemployed young men, ages seventeen to twenty-three years of age. At first the boys lived in army tents, then built more permanent buildings in 1935. It was run by the Army but the U.S.D.A. Forest Service provided work projects. The boys set to work controlling the bark beetle infestation and spruce bud worm, by cutting and burning infected trees. They cut and peeled logs for a buck-and-pole fence at the Wapiti Ranger station, their first major project. Crews responded for fire suppression, and they built and improved campgrounds. After the Blackwater Fire, they built fire lookouts on Clayton Peak and Beartooth Peak. Newly married Morris Simpers was camp foreman the first year and then promoted to Superintendent, until the camp closed in 1942. The CCCs, also built a bridge across the North Fork over to Kitty Creek in 1940, and got logs from Kitty Creek for many uses. They built the large stone pillars on each side of the road at the entrance to the Forest Reserve, which were later removed.

Above: Canyon Creek ranger station after the 1923 flood. Helen Spencer photo used by permission of the Park County Archives.

Below: Canyon Creek ranger station garage destroyed by the 1923 cloudburst. Park County Archives photo.

The tragedy of the Blackwater fire, August 20, 1937, occurred during the days of the CCC camp, the enrollees fought the fire but escaped the fatal entrapment that killed ten enrollees from Ten Sleep. Early civilian employees were Ralph Yates, W. S. Widdous, Alby Russell, Don Huntington, Bryan Sullivan, Carl Buckingham, the mechanics were: Frank Kellener, and Harry Johnson.

Married men of the supervisory staff lived off the camp. Besides Captain Watkins and wife who stayed at Mountain View Lodge, Morris and Ruth Simpers at first lived in a three-room cabin with bath at Nameit Creek Lodge. They later moved to the Frost and Richard Ranch for a few months and then to the ranger station. One camp doctor, Dr. Luperello and his wife Ruth also lived at Nameit Creek. At this time Frank Morris (no relation to Leonard Morris, owner) and his wife Faye and son Glenn were caretakers at Nameit Creek. The administrative staff socialized for entertainment.

The camp was incorporated into the life of the North Fork. Young Jess Frost remembered it was his chore to drive an old truck up to the camp and haul the garbage down to the Frost and Richard Ranch to feed the hogs. Enrollees attended the Cody Stampede. Careful to foster their spiritual needs, priests, ministers, and preachers from area churches took turns conducting services at the Camp. When Simpers went to the CCC Camp at Dayton, Wyoming, Forest Service employee Wiley Thomas temporarily replaced Simpers as foreman at the camp, from 1939 to 1940. Thomas married Eileen Freeborg, a Cody girl. Jim Witzeleban, a camp enrollee who drove an ambulance during the Fire, married Frances Shull of the North Fork.

In January 1942 Morris Simpers closed the camp and removed all buildings, the lumber and materials were moved to the Heart Mountain Relocation Camp, which was then being built.

NOTES

1. Nelson, *My Early Days in the Forest Service,* Park County Archieves.

2. A.D. Chamberlain , January 8, 1899, letter to Congressman Frank W. Mondell. Letters courtesy of Shoshone Forest Service office, Cody, WY.

3. A. D, Chamberlain, letter to Wyoming Governor De Forest Richards.

4. C.G. Poole was District Ranger for North Fork District 1906 through 1908 and Dr. Lane rode up from Cody to deliver the Poole's baby daughter, September 1, 1907. She was born in the ranger station and could be the first white child born within the Shoshone Forest Reserve.

5. Bill Barnhart in his book *The North Fork Trail* has a picture of the tablet. *The North Fork Trail* contains an excellent selection of pictures.

6. Interview Helen Spencer to Joy Hall in March of 1979.

7. Interview Helen Spencer, November of 1993, with Ester Johansson Murray,

8. Spencer interview.

Law Enforcement

Law enforcement on the North Fork of the Shoshone valley was roughly divided between the Park County Sheriff, the ranger of the Wapiti district and the game warden. During Prohibition, federal and state agents became involved in finding and arresting the moonshiners. Occasionally the prosecuting attorney was also involved. Usually they worked separately, but on some cases several different departments worked together.

The first deputy sheriff in 1893 for northern Fremont County was Jack Price of Embar, a ranch a long distance from the little group of settlers in the Marquette area. In 1895 there was a Justice of the Peace over on the South Fork, William P. Webster. After Big Horn County was established, J. J. Fenton and T. J. McClung were Deputy Sheriffs. In 1903, Felix Alston was Deputy Sheriff for Big Horn County, in 1906 he was elected sheriff. These deputies served to kept the peace in the northern ends of the county. In 19ll, Felix Alston resigned to accept the warden's job at the State Penitentiary in Rawlins. Sometime during the late 1920s and early 1930s, William T. Borron was Justice of the Peace on the North Fork. He presided at the marriage of two neighboring ranch employees. Borron and Hollister performed the wedding in the living room at the Hollister ranch, and all the neighbors were invited. The groom performed slight-of-hand tricks, immensely amusing to the youngsters.

Henry Dahlem was Park County Sheriff from 1911 until 1915; E.S. Hoopes, 1915 through 1919; W.T. Barber, 1919 through 1921; C.A. Davis 1921 through 1923 and Sheriff Loomis, served from 1923 until 1925. Henry Dahlem finished out Loomis' term of office from 1925 until 1926, and when Loomis was convicted of taking a payoff from a bootlegger, Sheriff Frank Blackburn served from 1926 until 1960. During Prohibition they waged a mostly unsuccessful battle with the North Fork bootleggers. In January 1912, B. G. Neeland of the North Fork was arrested for baiting his traps with grouse. He went free because he was not caught in the act.

An interesting case reported in the *Northern Wyoming Herald* for May 8, 1914, involved the United States versus Sam Berry, Hardy Shull, and William Hawkins. These men were accused of killing elk in Yellowstone Park in November of 1913. Forest Ranger R. W. Allen was the chief witness. Sam Berry could not be apprehended, so when the case was tried Shull and Hawkins were found not guilty because Berry shot elk, and the others only helped transport it.

In June 1918, the newspaper reported a black boy from Pryor, Montana, rode into Cody on a buckskin horse, and headed up North Fork. He stopped at the Rhoads ranch on Rattlesnake Creek and stole some guns and looted Elias Martin's cabin. His next stop was at Canyon Creek, where he looted Jimmie Osborne's cabin. He got no farther than Libby Creek, where Billy Howell captured him "in the act of stealing in the Holm Lodge stable." His name was Henry Cody and the buckskin horse he was riding had been stolen in Montana. Judge Metz sentenced him on grand larceny and Deputy Sheriff E. S. Hoopes took him to Rawlins to the penitentiary.

In 1918 the local sportsmen protested the killing of elk on the North Fork. Killing game out of season was illegal, but law officers seemed to target moonshiners for poaching more than other people living on the river. One time law officers found a piece of paper with the name "Shull" on it, where an elk had been killed. The *Northern Wyoming Herald* for February 27, 1918, stated Bill Herrick, an "attache" of the Shull ranch pled guilty and was fined $25.

Some attempts by the law officers to enforce Prohibition verged on the comical, one wonders if the participants felt they were playing games. It was hard to nail the moonshiners, but sometimes it was easier to catch the poachers. According to the *Cody Enterprise* of October 3, 1928, Game Warden Dwight King arrested Lonnie Royal for hunting elk on the Game Preserve, along with his companion, a minor. Lonnie was fined $75, but the fine was remitted except for $10 court costs. His companion received a thirty-day jail sentence which was suspended on good behavior. "They promised to walk the straight and narrow."

Then, in December of the next year Bill Herrick and Chet Freeman were charged with poaching deer out of season on the game preserve. Herrick was found guilty and fined $25 in January 1930.

With nothing much going on until tourist season started, the exploits of moonshiners and game poachers gave everyone something to talk about. The *Cody Enterprise* for January 4, 1933, stated that Hardy Shull and Bert Allen were acquitted of killing elk on Horse Creek. Ranger Spencer followed their trail to where they cached the meat. When Shull and Allen returned, Spencer arrested them, but in the dark they gave Spencer the slip. At the trial, Jack Spicer swore Shull and Allen had been with him at his home all afternoon. Judge Marston turned the defendants loose.

On one occasion the Prohibition Officers posed as oil men. They stopped first at Hardy Shull's, where they revealed their identity and purpose. Shull cooperated and they gave the entire place a thorough search but found no liquor. Other Northforkers were not so lucky. Sheriff Loomis, Undersheriff Pully, John Nelson, and Prosecuting Attorney Ernest Goppert in a hip pocket raid at a dance arrested Carl Buckingham, Earl Hayner, and Vernon Spencer on charges of possessing, transporting and selling intoxicating liquor.[2]

The Earl Durand story has connections with the North Fork too. Summer cabins were broken into, elk killed, and one of rancher John Yeates' young cows was butchered, some of Durand's depredations. The posse caught up with Durand in the Canyon and Leonard Morris got the drop on Durand, he was captured and jailed in the Park County Jail. The rest of the Durand Story has been retold often and embellished with myth and imagination.

NOTES

1. *Northern Wyoming Herald,* July 17,1918.

2. *The Cody Enterprise,* September 12, 1923. Law officers used "hip pocket raids" to frisk the men to see if they had a bottle concealed on their person.

Moonshining And Bootlegging On The North Fork

During the Prohibition years (1919-1933) the following type of news item appeared often in Cody's newspapers. "Sheriff Dahlem and County Attorney Joseph E. McElvain raided a moonshine operation at the head of Green Creek. The still house was cleverly hidden. They have an idea whose operation it is but due to the small amount of evidence they can issue no warrant. The moonshining equipment was of the best quality and well cared for." This quotation from the *Park County Herald* for February 10, 1926, is typical of the news stories during the years of Prohibition. The Herald was for Prohibition, taking a stand on the side of the law, as opposed to the *Cody Enterprise* another weekly, published by the flamboyant Caroline Lockhart who was vehemently anti-Prohibition. She wrote an ironic column each week for the front page called "As Seen from the Water Wagon."

The following research will help answer such questions as: Why couldn't the sheriff and county attorney of Park County, Wyoming, issue an arrest warrant? Where were these well-hidden stills in the North Fork valley of the Shoshone river? Thanks to Lonnie Royal who remembered where they were, we can place their location on a map. And lastly, why were the law enforcement officers so ineffective? It will be noted how this remote area of Wyoming fit into the bigger picture of the law breaking of the 18th Amendment—the Prohibition Amendment—throughout the United States.

In simplistic terms, moonshining was the illegal manufacture of an alcoholic beverage containing more than one-half of one percent of alcohol by volume. Bootlegging involved the sale and distribution of the illegal drink. Both were part of the extensive and uncontrollable law breaking throughout the nation, and began before the 18th Amendment of January 1919. Examples in Park County would include "Doc" Wilkins, a Cody veterinarian, who had an illicit operation below and east of the Upton place on the North Fork. Jack Spicer had an operation going on Pat O'Hara Creek by 1914, before he moved onto the North Fork.

To review briefly, the growing misuse of liquor during the first decades of the 20th Century was devastating family life and individual health. At first, most people wanted to curb the ubiquitous saloon, not necessarily the drinking of alcoholic beverages. The strongest force among many trying to solve the saloon problem was the Anti-Saloon League, but as this well meaning group became more and more powerful it drifted away from its goals to curb the proliferation of saloons. "The conversion of the Anti-Saloon League into an anti-drink pressure group further suggests that real radicals had captured the most powerful political machines ever fashioned in American life."[1]

As the political forces got the necessary power their first legislation was the Lever Food and Fuel Control Act of August l, 1917, which forbade the use of foodstuffs for distilling liquor, purportedly to help the World War I effort. This was followed by the infamous 18th Amendment to our constitution of December 22, 1918, (ratified January 1, 1919) and implemented by the Volstead Act of September 1919, giving our Federal Government control over the manufacture, sale or transportation of intoxicating liquors. This was beefed up by the "Jones Five and Ten Law", amending the Volstead Act and raising the first liquor offense from six months jail or fine of $1000, to five years in jail or $10,000 fine.

In the area of the North Fork of the Shoshone river, there were relatively few convictions of law-breaking. In the successful convictions the fines were a few hundred dollars and county jail terms were 90 days or less. Only one man, Martin Jobe, was sentenced to the State Penitentiary at Rawlins.

Finally, after thirteen years of futile attempt to control the morality of the nation, the 21st Amendment of 1933, repealed, state by state, the failed 18th Amendment. Caroline Lockhart was no longer editor of the *Cody Enterprise* vilifying Prohibition, and the *Park County Herald* was no longer published. The Great Depression superceded Prohibition as the all important national problem. In the same month "3.2%" alcohol content became legal, Park County's most notorious bootlegger died in a gun battle.

In reference to our first newspaper quote, why did the sheriff give the still and equipment such high praise? This can be explained by the fact from 1910 on, a dozen related members of several families from Allegheny County, North Carolina, and Tennessee areas of the Blue Ridge Mountains, settled around Cody and Pat O'Hara taking up homesteads and working on ranches, mostly herding sheep. They were the Woodruff, Spicer, and Royal families.[2]

These men brought with them the knowledge and skill in the manufacture of alcohol and proficiency in concealing their stills. Jack Spicer took a job herding sheep, but his expertise lay in making good whiskey. He set up his first still with a six-horse power steam engine in a natural cave on a steep side canyon on Pat O'Hara creek, four miles below the Allison ranch. Ray Prante recalled, "My sister, Jessie Lowe, had a homestead on upper Pat O'Hara and she ran into one of Jack Spicer's stills up there. It was in one of the best locations for a still, just beautiful, under a shelf of rock."[3] The *Northern Wyoming News,* a Cody paper, printed a story July 17, 1914, under the heading, "Wyoming's First Moonshiners." It is questionable if they were the first, but possibly were the best of the first in Wyoming. The article stated, "One thing to commend the moonshiners, they were making pure whiskey."

However well this still had been concealed, a Federal Revenue officer arrested Arlie Spicer and Luther Spicer, young men only eighteen and twenty years old, who were working for Martin Jobe at the Allison ranch. According to Prante, "Finley Goodman turned them in." The young men said the still cost $40.00 in Miles City, Montana, and they had $250.00 invested in the plant. The still had the capacity of seven gallons per day. The officers found 40 gallons of finished product. After sampling it they dumped it in Pat O'Hara creek.

Arlie Spicer was put in the Park County jail in Cody and Luther was released on $1500 bond. A few days later Arlie escaped from the Standard restaurant in Cody where he was taken for his meals. Major E. S. Hoopes, a deputy, usually had the duty of escorting the prisoner, but on the day of Arlie's escape, Sheriff Dahlem was watching the prisoner. The sheriff stepped out on the street for a minute and Arlie escaped through a rear door. Or, as the paper stated, Arlie took "French leave". [4] There are no court records of this arrest.

Another pre-prohibition moonshiner was a Cody veterinarian, "Doc" Wilkins, who had a still in the willows on the river bank just east of the Lee Upton ranch, lower Wapiti valley, on the south side of the river. When Wilkins got things working in his still, he would spend a lot of time sitting on the river bank holding a fishing pole and keeping a sharp eye out for unwelcome visitors. "He left before Prohibition and went back to the Ozarks, probably," according to Francis Hayden.[5]

Pat Kelly lived on the north side of the river below the mouth of Jim Creek. His still was in an old log building below the bench and closer to the river and couldn't be seen from the bench above the river bottom. Pat Kelly sold his product through his partner, Nick Reinicker, owner of a pool hall in Cody. Pat Kelly often went to Cody carrying a suitcase, his method of transporting the liquor.

One time Pat Kelly and Nick Reinicker called on Ben Simpers and spent almost all night trying to persuade Ben to go into partnership with them and set up an operation near the mouth of Whit Creek.[6] It was a bold attempt but proved in vain, perhaps because Ben had no inclination for law breaking, besides, Bertha Dahlem, wife of the Sheriff, was Ben Simpers' sister.

In picking up the story of Jack Spicer, the law caught up with him in 1921, when he lived in the Pat O'Hara country. He was apprehended December 1, 1921, for manufacturing, possession, and sale of intoxicating liquors. This case, number 354, dragged on until March 8, 1924, and was dismissed the same time as court case number 357, discussed later.

Before Jack Spicer moved over to Canyon Creek on the North Fork, he made the news in March of 1922, and established his reputation as a gunman. According to the paper, at this time Spicer had a "bootlegging partner" named Joe Hill. The two had a falling out at their cache in the Monument Hill country. Spicer accused Hill of "lifting the cache", whereupon Spicer took Hill's . 32 calibre Savage pistol and threatened Hill. Hill tried to get away on horseback but Spicer took four shots at him, one shot hit the borrowed horse, one shot went through the cantle of the saddle and one hit Hill in his side. According to the newspaper account, "Spicer and his wife skipped so could not be apprehended." [7]

During Prohibition, Park County had three sheriffs: Henry Dahlem, William Loomis, and Frank Blackburn. Dahlem was sheriff when Prohibition started; William Loomis of Powell ran for sheriff in 1922, on the Democratic ticket against E. S. Hoopes, Republican, of Cody and won the election. According to Will's nephew, Gordon Loomis, "Uncle Will was kind of a wild young man, he loved hunting and fishing and all kinds of sports and at one time was Minnesota champion wrestler." [8]

Shortly after taking office, Loomis followed up on a hot tip and raided the Morris dude ranch twenty two miles up the North Fork from Cody. Morris was charged with moonshining in January of 1923. It was determined John Borgham, aka "Pontoon Johnny", had falsely placed items on the ranch and informed the sheriff. Sheriff Will Loomis found a keg of whiskey containing three gallons of moonshine which he destroyed.[9]

In September of 1923, State prohibition officers descended on the North Fork "posing as oil men". Their target and first stop was Hardy Shull's place. Shull cooperated and the entire place was given a thorough search but no liquor was found.[10]

Sheriff Loomis, flanked by the prohibition officers, Park County undersheriffs, and Prosecuting Attorney Ernest Goppert, made an unannounced raid at a dance. They nailed three well-liked North Forkers, Carl Buckingham, Earl Hayner, and Vernon Spencer of possessing intoxicating liquor. These court cases were dismissed February 14, 1924. It was called a "hip pocket raid" when law officers checked men at a dance to see if they carried a bottle of moonshine concealed in their clothing.

B. G. Neiland, aka Neeland, ran a small moonshine operation in Porcupine Neiland Draw on the west side of Rattlesnake mountain. (At the time the Shoshone Dam was being built in the canyon, it was known as John Henry Martin Draw.) Sheriff Loomis caught Neiland transporting five gallons of moonshine by packhorse. He had almost made it into Cody before being apprehended. Neiland pled guilty on May 7, 1924, according to Court Case 410, and he was sentenced to ninety days in the county jail and paid a $500 fine.

Apparently Loomis' philosophy regarding Prohibition did not coincide with the requirements of the job. After two years in office he was found guilty of taking $225 protection money from a moonshiner, not a North Fork moonshiner. When Nellie Tayloe Ross, Wyoming's first lady governor, (January 5, 1925 through January1927) took office her first official duty was to have Loomis arrested. The question came up, who should arrest the sheriff and the task fell to the Park County coroner.[11]

Ex-sheriff Dahlem was appointed to fill out Loomis' term of office. He carried out the duties of his office in a creditable manner without coming down too hard on the moonshiners. Prohibition proved unpopular with most of the people as shown in the November 1918 election on the North Fork when 18 voted for Prohibition and 27 voted against it. Those hit by the law officers sometimes retaliated. After a dance at the Wapiti school house in January 1926, Sheriff Dahlem found his car had been tampered with and he had to send to town for a mechanic to repair it. Friends passed the hat to cover the expense.[12]

The next big crackdown came in February 1926. The search revealed a still on the south side of the river at the head of Green Creek. The still house, as usual, was cleverly hidden. Law officers found thirty sacks of sugar, seventy three sacks of chopped corn and oats, and 375 gallons of mash and the fifty gallon still. The sheriff packed the evidence out to where it could be trucked to town. Since it was winter time it was difficult to hire a pack outfit, but Dahlem finally obtained nine pack horses and two saddle horses wintering at the J. F. Kelly ranch. The ride up Green Creek was not easy, but the officers reached the still about noon. Fresh tracks led up the mountain, the Sheriff followed the tracks for an hour but finally gave up because of deep snow. No doubt, discretion entered into his decision. It was neither wise nor prudent to track these lawbreakers too far into the hills. Sheriff Dahlem dutifully wrecked the still and packed out the equipment and supplies. He had, of course, a good idea whose operation it was, but "due to the small amount of evidence" he could issue no warrant. The confiscated sugar was sold for $119.10. The newspaper noted the sheriff lost some of those borrowed pack saddles but "was willing to trade for bedding he confiscated."[13]

In an interview with Mrs. Emma Kelly she recalled: "One time the sheriff cleaned out a still and brought out a bunch of stuff and put it in our horse stall in the barn because he couldn't take it all to town. The next morning some of it was gone. Mr. Kelly came in and said, 'They didn't take it all, but they took what they wanted.' If we had heard them we wouldn't have jumped them. The only thing to do was keep out of it. They controlled the North Fork. People were afraid of them."[14]

The next North Fork raid came in May 1926. Sheriff Dahlem, while riding in the rugged Big Creek area "stumbled" on a trail which led to a well camouflaged fifty gallon capacity still. He arrested Harry Johnson on the spot, Johnson claimed he was making just a little liquor for his own use. He was fined $900 and 90 days in jail according to Court Case 483.[15]

Sheriff Frank Blackburn, an exemplary law officer, was elected in 1926, (he took office 1927 and served until 1960). Blackburn and two federal agents, Charles Davis and Ted Denny, made a successful raid on a still on upper Big Creek in October 1928. There were "barrels and barrels of mash" and 200 gallons of finished product in kegs lined up along the trail ready to be taken out. Martin "Mart" Jobe was in charge of the operation and was asleep when the 2:00 a.m. raid occurred. Although this was definitely a Hardy Shull operation, the evidence against him was "inconclusive". Martin Jobe pled guilty April 1, 1929, and was sentenced to two to three years in the State penitentiary.[16] So Mart Jobe, like Harry Johnson previously, did time for being the one who got caught. More times than not, the law officers were unsuccessful. Bud and Chella Hall ran the Circle H cattle and dude ranch on Big Creek, and Chella drove the North Fork stage for many years. She said, "I never hauled any whiskey to town. Sometimes I had law officers hid in the back of my Dodge pickup, they were covered up with tarps. They would go on up country and stay out overnight and then make a raid on Jack Spicer's still. One time they got there and found a note, 'Just a little too damn late.'"[17]

At one time Spicer had a still up Hardifer Draw on the East Fork of Big Creek. At this time the law officers also raided Hardy Shull's home, but no evidence (liquor) was found. Frances Shull Witzleban, daughter of Hardy Shull said, "(Certain neighbors) were always trying to catch Dad with his whiskey. They would come over on our hills and just sit and watch and wait for something to catch us at. Dad was too smart for them. Later when Frank Blackburn was sheriff, he came up because he had heard Dad had some whiskey there. So Dad said, 'Come on in and search the place.' They came in and searched the house and never found a thing. Do you know where that two gallons of whiskey was? It was between my sister and me in bed and we were sound asleep. Dad was the only one who could go out and draw whiskey out of the bank of the creek. He had his barrel buried in the bank and he could go out and tap a bottle of whiskey. They even came in with airplanes and got some of Dad's whiskey. There is still some buried up in the canyon." [18]

In February 1928, two popular young men, Ernest Rueger and Irving Meryhew, were batching at the Jud Weston place up "Britisher" (Breteche) creek on the south side of the valley. Farther up the creek, in a canyon, a still was found. The men's testimony of disclaiming ownership and their plea of "not guilty" held up in court in October. The court ordered the still destroyed.

Chella Hall, during her years of driving the North Fork stage, said she hauled sugar for Hardy Shull and delivered it to the Jenkins' store. E. H. Jenkins built Mountain View Lodge, a small tourist and mercantile business between the Trail Shop and just west of Jack Spicer, but went broke during the Depression.

Even over 65 years after these events, the trauma of going through the prohibition era is sharp and painful to some family members still living. Josephine Brown of Denver recalls vividly the pain, humiliation, and feelings of shame and disgrace her mother endured during those times, also the tears that were shed and the fervent prayers as they kneeled together at bed time. Josephine, being the oldest daughter, said she felt ostracized in school and looked down on by neighbor children. No doubt the father was trying to earn a living for his family and chose to do so by doing what he had expertise in. Josephine wished her father could be remembered for “all the good things he did.”

Frances Witzleban said the “grub line riders” always could be sure of food and shelter with Delia and Hardy Shull for as long as they needed it--a few days or all winter. Hardy was a soft touch for the broke, the homeless, and orphans of Saint Joseph Orphanage in Torrington, Wyoming.

Ray Prante, who in his younger years did a lot of freighting and hauling by truck, recalled in an interview in December 1984, "Jack Spicer didn't waste words." Prante would meet him on a Cody street and Jack said, "tonight", or "Thursday", or whatever designated day he wanted Prante to go to the Cody Trading Company and pick up the load of sugar, usually ten-100 pound sacks. From the location of Spicer's house on Canyon Creek on the North Fork, he could see the truck lights as Prante drove out of the Shoshone canyon and he could judge what time to expect Prante. There wasn't all that much traffic in those days. He had instructed Prante to drive into the yard and not get out of the truck, but to sit and wait. If Spicer did not come out within an hour, Prante was supposed to leave. Usually after half an hour Spicer came out and Prante drove into a shed where Spicer unloaded the sugar. Spicer always paid in cash and one pint of whiskey.[19] Morris Simpers, another early day North Forker, said when they lived on Whit Creek the road went by quite close to their house. "The old log bridge would go bumpity-bump when a truck drove over it. Sometimes at night we would hear a truck go over the bridge and figured it was Chet Freeman or Ray Prante with a load of sugar and supplies for the moonshiners."[20]

As the final years of Prohibition ran out, the law came down harder. In Wyoming, in 1928, 393 persons were arrested for violating the federal prohibition laws, in 1929, 425 were arrested. In 1928, 58 stills were confiscated, in 1929, 80 stills were confiscated. In 1928, 3,849 gallons of whiskey were confiscated and in 1929, 7,096 gallons. (By 1931, five stills were confiscated in one week in June).[21]

Jack Spicer never served any time in jail, but Hardy Shull was convicted of moonshining and served thirty days in Park County jail in 1929. This met with general public disapproval and neighbors pitched in to put up Hardy's hay crop.[22]

Lonnie Royal, a hale and hearty eighty-nine-year-old in 1992, and living alone in the family home on Canyon Creek, explained how they made the brew: "When the mash, composed of chopped grain, sugar, water, and yeast, had fermented about three days, it would be transferred to the 50 gallon still, often made of copper. I didn't like to use copper, however I got a copper still once from Emil Bloom, brought it up here and cached it, but someone found it and stole it."[23]

Fire under the boilers heated the water and caused steam to rise which was bled into the still. The steam stripped the alcohol out of the mash, then traveled through a condenser and ran into an oak barrel. The 80 proof alcohol was triple stilled to get the best 100 proof.[24]

Besides using grain mash, Lonnie sometimes used honey and sprouted barley, "Spouted barley and honey makes the best whiskey," according to Lonnie. One time a brandy operation had been set up at the still on Post Creek with Clarence Wood hauling apples up from the Powell community and Lonnie making apple brandy.

Lonnie laughed when he recalled how the "works" blew up one time in 1928, but at the time it wasn't funny. "Old Bill Herrick stayed over there and cooked for me, and he was supposed to watch the operation while I went with Clarence for another truck load of apples. When I came back he was lying in bed, drunk as a hoot owl, with a dipper and bucket of whiskey by his bed. I had to get rid of him because we never drank on the 'job'. We had built a shack to keep the mash warm, when I got back I thought the gasoline engine had blowed up, plums and apples were all over everything. The apples and plums got plugged up there somewhere, blowed the whole top out of it. If I had been there it wouldn't have happened because I could tell by the sound if everything was working smoothly."[25]

When things went well, Lonnie had worked out an efficient system for moving out the finished product. Much of the work was carried out under the cover of darkness. Lonnie said, "I loaded up six pack horses with five gallons in a pannier on each side and a keg as a top pack. I had a dog named Shorty, he was half coyote and very smart, I got him from Pat Kelly. After a few trips I would lead out and the dog kept the horses on the 'crooked and narrow path'".

For awhile in 1929, Jack Spicer again worked over in the Pat O'Hara country. Howard Royal operated the biggest still they put into operation, located up under Table Mountain on Whit Creek, on the south side of the North Fork river. In July of 1929, law officers made a raid up Whit Creek and seized a large still, with ten gallons of finished product and nine barrels of mash.[26] The newspaper account said a forest ranger stumbled on the still while riding the range and he warned the operator to get the outfit out. Later, when the sheriff checked, the still hadn't been dismantled and he "made the raid."

Howard Royal, a nephew of Jack Spicer, claimed the still belonged to Charlie Krause, but Krause said he was working at the Two Dot and disclaimed ownership. Royal said Jack Spicer built the still. Royal escaped and with two brothers left the country.[27] There is no record of a court case.

According to folktales, Waldemar Petermann, a conscientious employee of the Forest Service found the still. "He double crossed us and turned my brother in," said Lonnie. "He got shot in the rear one time at a dance in the old Masonic Temple in Cody."[28] The wound was not serious.

Jack Spicer chose a location on Wall Creek, on the north side of the river, for his last still in 1931. In this operation he was using beet pulp which he hauled up from the sugar factory at Lovell, Wyoming. Lonnie believed the whiskey from the beet pulp made Jack crazy, and he wouldn't touch the stuff himself.[29]

Time was running out for the Prohibition Era, but looking back it was interesting how each of the two main moonshiners had settled on the North Fork. Hardy Shull had been in the area for ten years when he bought the William Edwards homestead on Half Mile Creek in 1916. This was the last homestead location on the north side of the North Fork River outside of the Forest Reserve. Across the river on the south side, Jack Spicer bought the Jimmy Osborne place on Canyon Creek in 1923. Actually the deed was to Etta Spicer, nicknamed “Jake”, and the deed transferred to Jack in 1927. [30] There were two more places west of Spicers, outside the Forest Reserve boundary, Mountain View Lodge and Sherwin’s Trail Shop. Folk tales tell that Jack Spicer taught Hardy Shull how to make whiskey and they worked together at first on some of the operations on Big Creek.

Hardy’s old time neighbors remember him as jovial, sociable, with an outgoing personality. Hardy’s daughter Frances, described her Dad as ”big, stout, and TOUGH.” Frances said, “Everybody respected my Dad, even Jack.”[31] Josephine, the oldest Shull daughter, cherished a deep almost reverential respect for her father and hated having his memory tarnished in anyway.

Perhaps no person on the North Fork ever made such a strong impression as Jack

Spicer. Most people were half-way afraid of him, at least they didn't want to tangle with him. He did tend to foster his villainous, steely-eyed appearance, seldom traveling unarmed. "Always had two guns and a knife, no matter where he went," said Frances. "My Dad was the only one who dared to cross him."

Those who didn't like him gave him the nickname "Snake", but were always careful where they used the term, according to Ray Prante. Morris Simpers remembered Jack as a tall, muscular man, clean shaven with piercing blue eyes, and not given to frivolity, but he did entertain occasionally with a clog dance at Wapiti school house dances.

"I remember Jack wore Army type pants tucked inside high-laced boots, and a western hat," said Clark Lawrence.[32]

How were these moonshiners accepted on the North Fork? That would depend on whether you were for or against Prohibition at that time. Lonnie Royal said, " I can remember everyone pitching in together and helping each other, it was a community deal, putting up ice or putting up hay." Nina Sherwin remembered the men putting up ice and the women cooking the meals. In 1932 Jack Spicer proved acceptable for jury duty on the Primm case. He also bid on the North Fork mail contract one time, but his bid was too high. The Spicers loved children but had none of their own. Brooks and Huldah Borron, neighbors, had six children, so the Spicers tried to persuade them to let them adopt daughter Ruth.

Huldah also attested to Jack's speed and proficiency with a hand gun. One time the Borron family visited the Spicers and were invited to stay for supper. "Jake" (Etta Spicer) sent Jack out to kill a chicken and he asked Huldah "Which one should I kill?" Huldah pointed out one and "quick as anything Jack pulled his gun and shot the chicken's head off."[33]

Frances Shull Witzleban said, "We were best friends with Jack and "Jake" and we (Josephine, Frances, and Rita) just loved it when we could go over there and spend a night with "the Spicers."

Morris Simpers recalled, "All of them (the moonshiners) had people operating the stills who were imported from the Carolinas, professional moonshiners. Then, in the summer time they worked in the hay fields. I do remember one thing, they were always very gentlemanly around women. And they all liked kids. One I remember was a peg leg." [34]

The Women's Club provided a unifying contact on the North Fork and almost all the North Fork ladies belonged. According to Frances Witzleban, her mother Delia Shull went to the meeting at first, but she did not feel comfortable with the gossiping that went on so she did not belong. Etta Spicer took snuff so it was inconvenient for her to attend meetings.

The dances at the Wapiti school house helped unify the community to some extent. On the other hand, John Yeates, who grew up on the North Fork and attended the Wapiti school, said, " There was quite a clique of people who liked Saturday night dances and insisted on using the school house. They had no children in school and were not much concerned about the conditions they left behind. This was quite a bone of contention for the school board. Occasionally on Monday morning following one of these dances we kids would have a whiskey-bottle-hunt. . . The collection might result in four to six empties."[35]

Sale for profit motivated the manufacture of whiskey and there were various ways of handling the sale and distribution. Some was sold directly from the homes of both Hardy Shull and Jack Spicer. Frances Witzleban said her Dad had a rule of no drinking on the place. Buy it and leave. One time when Hardy was gone, two men came, bought and started drinking. Frances said, "My mother couldn't do anything about it, the two men got in an argument about who had the most powerful car. They hooked their cars together to see who

Lonnie Royal outside bunkhouse where Artis Royal stood in gun battle with Jack Spicer. Bullet holes near door jam. Sept. 1994

could outpull the other. When my Dad came home they really scooted."

Spicer at times sold "wholesale" to the Green Drug Store in Cody. Here the 120 proof was cut to 100 proof and after being bottled, Canadian labels and tax stamps were glued on and then it could be sold as prescription medicine, legally. Spicer sold it for $20 a gallon wholesale and it retailed for $5 a pint at the drug store.

Morris Simpers went with his Dad one time up to Shull's to buy some whiskey. "We went up the creek a little ways, Hardy brushed some leaves away and stuck a piece of hose in one of the two barrels he had dug into the bank and he siphoned out what we needed. He covered it over afterwards and you'd never suspect or find his cache."

Business was cash on the barrel head, very few customers got credit, although Morris recalled at one time Dwight Hollister owned Hardy Shull $1400 for booze.

For some customers Spicer delivered in person. "Jack would come walking right down main street (in Cody) with a gunny sack over his shoulder with two gallon jugs in it, and leave Doc Kinne one and come on down to Mike Clark's (filling station) and leave him one," said Clark Lawrence who worked for Mike Clark at the time.

Nick Donko in a *Cody Enterprise* interview, reported, "it was during the Prohibition and I knew a guy who made whiskey and could give (sic) me a pint of whiskey for $3. The man (was) a mean one you didn't want to mess with." [36]

Lonnie said he hauled whiskey to more distant outlets such as Miles City, Forsyth, and Billings, Montana. According to Huldah Borron, her husband, Brooks, drove a new Ford to Powell with a load of whiskey to be picked up by a Billings contact. Brooks did not like that kind of job so made only one run.

The above covers the illegal manufacture of moonshine. It was common practice for almost every household to make home brewed beer and sometimes wine out of dandelions, chokecherry, or berries. This was legal if the beverage contained no more than one half of one percent alcohol by volume. Neither producer, consumer, or law officers ever ran tests to verify its alcohol content.

The Prohibition era on the North Fork of the Shoshone ended with a tragic gun battle between Artis Royal and his uncle Jack Spicer the morning after they had hosted a Saturday night dance at the Wapiti school house the end of March 1933. Nina Sherwin recalled Artis and Jack got into some kind of argument, maybe over the music. [37] Artis and Lonnie went into town after the dance instead of returning to Spicers where they made their home. Artis came back early the next morning, planning to slip into the bunk house and get his things out of there, only to discover Jack waiting for him gun in hand. Artis made it to the bunk house and got his gun and shooting began. The *Cody Enterprise* for April 1, 1933, stated, "A gun fight between Jack Spicer and his nephew Artis Royal, resulted in Jack Spicer being killed from a bullet through the heart, and one shot in the lower body. Artis received three bullet holes in his chest, one through each lung and one high in the chest. Artis emptied his gun but only two of the five shots hit Spicer. Spicer fired three times."

The paper stated Spicer lived in the Cody area for twenty five years. "All were rough and ready type and seldom go unarmed. They settled their differences the way the mountain folk of the Carolinas had always done." Lonnie had a pair of chaps hanging in the corner of the bunk house, he said they were "ventilated with numerous bullet holes."

Artis spent six weeks in the hospital and miraculously recovered. Clark Lawrence said, "Dr. Dacken was telling me about it one time. Dr. Dacken said, 'I didn't think he would make it. He would lay on his stomach and you could look right in his back and see his lungs working.'" Artis slowly recovered in the Cody Hospital which at that time was in an old private home, 901 Rumsey Avenue, near the Girl Scout house.

Most of the North Fork neighbors paid their respects by attending Jack's funeral. Charges of first degree murder were filed against Artis, but he was acquitted on self defense.

Hence, Prohibition ended in February 1933, the 18th Amendment repealed by the 21st Amendment of 1933, and less than two months later one of the most notorious characters connected with moonshining and bootlegging on the North Fork died in a gun fight. Maybe the product of the beet pulp operation from that last still on Wall Creek did make Jack Spicer crazy.

North Georgia Type Still

A unique type of still, quick to set up and very productive for a medium-sized operation. Steam is utilized by means of a boiler (sometimes this unit is portable and on wheels for quick removal). Steam is used to heat the connected units to the boiling point, forcing vapor into the third mash barrel. This vapor and the water that it becomes is high strength and is further intensified in the doubler before condensing in the double walled condenser. Three mash barrels rather than one assures a much higher proof of alcohol.

Stills were hidden in places, under overhangs, in dugouts, or among trees to help disguise any smoke rising from the operation.

From *The Second Oldest Profession , The Infromal History of Moonshing in America. Carr, Jess, Published by Prentice-Hall, New Jersey, 1972.*

A map of the locations of Stills on the North Fork can be found at the end of the book.

NOTES

1. Norman H. Clark, *Deliver Us From Evil*, New York, W. W. Norton & Co., Inc. 1976. p. 120
   For general background material: Larry Engelman, *Intemperance-The Lost War Against Liquor*, The Free Press (MacMillan) 1979
   Alec Wilkinson, *Moonshine, A Life in Pursuit of White Liquor*, Thorndike Press, Thorndike, Maine, 1952

2. According to Lonnie Royal, the first to come to Wyoming were Billie and Johnnie Woodruff and cousin Ernest Spicer. These men went into the sheep business. Next to arrive were Jack, Arlie, and Luther Spicer- three brothers who were cousins to the first three. Morgan Royal and son, O. A. Royal came to Powell in the early 1900's. Lonnie and Artis Royal, nephews of Jack Spicer and Joshua Spicer, Jack's brother, came in the 1920's.

3. Ray Prante, Oral Interview, Cody, Wyoming, September 28, 1985.

4. *Northern Wyoming News*, August 7, 1914.

5. Francis Hayden, Oral Interview, Cody, Wyoming, March 1984

6. Morris Simpers, Oral Interview, Cody, Wyoming, Nov. 11, 1990

7. *Cody Enterprise,* March 22, 1922

8. Gordon Loomis, Oral Interview, Billings, MT July 25, 1990

9. *Cody Enterprise,* January 21, 1923

10. *Cody Enterprise,* September 12, 1923

11. Morris Simpers, ibid

12. *Park County Herald,* January 6, 1926

13. *Park County Herald,* February 10, 1926

14. Emma Kelly, Oral Interview, November 11, 1990

15. Court Case 483 was against both Harry Johnson and Hardy Shull. The case against Shull was dropped November 20, 1926.

16. Court Case 578

17. Chella Hall, Oral Interview, Cody, WY August 14, 1989

18. Frances Shull Witzleban, Oral Interview, Cody, WY July 1984

19. Ray Prante, Oral Interview, Cody, WY December 1984

20. Morris Simpers, ibid

21. *Cody Enterprise,* January 15, 1932

22. Court Case 581, State of Wyoming versus Hardy Shull and James Osborne on Bootlegging, March 9, 1929. Osborne was judged not guilty but W. H. Shull was sentenced to jail. He appealed his case and lost and was sentenced to 90 days in jail and $750 fine. He was a "model prisoner" and after serving part of his jail sentence and paying $375 fine, Judge Metz decreed the "Defendant be paroled pending his good behavior.", December 10, 1930

23. Lonnie Royal, ibid

24. Wilkinson, *Moonshine* p. 30 states: Yeast converts the sugar to alcohol and carbon dioxide. An average batch would consist of 50 lbs. of mash (45 lbs. of meal; 30 lbs. of sugar; 1 lb. of yeast, and water poured over the ingredients to kick off fermentation.) In the still the mash separates from the meal "mammh". The meal is heated over a fire to about 173 degrees when the alcohol vaporizes, then vapor cooled and condensed into liquid. According to Richard Perry Hatch of Idaho Falls, ID some people cooled the liquid by running it through coils submerged in cold water, then filtering the liquid. There were regional variations.

25. Wilkinson, p.31, also explains about the importance of knowing the tone and cadence of the sound of the fermentation.

26. *Cody Enterprise,* July 24, 1929

27. *Cody Enterprise,* August 28, 1929. There is no record of a court case.

28. Lonnie Royal ibid

29. John A. Murray, during the 1940's, was a chemist at the Great Western Sugar Factory in Worland, WY. he states processed beet pulp contains only one tenth of one per cent sugar, an amount insufficient to cause fermentation. Oral Interview, Billings, MT May 17, 1992

30. From Records in County Clerks Office Park County, WY

31. Frances Shull Witzleban, ibid

32. Clark Lawrence, Oral Interview, Cody, WY May 31, 1989

33. Huldah Borron, Oral Interview, Cody, WY July 1984

34. Morris Simpers, ibid

35. John Yeates, letter, November 1991

36. *Cody Enterprise,* January 18, 1989

37. Nina Sherwin, Oral Interview, Wapiti Valley, July 16, 1985

Early Deaths on the North Fork

From the 1890s to the early 1940s, many deaths occurred on the North Fork from both natural and tragic circumstances. "There appears to have been an attitude factor prevalent then towards accidental deaths that has changed nowadays. It can be described in the phrase 'high acceptable level of risk' and it helps to explain some of the accidents." According to John Yeates steep wagon roads, snow and mud, deep river crossings, long hauls and heavy loads frequently stressed teams and equipment. The old-timers accepted such risks as part of their day's work. " Applicants for work were expected to already know their job skills, and many, eager for work or overconfident of their ability, would not risk lowering their dignity by asking questions," remembered to John Yeates. When a farmer or rancher needed a hired hand, he would go to the local saloon, or during Prohibition, pool hall, and pick up a temporary worker, there being no employment offices.

During this period, lives were lost to forest fires, automobile accidents, construction and logging accidents, drowning, homicides and suicides. The first recorded death on the North Fork was that of Mrs. Wesley Bloom, who with her infant daughter, drowned in the Shoshone River during high water on July 21, 1893. The Bloom family included two older children, Johnny and Lena, and the baby, whose name we do not know. The family had recently moved from Trail Creek to near the mouth of Trout Creek. At this time there were no bridges across either fork of the Shoshone River, so travel from Trout Creek on the north side of the North Fork required fording the river to reach the Marquette Store and Post Office. Continued travel around Cedar Mountain required fording the South Fork too. The depth of the rivers during June and July varied from week to week, depending on the temperature and melting rate of snow high in the mountains, and these months were the times of the highest flow rates.

While fording the North Fork with a wagon-load of animal hides the Bloom's wagon encountered deep, fast water. Upright bows supported a canvas cover over the wagon, although this cover was not in use at the time. The depth, velocity and force of the river probably floated the wagon and partially overturned it, leaving the running gear submerged and in place. Johnny and Lena clung to the wagon bows, however Mrs. Bloom and the infant were washed away. Wesley Bloom also stayed with the wagon and reached the farther river bank. Searchers found the body of the infant downstream, buy they could not find Mrs. Bloom's body.

On November 1, 1902, year-old Irvan McClure, son of F.H. and Alma McClure, died at Wesley Bloom place at Trout Creek. He died from scalding water burns. The family had returned from the 40 mile trip to town and back, and the baby got a hold of a cup of boiling water prepared for the tea at 8:30 Friday evening and died four hours later. The mother wrote a letter of explaination to the *Wyoming Distpatch,*November 5, 1902 edition and composed a 40 line poem in memory of Irvan McClure.

"Jack Rabbit Charley" Brennin was thrown by a bronc and killed at the Ed Grinder place, Marquette, on July 9, 1905, and buried there.

The narrow North Fork wagon road, and later the road through the canyon, did not allow for careless driving either with horses or in a motor vehicle. A few guard rails, or in places only large boulders along the edge of the road stood between the travelers and a precipitous cliff. Early newspapers carried frequent stories of runaways and overturned vehicles.

Maud Murray [1]told about a buggy trip through the canyon in 1909 when an empty rig pulled by a runaway team of frisky black horses tried to dash by in the box canyon section. The space was too narrow, buggy wheels locked and Maud picked up baby Margaret and jumped out. No one was seriously injured in this potentially dangerous wreck.

Intoxication contributed to a number of automobile accidents; and heavy drinking and depression caused some of the suicides.

Unlike the South Fork, the North Fork had no cemeteries, nor any churches or chapels until later years. Most who died were buried in Riverside Cemetery in Cody, some who became sick moved from the North Fork and died somewhere else, and many of the elderly from Poverty Flat, Marquette area, and Wapiti valley died elsewhere. Thomas Trimmer, well known and active in the community, died in Cody of pneumonia on February 11, 1908 at the age of forty-nine. He had bought the Charles Green property just west of the canyon. Another person who moved from the North Fork to seek treatment was Mildred Huntington Sherwin, thirty-two-year-old wife of Wylie Sherwin. She died of tuberculosis on May 5, 1927, while under family care in Lovell. She had taught school at Crooked Creek before her marriage to Wylie in 1915. Besides her husband, she left four children, Virginia, Betty, Ted and Clifford. They lived at Trail Shop.

Later, the Smith Murrays lived at Trout Creek. In June 1903 Mrs. Smith Murray committed suicide by drowning herself in Trout Creek. According to the *Wyoming Stockgrower and Farmer* she had previously shown signs of being of an unsound mind. A neighbor, Thomas A. Trimmer, went to Cody to report the death and to notify Smith Murray, who had gone to town, but Murray had already started home via the Rattlesnake Mountain trail. Parts of this trail were extremely steep and suitable only for horseback and foot traffic, but it was the only way to avoid fording the dangerously high rivers. Judge M. O. Newton filled the office of coroner. Due to the high water there was no choice but to bury Mrs. Murray on the ranch, and the location of the grave has been lost.

The September 22, 1904 issue of the *Cody Enterprise* noted that the body of Tom Williams had been found. Williams, a carpenter working on buildings at Pahaska Lodge, disappeared a year or so before. The July 27, 1905 issue of the *Cody Enterprise* listed the drowning of John

Rice. This accidental drowning occurred during a river log drive and they recovered his body in the Shoshone Canyon. The paper stated "Rice was of Hispanic ancestry and had no known relatives."

On September 18, 1905 George Grupp Jr., age thirteen, died of a gunshot wound from a .22 rifle while scuffling with his brother Frank, two years younger. The George Grupp family was camped at the Rattlesnake Creek ranch of John Henry Martin (no relation to the B. F. Martins). Six of George Jr.'s young friends served as pallbearers.

A tragic accident involving eleven men occurred in early June of 1906 on the North Fork river at Devil's Elbow. The Wallop-Moncrieffe Lumber Company had brought these experienced river runners from the Midwest to float logs from the upper North Fork to the company sawmill at Trimmer's Ford, a few miles upstream from the canyon. The loggers, in a bateau style river boat, attempted to dislodge a log jam. Although this was a typical operation on log drives, the extremely swift current made the work especially hazardous. The raging water forced the boat against the log jam and it immediately capsized. Seven of the eleven men in the boat drowned, but the paper listed only five names: Joe Redding, of Green Forest, Arkansas; Robert Hendrickson, of Hope, Indiana; John Hartley; John Finnican; and Joe Karry.

John K. Rollinson recalled the tragedy. At the time Rollinson worked for the Forest Service as a guard and later a ranger. He tells that the river was "nearing its height in floodwater from melting snow. . . . A bateau was used to pole the men from one side of the river to the other so that they could break up log jams, many of which had to be blasted loose."

One of Rollinson's jobs required him was to ride down to Marquette for the mail. On this particular day on the way back, he came to the camp which moved downriver each day following the crew. He wrote, "It was late afternoon and as I was hungry I thought I would stop at the camp and brace the cook for a handout." While the cook, a teamster, and Rollinson watched. Rollinson wrote, "suddenly we saw the bateau strike the logs. The force of the water turned it over so quickly our eyes could scarcely follow it . . . All were thrown into the swift current. Some clung to logs; others were sucked under the now floating island of timber, and those who had clung to the center were being struck by the hundreds of logs. . . at express train speed."

Two men reached the camp side of the stream and two others caught tree branches on the other side. Rollinson immediately rode down to the sawmill camp, bringing word of the tragedy. The men built fires along the river bank and around midnight. They located the first body and removed it from the river. Soon they recovered four more, but it took ten days to find the last two bodies killed in the great log jam.[2]

The July 26, 1906 issue of the *Wyoming Stockgrower and Farmer* carried the account of another fatal logging accident: Valentine Butile, a Frenchman, was killed instantly when a log shot down from a log chute, striking W. H. Dennis, foreman, and V. Butile. Dennis escaped death but Butile lost his life. This occurred on July 22, 1906 at a logging camp "near Wapiti." The inquest called it an accidental death and they buried the young man the next day.

On September 3, 1906, Arthur M. Plumb killed himself with a shot through the heart from a .45-90 Winchester rifle. Plumb still lived on the Frank Grinder ranch which he had just sold to H. B. Robertson (later the Frost and Richard ranch) and was despondent prior to the time of his suicide. The act occurred in the ranch bunkhouse.

From 1905 until 1910 crews worked on the 325 foot high Shoshone Dam. Stories of the dam construction contend eight or nine workmen lost their lives. In January 1910, during a final inspection supervising engineer W. H. Lincoln, age around twenty eight years, fell forty feet to the bottom of the spillway, he never regained consciousness and died. Contrary to folk tales, no bodies were entombed in the concrete.

On June 16, 1910, as the reservoir was being filled, four of five occupants drowned when their motorboat capsized on the reservoir. They were A. C. Downey, engineer, whose body was recovered on August 12, 1910; Adam Saul, carpenter, whose body was recovered on August 5, 1910; R. C. Soper, engineer, and Don Calkins, age twenty two, whose bodies were recovered at a later date. Calkins was the son of the J. K. Calkins, editor of the *Wyoming Stockgrower and Farmer.*[2]

Carl Johansson, worked as a carpenter on the dam and had planned to ride along across the reservoir and visit the Nordquist family on Irma Flat, but at the last minute changed his mind and saved his life.

From 1886 to 1916 Yellowstone National Park was under the administration of the United States Army, and one Army post was located at the East Entrance. The March 30, 1912, issue of the *Park County Enterprise* told of the shooting death of Private Frank Cunningham and the wounding of Private Frank Carol.

Aubrey Haines explains the circumstances prior to and the details of the actual shooting. Five men were stationed and mostly snowbound at the East Gate from October 1911 to May 1912, a hatred developed between Sgt. Brittain and Private Cunningham. The station log gives some idea of the dangerous nature of Pvt. Cunningham. Haines writes, "Early in January he went to Cody on a pass and while there got drunk and shot up the Irma Hotel for which he was fined $50 and costs. Unable to raise that amount Cunningham lay in the Cody jail for the rest of the month, returning to duty February 3, 1912 . . . the cleavage that developed within the detachment is evident in the fact the privates patrolled in pairs while the sergeant always patrolled alone."

Conditions worsened and on an early April patrol Sgt. Brittain started out as usual with his Colt .38 service revolver. A broken ski pole forced him to return to the station where a fierce confrontation broke out and Brittain pulled out his pistol and shot Cunningham between the eyes, killing him instantly. Private Carol advanced and Brittain shot him in the arm, nearly severing the large vein. A tourniquet was applied to the arm and it did not require amputation.[3] The body of Private Cunningham, age twenty one, was buried at Fort Yellowstone. In Cody a detail from Fort Yellowstone arrested Sgt. Brittain and Private Mutch and took them back to the Fort. Private May went back to Sylvan Pass station temporarily with Corporal Tex Wisdom and Private Gibson. Aubrey Haines finishes the story, "Sergeant Brittain was tried by a court-martial. . . at the Fort and found not guilty of homicide on the grounds he was justified in defending himself. The three surviving privates were subsequently tried for mutiny and found guilty; Carol, whose arm was permanently disabled, received a three year sentence and the other two received two years each."[4]

Sometime in June 1912, Pat English a teamster died in a wagon accident, while working for F.H. Garlow, manager at Pahaska.[5] English was driving a four-horse team pulling a wagon load of wood and coming from Mormon Creek it overturned on a steep and muddy downgrade.

On January 8, 1914, Clyde Pepper, a twenty-eight- year-old rancher, was dragged to death by a horse on the upper Pat Kelly ranch on Whit Creek. He had roped the horse and the rope had caught around his wrist in such a manner he could not release it. John A. Yeates, Sr. discovered him around noon and summoned the coroner.

Another fatal accident related to the East Entrance Army Post is recorded in the *Northern Wyoming Herald.* On March 21, 1914, twenty six year old Edna Durell died of exposure while walking between Pahaska and the army post. She planned to spend the winter at Pahaska and started out to visit a soldier at the post but when almost there she turned back. She traveled only a short distance before collapsing. Her clothing proved inadequate to the cold.

A September 1916 issue of the *Northern Wyoming Herald* carried an article about Charles E. Johnson who fell from a Cody-Sylvan Pass Motor Company bus enroute to Pahaska. He worked as a general utility man at Pahaska. He was buried in Billings, Montana.

On July 30, 1919, Mrs. Frank Medford, around twenty eight years of age, died in an automobile accident near the Rattlesnake Creek bridge. She was the wife of Reverend Medford of Greybull. The Medfords and their three year old son and Mrs. Medford's young sister, were en route to the park when the accident occurred. The car turned a somersault when it hit a boulder and landed in a gully. Mrs. Medford's sister and Reverend Medford sustained bruises but the little son escaped unhurt.

On December 3, 1919, George Dahlem, age thirty four, died at the deMauriac ranch. Henry Dahlem was foreman of the ranch at that time. Unable to speak for thirteen years, he had been cared for by Henry and his family. George and his brothers Henry and John had previously lived at Roberts, Montana, where George had been bucked off a horse and landed on some rocks, causing his severe injury. Paralyzed, bedridden and unable to speak, he had been cared for by Henry and his family for thirteen years.

Cecil Burton "Burt" Huntington, age twenty three, on August 15, 1920 died at the home of his father, C. J. Huntington, on the Thurmond place. Burt joined the Marines in 1917, surviving fierce drives on at least six fronts in Germany, before serving with the U. S. Army of Occupation. He contracted influenza and pneumonia at Koblenz and had never regained his health.

On December 25, 1920, William F. Simpers, age seventy one, father of Mrs. Henry Dahlem and Ben Simpers, died at the deMauriac ranch at Trout Creek, where the Dahlems were living, in May 1921.[6]

May 1921, a perforated ulcer caused the death of Gabriel (George) H. Slater, age about fifty, at the Hollister ranch on Rand Creek.[7] Slater, originally from Indiana, had been in the area for seventeen years.

A vacation in the mountains ended sadly when a lady guest, Louise J. Schneider of Philadelphia, died at Holm Lodge in June of 1921. No details are known.

Another tragic death occurred at Hanging Rock Campground in July 1922. Mr. and Mrs. A. S. Moore and three children were en route to North Dakota when the oldest, Helen, age six, drowned in the North Fork River. It appeared she awoke early, put on her bathing suit and tried to bathe in the river. Her body drifted several hundred feet downstream. She was buried in Riverside Cemetery in Cody.[8]

A ranch worker, Lee (Ole) Wright, age forty-three died, at the Flying Y ranch on Rattlesnake Creek.[9]

Another fatal automobile accident west of the Shoshone Canyon occurred on July 28, 1924. The *Park County Herald* carried the story of a small truck and a car with six

New Year's Day 1913. Sylvan Pass Soldiers Station. Left to right, Mrs. Dave Shaw, cook at Pahaska and at the Irma Hotel, Ranger Harry Miller, George Wallicker (came from Omaha), Mrs. Wallicker, 26 years old Edna Durrell, Jimmy Rooch, Pvt., Paul Wright, Sgt., James Brooks, George Hall and Pvt. Ozajke.

Edna Durcell taught school at Irma Flat. Sometime after this picture was taken she was found dead not far from Pahaska.

This picture is courtesy of Gladys Andren.

passengers plunging into the reservoir. Only one girl, age eleven, reached shore. Those who died were identified as the Junius Tanner family from Utah, and Willard and Sarah Welch from Cowley, Wyoming.

The North Fork community felt sadness and shock over the death of five-year-old Barbara Eleanor Kelly, daughter of the Joseph Frank Kellys who was instantly killed in an automobile accident on January 5, 1925. Mrs. Kelly and Barbara had ridden to town with Wylie Sherwin of the Trail Shop so Barbara could see a doctor. On the way home in the afternoon, a car driven by Jack Morrison tried to pass and in doing so swerved to the right, striking the left front wheel of the Sherwin car. This forced the Sherwin car into the ditch. The car door flew open and Barbara was thrown out, falling beneath the rear wheel which killed her instantly. The sudden stop of the car also threw Mrs. Kelly out but she was unhurt. Morrison drove on for a half mile, then looked back and seeing what had happened returned and took the occupants back to Cody. Charles Gawthrop, Lloyd Buchanan, and C. A. Evans at the coroner's inquest agreed Jack Morrison drove in a reckless and unsafe manner causing the accident and the death of Barbara. The May 16, 1928, issue of the *Cody Enterprise* stated that Jeff Chapman, age sixty-nine, had died at the Carl Buckingham road camp on the North Fork. His previous occupations included running the Alaska Saloon in Cody around 1910, and deputy sheriff.

And there was the mysterious disappearance of Pat Kelly in the 1920s. Whatever happened to him?

Another automobile accident attributed to drunken driving occurred in September 4, 1931. W. E. Fritz drove off the road near the J. F. Kelly lane killing Ed Holmquist, age sixty, and Edward Burdette, age twenty-one. Holmquist, a droll story teller with a Swedish accent, was a well-liked bachelor who worked as a general ranch hand and wrangler for various dude ranches. Ed had been in the area a long time. In 1906, along with most of the men around Marquette, he joined the Modern Woodmen of America, Camp 5910. Burdette came from the East and in previous years had been enrolled in the Valley Ranch Boys School. Driver Fritz was released from the charge of manslaughter in February 1932. Carl Johansson had the sad task of handling the affairs of his good friend after Ed's death.

Another alcohol-related accident happened in a bizarre manner. Long-time resident, Hurricane Bill Herrick, also met his death under the wheels of an automobile. Herrick, age fifty-six, had a crippled leg, played the violin and loved a good time. Once Al Clarke invited his friends to a drinking party at the Clarke Cabin on Jim Creek. After the party Al offered to drive Herrick home to the Johnson cabin, farther up the river and west of the Kelly lane. Because of the deep snow in the lane they decided to open a wire gate to the James Legg field and drive across the field to the cabin. Herrick got out to open the gate and as the car passed through he fell under and was run over by a rear wheel. Because he disappeared from sight Clarke backed up to look for him and ran over Herrick a second time. They took Herrick to the Hollister ranch but couldn't revive him and then to Cody.

The coroner's jury of M. E. Knight, Charles A. Vans, and S. Ross Yates determined that Herrick was knocked down and run over twice by the Chevrolet driven by Al Clarke. "He (Clarke) was in such an intoxicated condition as to render him incapable of possessing due responsibility." His driver's license was revoked.[10]

In contrast to these other deaths. Dr. Horace H. Hollister, age ninety-one, died peacefully on May 31, 1932, at the Dwight Hollister ranch. Dr. Hollister, the father of Dwight and Maude Hollister, had been a prominent physician and came west in 1930 to live with his son and daughter. They buried him in Rutherford, New Jersey.

On an early summer day, June 10, 1933, Elizabeth "Grandma" Upton died in her eighty-eighth year, at home, after living on the ranch at the foot of Sheep Mountain for 29 years. She and son Lee settled there in 1903. Three years later, March 7, 1935, after thirty-one years on the ranch, Lee died and his funeral was held in the picturesque old log ranch home.

Another violent death resulted from a gun battle. On April 2, 1933, Jack Spicer, age forty-seven, was killed with a bullet through his heart from shots fired by his nephew Artis Royal, at Spicer's home on Canyon Creek. Artis, also seriously wounded, made a miraculous recovery. Spicer was survived by his wife and numerous family members.

Again the community was saddened when it learned of the death of Arthur Royce and his three and one half year old daughter, Elizabeth. Royce while driving home from Cody on a Saturday afternoon at 5 p.m., the car left the road and plunged 225 feet into the Shoshone Canyon. A few years previous the Royce's had purchased the Stonebridge-McClain ranch. Art had served as clerk of the District 9, Wapiti School Board during 1931 and 1932.[11]

Dr. Charles and wife Bessie Rhoads were early settlers on Rattlesnake Creek. Bessie, age fifty-nine, died of heart attack in August, 1934, on the family ranch.[12] Dr. Rhoads had already died in Billings, Montana, March 13, 1933. Howard, Willard, and daughter Helen survived their parents.

Another car wreck near the J. F. Kelly ranch took the life of Loren A. "Pete" Stall, age twenty-four, on June 9, 1935. Stall worked as a dude wrangler at Holm Lodge. Fred Garlow and Pete had ridden to town with Louis Van Wezel, driving as fast as the Packard Straight Eight Sport Coupe would travel. Garlow chose not to ride back with Van Wezel, who tried to get the car to go even faster. Near the J. F. Kelly ranch the car left the road and hurtled seventy-five feet through the air ,Van Wezel survived.[13]

Sometime in early September of 1935, Ernest Rueger caught a ride from Cody to Jim Creek, got a short carbine rifle from the Al Clarke cabin, walked a little ways up Jim Creek, sat down, aimed the gun at his head and took his life. Four weeks later, Al Mensel, Vern Spencer, and Under Sheriff Joe Freeborg discovered the body. Rueger was buried in Riverside Cemetery in Cody. He came west as a young man, lived and worked on the North Fork as well as for Valley Ranch. Ernie had a pleasing personality and was well-liked. A tall and lanky cowboy, he wore his Stetson at a slightly rakish angle, and often had a hand-rolled cigarette between the fingers of his left hand. However, his alcoholism no doubt contributed to his suicide.

On May 25, 1941, thirty-five-year-old Garland "Curley" Lasater drowned while fording the North Fork near the Fred/Leonard Morris ranch. He was dressed in heavy coat, chaps and boots and riding a bronc. As the river got deeper, he lifted his feet from the stirrups and the bronc began bucking, throwing Lasater. Don Huntington, his companion was unable to rescue him so Huntington ran to the Morris ranch for help. Aiding the search were fifty CCC boys. They found the body two and a half miles downstream. Lasater, cow foreman at deMauriac ranch, had graduated from Oklahoma A & M college.

Dwight E. Hollister was born April 17, 1877, in Ridgewood, New Jersey, and on June 14, 1951, he put on his best suit, opened his Bible to a favorite passage and shot himself.

NOTES:

1. In a reminiscence *Up and Down the North Fork.*

2. John K. Rollinson, *Pony Trails of Wyoming,* The Caxton Printers, Caldwell, ID., pp. 324-325.

3. *The Wyoming Stockgrower and Farmer* March 30, 1912 The paper concentrates on the difficulty of the rescue operation. Dr. Waples traveled by Tex Holm's automobile from Cody to Frost and Richard ranch, then by horse and buggy to Holm Lodge where horses from the military post took them the rest of the way. The trip took twelve hours.

4. Aubrey L. Haines, *The Yellowstone Story,* Vol. 2, pp. 200-201.

5. F.H. Garlow married to Irma Cody, parents of Fred and Bill.

6. *Northern Wyoming Herald*, December 29, 1920.

7. *Park County Enterprise,* May 31, 1921

8. *Cody Enterprise,* July 19, 1922.

9. *Cody Enterprise,* December 20, 1922.

10. *Cody Enterprise,* February 3, 1932.

11. *Cody Enterprise,* August 16, 1933.

12. *Cody Enterprise,* August 3, 1934.

13. Coroner's jury decreed manslaughter, the family sued, Park County District Court Case #2206, for $54,392.50 due the family and $102,376.50 for alleged negligence. The case was removed to United States District Court in July, results of the case were not printed. *Cody Enterprise* June 12, 1935.

Blackwater Fire

The worst disaster on the North Fork was the Blackwater Fire of August 21, 1937. Fifteen men died and 38 required hospitalization and/or treatment. In terms of loss of life this forest fire is among the ten worst forest fires in United States history. Twelve Civilian Conservation Corp (CCC) enrollees, one Bureau of Public Roads employee and two Forest Service employees died. The fire destroyed 1,700 acres of Douglas and Alpine fir and Engleman spruce timber.[1]

During a storm August 18, 1937, lightning struck an Alpine fir and started the fire at the bottom of a canyon five miles up Blackwater Creek, 35 miles west of Cody, at an elevation of 7,600 feet . It was a dry season, the temperature was in the high 80s, and humidity was only 6 to 10 per cent.

From a deceptively unremarkable beginning, unpredictable fire blowups, spot fires, and sudden, erratic, high velocity winds spread the fire. Ninety-two hours elapsed between the discovery of the fire and its containment. Within two days after the fire, there were two investigations, one by Forest Service and the other by the CCC. Both concluded that human error did not contribute to these deaths. Crown fires, blowups, and high winds caused the entrapment and deaths.

On August 20, pilot Bill Monday was flying Carl Krueger, assistant to Ranger John Sieker, to investigate a Sunlight Basin fire and spotted the smoke to the south. About this time the column of smoke was observed by people at Pahaska and by Mrs. Tex Wisdom at Blackwater who reported it to District Ranger Charles Fifield at Wapiti. He checked it and requested a crew of equipped fire fighters from the CCC camp a few miles downriver. Some fifty CCCs arrived and more were requested from nearby camps. Late that night, Morris Simpers, CCC camp foreman, established a fire camp two miles up Blackwater Creek, and soon moved it two miles closer to the fire. Wylie Thomas, foreman for a CCC crew working in the Beartooth Mountains, had a day off and came to Cody. He was immediately recruited to take charge of the upper fire camp.

By Saturday morning the fifty-man crew from Tensleep arrived with foremen James Saban and Paul Tyrrell. Nine Bureau of Public Roads crew members under Bert Sullivan started working on an east side fire line, and Carl Buckingham and his crew of 12 enrollees worked on a north side line. Rangers Clayton, Post, experienced fire fighters, and Hale, tackled the advancing fire to the southeast, with Tensleep CCCs and their foremen Tyrrell and Saban.

All plans were working well until an afternoon wind shot through the area, causing two crown fires to come together.[2] Urban Post began to warn the fire fighters to escape to a northeast ridge. At about 4:00 p.m. David Thompson, Assistant Tensleep Company leader, arrived with the last communication from Alfred Clayton and the six men in his crew. The note read:

> Post—
>
> We are on the ridge in back of you and I am going down to spot in the "hole". It looks like it can carry on over the ridge east and north of you. If you can send any men please do so since there are only 8 of us here.
>
> Clayton

There was no possible way to save the trapped Clayton group when the wind turned the fire downhill. Post and Sullivan barely survived on a rocky ledge of the ridge, heroically keeping the enrollees from becoming panic stricken and running into the flames. Tyrrell tried to shield his group of boys lying on the ground, hence getting fatally burned himself. Only by lying on the rocky ledge, face down, and getting a breath of air occasionally as the winds shifted, did most escape death. Five men left the ridge and ran through the fire, only one of these survived.

Three hours later the worst was over. Survivors were coming out and rescuers were rushing in and searching for the burned and dead. At 10:00 p.m. forty men reached the first aid station. Seiker radioed for doctors, nurses, ambulances, and medical supplies.

Sunday morning the fire camp was moved back down. Pack outfits started bringing out the bodies, and the containment and mop-up of the fire continued.

The Official Roster of those who died:
Alfred Clayton, 45, Cody and Sheridan, Wyoming, Forest Ranger
Rex Hale, 30, Afton, Wyoming, Technician, Forest Service
Billy Lea, Sherwood, Oregon, Bureau of Public Roads employee
Paul E. Tyrrell, 24, Technical Foreman Tensleep CCC camp 1811
James T. Saban, 38,[3] Foreman, Hyattville, Wyoming, Tensleep CCC camp of 1811

Enrollees of Company 1811, Civilian Conservation Corp.
Clyde Allen, McDade, Texas
Roy Bevens, Smithville, Texas
Ambrocio Garza, Corpus Christi, Texas
John B. Gerdes, Halletsville, Texas
Will C. Griffith, Bastrop, Texas
Mack T. Mayabb, Smithville, Texas
George E. Rodgers, George, Texas
Earnest R. Seelke, LaGrande, Texas
Rubin D. Sherry, Smithville, Texas
William H. Whitlock, Austin, Texas

Four hundred and seventy five enrollees from six CCC camps, plus nine volunteers from Bureau of Public Roads and thirty one local volunteers, make a total of 515 fire fighters plus forty nine foremen and supervisors fighting the fire.

The tragedy of the fire and the heroism of the men was remembered in several ways. The newly organized American Forest Fire Medal Foundation awarded their first medal to Urban J. Post, and a second medal posthumously to Junior Forester Paul E. Tyrrell. They awarded a third medal to Bert Sullivan.

In the summer of 1939 Wapiti CCC enrollees built a roadside monument, 33 feet long and five feet high of natural red stone on a large, grey flagstone platform, west of the river from the mouth of Blackwater Creek. On this are inscribed all the names of the men who died. The dedication was August 20, 1939. After 55 years, vandalism and age are taking their toll of this memorial. Double Mountain was renamed Clayton Mountain and the "hole" where Clayton and crew were trapped was named Clayton Gulch. A memorial trail leads up Blackwater Creek to a black quartzite marker with bronze plaque at the site of the deaths and on to the rocky ridge where Post and Sullivan and crew members sought safety.

Rex A. Hale, of the Forest Service, died in the gulch entrapment and was honored by the naming of roadside Rex Hale campground north from Blackwater canyon. Hale was supervising the development of this facility when called to fight the fire. In Tensleep Ranger District of Bighorn National Forest, the winter quarters were named Saban Ranger Station and the summer quarters, Tyrrell Ranger Station.

Half a century later memories were revived by a fifty year CCC reunion and rededication of the Fire Fighters Memorial. The most enduring memory of the fire by survivors, witnesses, and anyone associated with it is the horrifying screams of the burning victims.[4]

NOTES

1. The most comprehensive account comes from The Tragedy at Blackwater Creek, by Lyle Hale, Afton, Wyoming, younger brother of Rex Hale, fire victim. He compiled all the official forest ranger reports and CCC foreman reports.
2. Crown fire is a term for when a fire moves rapidly through the tree tops.
3. An interesting example of the web of history: George Saban, one of the Ten Sleep raiders, was the father of James Saban, hero and victim of the Blackwater Fire, according to his daughter, Jean Saban Groshart of Worland.
4. This condensed account is taken from a more detailed research by John A. Yeates and is available at the Park County Archives.

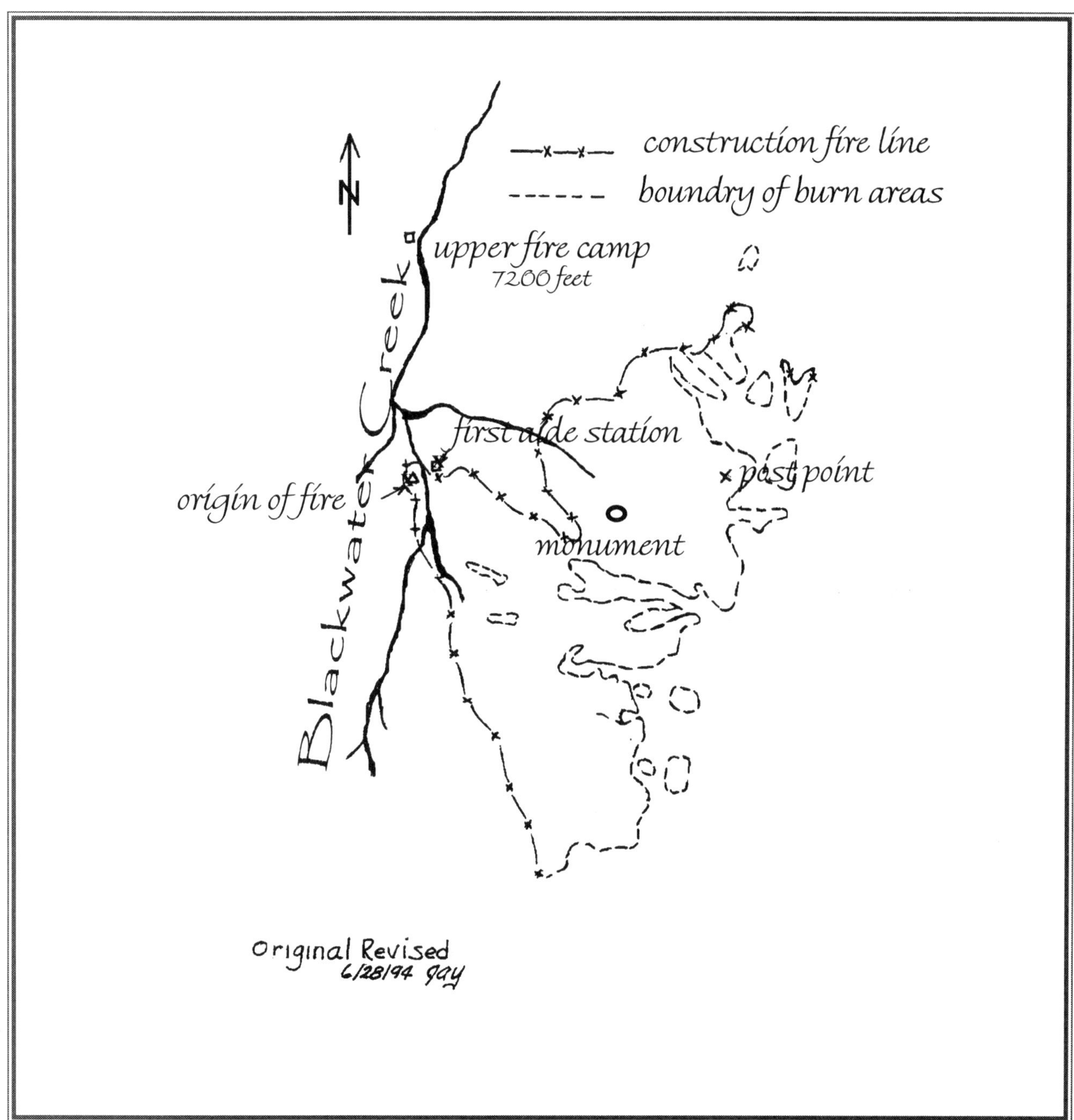

Map courtesy of John A. Yeates.

Arts and Entertainment

E. Farrington Elwell 1908 postcard. Photo courtesy of Park County Archives.

It is impossible to list all the talented and creative people who lived or worked on the North Fork, or who passed through as visitors, guests, or tourists, only a few can be mentioned. The first widely recognized artist on the North Fork was E. Farrington Elwell who came west because of his friendship with Colonel William F. Cody. Elwell met Cody in Boston where Elwell, at the age of seventeen did engineering work for the city of Boston and sketched and painted in his spare time.

In 1901 Colonel Cody invited Elwell to work on his TE ranch on the South Fork. Elwell was married, so Colonel Cody, always generous and kindly, offered the Elwells a salary, free board and room, and six saddle horses for their use. Elwell accepted the offer and continued his art work. He later created many of the Western scenes used in advertising posters for Cody's Wild West Shows.

By 1908 Elwell decided to move west. He chose the Charles H. Stonebridge ranch on the south side of the North Fork river, across from the Pat Kelly ranch, where he planned to raise horses and run a dude ranch. That same summer, Elwell, Stonebridge and Finley Goodman, who advertised in 1905 as "harness and saddle maker," took fourteen New Yorkers to Yellowstone Park on a pack trip. Elwell planned to raise Morgan horses but his timing was off. The "horseless carriage" displaced the horse and Elwell had to return to Boston to earn a living.

Charles Bradford, resident of the North Fork wearing one of Tex Kennedy's hand made leather vests.

E. Farrington Elwell did six color plates for the classic story, *The Log of a Cowboy*, by Andy Adams (1903). He also illustrated the *U P Trail*, by Zane Grey.[1]

Elwell had a kind face and a six-foot frame. He loved horses, rode well and mixed well with his North Fork neighbors. In 1909 Elwell joined thirty other well-wishers who helped Grandma Upton celebrate her sixty-fifth birthday, and he presented her with one of his oil paintings of a Western scene. During his early years on the TE ranch he made friends with Eli and Mattie Jernberg who worked there and they named one of their sons Elwell after him. E. Farrington Elwell died in 1962, in Arizona, at the age of eighty-eight after a long and productive life.

William Robinson Leigh, born on September 23, 1866 in West Virginia, came out to Cody in 1910 to go on a hunting trip with Will Richard, "a French-Canadian taxidermist." [2] His painting, *A Close Call* (1913) resulted from the 1912 hunt organized by J. D. Figgins, director of the Colorado Museum of Natural History, to find a grizzly for a habitat group. Leigh's *Foothills of the High Rockies,* shows a familiar eroded volcanic pinnacle on the south side of the North Fork above Breteche Creek. *Hunting Mountain Sheep* (1912) is a Wyoming setting as are *Mountain Landscape, Wyoming*, and *Grizzly at Bay* (1915) which shows two hounds and two airedales, owned by the Frost and Richard ranch, distracting a grizzly from a fallen hunter. The *Mountain Landscape* shows the influence of impressionism, as Leigh particularly admired the French impressionist, Monet. However, *Big Horn Sheep, Cow Creek* is a realistic painting of a young ram with a quarter curl (the horn grown 1/4 of a complete circle, or 90 degrees) proving to art critics his artistic ability. Leigh had difficulty making the transition from illustrator to artist, but is now an accepted artist. He died March 11, 1955, in New York City. His slightly curled, grey moustache and small patch of whiskers centered below his lower lip made him look very distinguished.

Frank Tenny Johnson had a log summer home and studio from 1931 until 1939, at the Rim Rock Ranch of Earl and Mildred Martin on Canyon Creek. Johnson's wife, Vinnie and Mildred Martin were cousins. Johnson was born June 26, 1874, in Big Grove, Iowa, and died

January 1, 1939, in New York City. He painted many North Fork scenes, excelling at night settings. His painting of the close-up view of the head of a *Wyoming Antelope* is realistic. Johnson used Earl Martin and other Rim Rock cowboys as subjects, his *Don, The Horse Wrangler* was posed by Don Huntington, a young North Forker. Johnson's clean-shaven, handsome features are reminiscent of Charlie Russell, perhaps because he parted his hair in the middle. The Trail Shop had Frank Tenny Johnson prints for sale, but none of the original oil paintings.[3]

Lawrence Tenny Stevens another Massachusetts native, came to the North Fork much later, in 1929. When Stevens lived in Bedford Hills, New York, he met a neighbor, N. P. deMauriac, who invited him out to deMauriac's Trout Creek ranch. Steve (Stevens) enjoyed hanging out in deMauriac's new lambing sheds where he amazed herders and ranch folk alike with his talent of sculpting the young lambs. Everyone liked him and admired his good looks.

His short visit on the North Fork introduced him to the West and he spent thirty days on a hunting trip with Ray and Don Siggins of the South Fork. In 1931 he married Priscilla Smith, an eastern widow with three daughters. On their wedding trip they all traveled west in an open touring car. In 1938 they bought the Double L Bar ranch on South Fork and spent several summers there until the Stevens divorced in 1944.[4] Steve sculpted a statue of Johnny Kirkpatrick, old Texas cowboy who had been deMauriac's cowforeman. The statue is called *Spirit of the West*, showing Kirkpatrick on his horse Monte and with his dog, Boy. Stevens sculpted a plaque with the head of William F. Cody to honor the naming of Cody Peak. This plaque was set in concrete and river rocks one mile below Grinnell Creek between the road and the river. By 1994 the plaque had disappeared.

Roy Glasgow, who trapped many winters on the North Fork headwaters, had considerable talent, painting outdoor western scenes and animals artistically and accurately.

Olive Fell, the only prominent early North Fork artist who was a native westerner, was born in Big Timber, Montana, in 1897.[5] Her family moved to Cody in 1902. She graduated from Cody High School, attended the University of Wyoming and the Chicago Art Academy. She settled on the P Bar P ranch on Jim Creek Heights and changed the name to Four Bear, or "Four Bar," an unfortunate choice since there already was Colonel Pickett's famous Four Bear ranch on the upper Greybull river.

She specialized in nature and animals and achieved her greatest satisfaction in etching. She reached her peak of artistic recognition between 1933 and 1934, and in 1933 exhibited in New York City with the Society of American Etchers. She found a profitable outlet with her famous *Little Cub Bear* cards and novelties for the tourist trade. North Forkers and Cody area residents admired her work. According to her obituary, "Without financial concerns, she might have been able to paint more for artistic expression than need."[5]

Tex Kennedy, an early ranch manager for Fred Morris ranch, was later appointed a game warden by Governor Nellie Tayloe Ross, and still later expressed his creative talent in tailoring. He made very warm shirts from army blankets. Morris Simpers remembered his mother bought one for his dad, Ben. Later, Kennedy, who always seemed to be smoking a cigar, turned to making leather vests and jackets and the *Cody Enterprise* called him a "leather worker artist." Jim Montgomery said Tex became allergic to wool, so he turned to working with leather.

Hans Snortland, a Norwegian craftsman, did outstanding work with peeled logs. He first came to Cody in 1924, and died in Cody on August 17, 1970, at the age of 83. He

Above: An example of Olive Fell's greeting cards.

worked with log construction in Yellowstone Park, Cooke City, and around Cody. He and Jim Wilson built the main lodge at Red Star Camp, 1935 through 1936, later called the Shoshone Lodge.

The dining room furniture is made of small pine poles in simple, classic lines. The chair seats and backs are of woven rawhide, six vertical strips of light tan leather thongs laced with six strips from side to side, and the chair seats are the same pattern. Sofas are of peeled, small diameter logs, and other pieces of furniture have the same clean-cut appearance.[7]

Besides woodworking craftsmen, master stonemasons left enduring examples of their handiwork, much of which will be lost when the North Fork highway is reconstructed. These craftsmen built artistically designed culvert-type bridges over many of the smaller streams, also headwalls, retaining walls, stone paving for drainage along the road and stone guardrails. Alexander Halone and son Eugene Halone of Thermopolis were master stonemasons, Eugene later settled in Billings Montana. Others were George Kochas and Charley Strom. The Halones used Portland cement and sand and mixed the mortar right on the job, according to Halone.[8] The Halones first worked for Taggarts on the 1923 road project from Canyon to Rattlesnake Creek.

Creative individuals in other fields would include Mildred Martin who had a special knack for making objects using materials found in nature. She also wrote North Fork news for the column "Wapiti Wallops" in the *Cody Enterprise*. Sometimes during the long, boring winters of the Depression years, she composed the Wapiti news in rhyme: "Sherwins went to Cody Monday, quite early in the morn, And came back home that evening amid a spring snow-storm." [9] A couple years later in a February 20 issue, the column was again written in rhyme: "Summertime the North Fork natives - Are so busy making hay, Wrangling cows and dudes and horses That there's no time left for play; And so when winter comes along, Old friendships they renew - At dances, club and dinners and at parties not a few." The column lapsed in the summer, dude ranching and farming kept everyone too busy to write the news. Mildred wrote *The Martins of Gunbarrel*, telling her experiences as a young bride at Absaroka Lodge, where the Martins first lived before establishing the Rim Rock Ranch. [10]

Hal Evarts is the most famous early North Fork author. He first came out to the Frost and Richard ranch in 1914, and later briefly homesteaded on Green Creek. After his marriage he attempted to start a skunk ranch at the Fred Richard place on Green Creek. He returned briefly after World War I. His story, *Elk of the Shoshone,* was published in the *Saturday*

Evening Post in 1919. Later stories were *The Yellow Horde* and *The Cross Pull.* The latter had a North Fork setting and one of the characters was modeled after Dwight Hollister.[11]

Helen Ogsten, wife of Yellowstone Park ranger Ted Ogsten, used her experiences to write *Piney Bear,* a juvenile tale published in 1948.[12] The story tells the life of a young bear during one year. Helen also wrote other nature stories. *Sincerely, Mary S.* are the reminiscences of Shawver who, with Billy Howell owned and managed Holm Lodge for thirty five years. The book gives the color and feeling of an early North Fork guest lodge or resort.[13]

Above: Rockwork at Nameit Creek.

Below: Rockwork at Pagoda Creek.

Roxielettie Yeates, wife of John Yeates Sr,, had studied music and graduated from the Louis Conrath Conservatory and later studied under Ernest Kroeger, composer and pianist in St. Louis, Missouri. She taught piano on the North Fork from 1917 until she moved to Cody where she continued to give lessons until 1969.

Ben Hammond had studied piano and expertly played the baby grand piano in the new home Mr. deMauriac built for his daughter Alice and her husband Ben at Trout Creek ranch.

There were many fiddlers in later years, but at first Uncle George Marquette played for most of the dances in the northwest part of the Big Horn Basin. George Logan played violin, as did William T. "Bill" Borron, who also came in the early 1880s. He could also play tunes on the melodian, piano, and coronet. He had had some experience as a bandmaster in Sheridan and he enjoyed organizing dances and the music for them with one or two other fiddlers. He called his group the "*Pioneer Orchestra*," or sometimes the "*Corn Stalk Fiddlers.*" Early Cody photographer Faye

Hiscock shared his talent on the violin and George Williams also played with Borron. "Hurricane" Bill Herrick called square dances and played fiddle. He sometimes borrowed a violin and had the habit of tightening the strings to raise the pitch, often the strings broke. Dances were held wherever there was adequate space and a tolerant and agreeable host to share it. Many dances were held at the Fred Morris ranch, when sometimes Fred contributed "vocal selections." Mary Martin Ebert recalled riding horseback with the Martin girls, her cousins, all the way from the South Fork to attend a dance at Morris ranch. The Thurmonds, just east of Trout Creek, had a new barn and gave a dance there in 1911.

Hans Snortland's furniture graces the dining hall of Shoshone Lodge.

In those days visiting and sharing meals satisfied the need for social interaction. At Christmas time in 1928 Denny Start and Verne Spencer skied down from Canfied Creek and Roy Glasgow skied from Red Creek to celebrate and enjoy Mrs. Pike's good cooking at Holm Lodge.

In 1992 Mrs. Robert Boyle wrote a history of the Wapiti Women's Club. She explained because the women were *"Landlocked in 1927"* by a rock slide in the Canyon, "the women of the Wapiti Valley formed the North Fork Women's Club to combat cabin fever, get out for lunch, and escape restless husbands for a few hours." Helen Spencer was first president. For the first three years of its existence, the group was purely a social gathering, with members taking turns preparing and hostessing midday dinners of meat and potatoes, while others carried in the vegetables, rolls and desserts, according to Nina Sherwin, who joined the club in 1930."[14] At this time the group became a Homemakers' Club of the Wyoming Agricultural Extension Service with educational demonstrations. The club "served in its early years as the hub of the community" and it continues to provide support and sociability to its members.

On the North Fork dances have always been the entertainment of choice. Pat Kelly had adequate room in his "new" house and sponsored both private and public dances. After the Wapiti school house was built, it provided an ideal mid-valley location for community dances and social events. If the school board and current teacher were so inclined, it could be used for various social gatherings. In 1912, donations received at a dance helped to pay for furnishings for the new school house. Faye Hiscock and Bill Borron supplied the music for the dance and Harry Williams gave a demonstration of cowboy dancing. Grace Miller (Mrs. Harry, the Ranger's wife) was "floor manager." In later years, bootlegger Jack Spicer, if in a good mood, would entertain with a clog dance he had learned in North Carolina.

In the mid 1920s, Charlie Sullivan and sons Bryan and Bert made up a popular orchestra. Charlie played fiddle, Bert chorded on the piano, and Bryan, who played banjo could also "act out stories." John Yeates, Jr., remembered them playing "*Irish Washerwoman,*" "*Rye Waltz,*"and a schottische called the "*Flop Eared Mule,*" which incorporated sounds like a donkey braying.[15] Jack Steen played violin for dances. Later Hank Hlavacheck was a popular fiddler. Nina Sherwin recalled there were four couples among their closest friends, who got together almost every Saturday night for fun. They were sometimes called the "*Silk Stocking Crowd.*" There did seem to be an up-the-river group and a down-the-river group.

In earlier times, the well-liked little Belgian World War I veteran, John Borgham, known as "Pontoon Johnnie, "played the accordion. Bertha Dahlem (Mrs. Henry) sang. Bertha often sang in a duo with Mrs. Vogel, at church or for funerals, never at dances. Bertha could whistle expertly too. Emma Kelly, (Mrs. J. F.) had a remarkable soprano singing voice although she had no voice training. Occasionally at gatherings she would sing "Songs My Mother Taught Me," accompanied by Roxielettie Yeates. In later years, Bob Rumsey could always be relied upon to play the drums at the dances.

Everyone admired the riders in Buffalo Bill's Wild West show, so rodeos provided great entertainment. The first were held at Marquette. Dewey Stilley Riddle, young bronc rider said, "We Saddled 'em down and rode 'em up." Carly Downing and the Holman boys were other young bronc riders. In 1913 Fred Morris entertained the neighbors with a bucking contest at the Morris ranch. A few years later the dude ranch rodeos were held on the Libby Creek meadows, called "The Flat." Again local horse wranglers showed off for the summer dudes. Orilla Downing Hollister no longer participated in these rodeos but she had been a bona-fide cowgirl with Buffalo Bill's Wild West shows. When he worked on the North Fork, Art Holman, another of Colonel Cody's riders, showed off his skill of horsemanship.

Lloyd Coleman of the Flying W ranch (later the Mooncrest ranch) at the head of Rattlesnake Creek , one-time champion bareback rider of the world, later had a career in Hollywood movies in the late1927 era. Lloyd was Gertrude Vanderbilt Whitney's model for the statue Buffalo Bill, the Scout. The horse he posed on was "Smokey" owned by Monte Jones.

Leonard Morris, only son of Fred and Maggie Morris, had an extensive career in the movies. According to a letter from his widow, Dottie Morris, Leonard did dangerous jumps on horseback as a stunt man in the film *Squaw Man*, starring William S. Hart. During the 1930s and 1940s he continued to play bit parts, as in the film *Strangers May Kiss*, with Norma Shearer. He worked with Wallace Beery in *Secret Six*, and in other films with James Stewart, Spencer Tracy, Lionel Barrymore and Clark Gable. Lillian Dixon recalled, "Leonard had rusty-red hair and a beautiful singing voice. I can remember him singing 'Wagon Wheels.'"[16]

At the yearly Cody Stampede rodeo celebrations, North Forkers were well represented.

Jimmy Tuff, the ultimate horseman, loved to race, his specialty was the Roman race, guiding a pair of horses as he stood with one foot on the back of each. For this stunt he shed his cowboy boots for soft-soled moccasins. Not only kids and dudes found this pretty exciting to watch, but everyone who had ever ridden admired his ability even though they disapproved of his horse stealing and dealing.

John Kirkpatrick, seventy-three years old, roping a calf. Photo courtesy of Park County Archives.

The contestants took their share of knocks and broken bones. In the 1920 Stampede, "Bad Medicine" bucked Earl Hayner off and Earl broke a few bones. George Coleman broke his shoulder in the 1922 Stampede. Earl is best remembered for his clowning; he wowed the audience by riding a bronc with a rocking chair for a saddle, and did he do it facing backwards? Tall, picturesque Johnny Kirkpatrick often won in roping contests over youthful ropers half his age, and was loved and respected by all.

It wasn't all work for the North Forkers, but the play and recreation were fairly simple, wholesome, and rated low on sex and violence.

NOTES

1. Farrington also produced many more illustrations, paintings, posters, post cards and other pieces of art in his long and prolific career.

2. The two kept in touch and Leigh returned in 1911, 1912, and in 1921.

3. According to Ted Sherwin's memoirs.

4. Letter from Roz Siggins, one of Priscilla's daughters, who married Don Siggins,

5. The 1910 census lists Olive as age 13.

6. According to Morris Simpers.

7. The famous "Molesworth" furniture, a heavier style with leather or Navajo-type blanket seats and backs, created and manufactured by Thomas Molesworth in Cody became very popular in both North Fork homes and dude ranches. Ed Grigware painted many North Fork Scenes and Stan Kershaw photographed the North Fork, but, along with furniture artist Molesworth, all fall in a more recent time period than this history.

8. Halones , interesting, but unrelated to the North Fork, Alexander Halone was head quarryman and setter of the granite base of the Buffalo Bill Statue.

9. *Cody Enterprise,* March 30, 1932.

10. Her book was published by Caxton Printers, Caldwell, Idaho, 1959.

11. According to the Three Roberts in their *Wyoming Almanac* (1990): His best known work, *Silent Call* was set in Wyoming. Later the story was scripted into a movie.

12. Published by Robert M. McBride in 1948.

13. In the early days these were referred to as "dude ranches" and the guests were known as "dudes" with none of today's meaning attached.

14. Interview with Nina Sherwin

15. John Yeates memoirs

16. Lillian Dixon interview

Goverment Services

Perhaps more than most areas in the West, several federal agencies had an early and lasting impact on the North Fork. Four of these were the National Forest Service, the upper half of the the river valley lay in the forest reserve and the lower part was bordered by government land. Second, the Bureau of Reclamation changed the lower valley from farm land to reservoir when the river was dammed in the Shoshone Canyon. The National Park Service controlled Yellowstone Park and that scenic playground was easily accessible during summer months. Also, the unhunted animals spilled over and replenished the forest reserve. For many years the Yellowstone Park Transportation buses traveled twice daily in summer between the Burlington Depot in Cody and the Park. Finally, the Bureau of Land Management, a latecomer, organized grazing allotments and range management.

There were other government, and quasi-government services of less magnitude for the people but with perhaps greater daily effect on every person. Those included the postal service, law enforcement, and elections. Also included is a brief account of the effect of World War I. The federal government called up draftees and accepted volunteers from North Fork Males. However, there were not more than twenty or thirty men in the Wapiti valley at the time. Like elsewhere in the West, many of them were single and mobile.

Early Elections on the North Fork

In 1887, the first election in the Marquette district of Fremont County listed seven ballots cast. The November 3, 1896 election, the first in Big Horn County, listed Marquette having forty-nine voters compared with thirty voters at Ishawooa. According to the 1910 census, there were 97 living on the North Fork. Big Horn county divided in 1909 and in 1910 Big Horn and Park County operated as separate counties. Good-looking Dwight Hollister was the Republican candidate for the State Legislature in 1910 and won with a total of 959 votes.

Wapiti voting district was number 16, and in the upper valley was number 24. In 1914, in the Primary election, 19 voted in district 16. They voted at the Wapiti school house and the judges were William T. Borron, Dwight Hollister and Lee Upton. In the November election, 43 voted, and B. C. Rumsey, running for the State Senate, got four votes. In 1916, fifty-three voted and in 1918, forty-nine voted, and eighteen were for Prohibition and twenty-seven against it.

In 1920, Bob Rumsey ran as an independent candidate for the state senate. He ran on an anti-Prohibition ticket from 1920 to 1930, and his friend, Caroline Lockart, editor of the *Cody Enterprise*, also strongly against Prohibition, said he was "straight forward and wet." In 1924, the Wapiti district favored Calvin Coolidge.

In the 1928 election there was a Republican landslide nationally, but at Wapiti the votes ran, Herbert Hoover forty-four, and for the Catholic Democrat Al Smith, seventy-two votes. In 1932 there were a total of 146 voters at Wapiti. Those who voted for Hoover were seventy-one, and for Roosevelt, seventy-one. B. C. Rumsey was finally elected to the State Senate and had the pleasure of introducing a joint resolution for repeal of Prohibition in Wyoming . It passed in February 1933. Another of his favored pieces of legislation, the Game Protection Bill lost. In May 1933, Wyoming "Went Wet".

In 1932, Lee Upton was an election judge as were Ben Simpers and John Yeates. These three earned $3. for the day's work, but Fred Richard earned $11. for being chief judge, picking up and delivering the ballots to the Court House.

In 1934, 27 voted in the primary election at Wapiti, and in the general election in November there were 138 voters. That election was a Democratic landslide.

The North Fork and World War One.

In Park County, of the approximately 733 men registered for war service, these were registered on the North Fork: Harry G. Evarts, Robert M. Patton, Detatee White, John Philip Siebert, Earle Linde, Henry Westerman, and Louis Smith. Later registration included Joshua Bryan Sullivan. The *Park County Enterprise* for September 22, 1920, stated Roy Lehman returned home after four years in the United States Navy. The newspaper stated he returned a "190 pound husky".

Manly E. "Budd" Hall at age twenty-two joined the 361st Air Service Squadron. John and Carl Bloom, who sometimes called Jim Creek Heights home, went off to war. Lawrence Nordquist got as far away as Razdonia, seventy miles from Vladisvostck, with Supply Company L, 31st Infantry Division, American Expeditionary Forces. He returned, a corporal, in January 1920.

Cecil Burton Huntington, aged twenty-three, died August 15, 1920, at the family home, (The Thurmond Place). He had been active in World War I, had influenza and pneumonia at Coblenz and had never regained his health.

In July 1917, all women in Park County were to be registered for Food Conservation for the War Effort. Bill Borron was appointed to register the North Fork women.

In November 1917, the Dwight Hollisters gave a dance at their home to collect money for the Red Cross. North Forkers did their share to support the war effort buying Liberty Bonds and raising victory gardens.

Other men who, at one time or other, were associated with the North Fork and were in the service were: George Cleas, Art Royce, Bill Fell, Dave Powell, Roy Glass, Clifford Spencer, Burton Marston, and Walter Goodman. Undoubtedly many names have been missed.

North Fork Postal Service

The first post office on the North Fork dates back to April 25, 1904, when the ranger station at Wapiti was established as a post office with Clarence Woods first postmaster.[1] Records are sketchy but it probably ran no longer than 1909 as it received its mail from the Marquette Post Office which was discontinued September 15, 1909.

Very few people lived permanently on the upper North Fork inside the Forest Reserve and required regular mail service. Those who lived in the middle and lower valley rode down to New Marquette, or the second Marquette Post Office.[2] The Shoshone reservoir would soon be filling and flooding the area, so after that date they had no post office and at great inconvenience had to travel through the canyon to Cody for mail.

In order to establish a post office the residents had to present a signed petition to the Postal Department indicating a need. Fred Morris contacted Senator Frank Mondell for the petition form and when it came Mrs. Fred (Mary) Morris rode horseback to each ranch to get signatures. It was a cold February day and she nearly froze, but when she came to the Ralph Millers at Trout Creek she later wrote,". . . they took me in and warmed me after my long ride."[3] The next day, again a bitter cold day, Mary Morris rode horseback to Cody Post Office with the required signatures and on September 18, 1913, Morris Ranch Post Office was established with Mary Morris first postmaster.

The Fred Morris family did not live permanently at their ranch because Fred was connected with the Philadelphia shipyards during World War I. Due to the fact they often were "back East" the post office facilities were moved from Morris Ranch to Hollister ranch, hence it could no longer be called Morris Ranch and was called Wapiti. It is assumed this went through proper legal channels although it is not recorded in Wyoming Post Offices, 1850-1980, by Gallagher and Patera. Lee Borron served as postmaster for awhile and the last in the 1920's was Orilla Downing (Hollister). Morris Ranch is listed from September 18, 1913, to November 15, 1923, when it officially was transferred to Trail Shop and continued to be called Wapiti.

Nina Sherwin recalled, "The mail came twice a week at first, Tuesday and Thursday. It was a real chore because you had to be there every mail day without fail. We had a lot of cubby hole boxes for the mail in our kitchen. Even Jimmy Tuff got his mail there at times. I had to learn that mail addressed to Norman Price was for Jimmy Tuff." [4] Sherwins had the post office until 1936, when "Simpers took it down at their Wapiti Lodge." Mail is still received at the Wapiti Post Office.

Besides the post offices, the United States Postal Department submits contracts for rural delivery on various Star Routes. These contracts are bid on by private contractors for periods of four years, then the route is up for bids again. Senator Mondell helped to get a Star Route for the North Forkers. Will Richard had the first contract dated May 16, 1913, and delivered twice a week to the residents on the mail route. He also carried the mail to the designated post offices on his route. This service proved much better than the previous volunteer carriers.[5]

Even after motorized vehicles took the place of horse-drawn stages the trucks or cars carrying the mail were called "the stage." The office for the North Fork stage in the early days was in the Wallop-Moncriefe Lumber yard in Cody, where the Elks Club stands in the 1996.

Contractors often subcontracted the driving job. For instance, Chet Freeman was an early contractor and he hired Jud Weston from Bretche Creek to drive. Elsworth Jenkins was remembered as an innovative mechanic and driver and W.S. Widdows drove in the 1930s. Budd Hall was a successful bidder on the mail contract in 1926 and his wife Chella drove the stage during those notorious Prohibition days. After the Halls, Louis and Jessie Lowe drove for a number of years.

Mail was dropped off in the mail box at each ranch in their own bag, usually a canvas sack, often a grain or feed sack, with a draw string to close it. Some ranches such as Rumseys and deMauriacs had locked pouches, a canvas bag closed with a leather band at the top that was sealed with a small padlock. Besides mail, the stage driver would haul parcels and groceries from the stores, and occasionally passengers rode on the stage.

To accommodate the influx of tourists and seasonal residents on the upper North Fork, a post office for the summer months was established at Holm Lodge. It ran from May 28, 1926, to July 31, 1950, during summers only. This summer post office was transferred to Pahaska August 1, 1950. Mary Shawver was first postmaster of Holm Lodge and held the position for many years and wrote about the visit of the Post Office Inspector. "The inspectors are human and helpful, but they have to count dollars and dimes, check records and receipts, but this particular time, something new was expected. He had to take my finger prints. Evidently, I looked doubtful, for he took them twice and then asked my age—such nerve!" [6]

Whether the stage driver dropped the mail off in the mail box by the side of the road, or a person picked up her or his mail from a cubby hole at Wapiti, regular mail service was a valuable link with the world beyond the North Fork.

NOTES:

1. *Wyoming Post Offices,1850-1980* by John S. Gallagher and Alan H. Patera, published by The Depot, Burtonville Maryland, 1980, pp.101-102
2. April 8, 1903 to September 15, 1909
3. Letter from 95 year old Mary Morris to Ethel Montgomery, around mid 1960s.
4. Oral interview with Nina Sherwin July 1985.
5. *Park County Enterprise* for May 1913.
6. *Sincerely, Mary S. by Mary Shawver,* Prairie Publishing Co., Casper Wyoming, no date, p.67

Brands on the North Fork of the Shoshone River

When ranchers registered brands with the state, they stated where they placed their brands on the animal. Early brands were placed on ribs, thighs, or hips of cattle. Horses were branded on shoulders, hips, or thighs, never on ribs or sides. Shoulder brands were favored as easier to spot in a bunch of horses. Later, brands on thighs were preferred. George Logan branded on "any part of cattle and horsest"

Brand	Name	Post Office	Date
	Henry Champman	Corbett	July 25, 1884
	Wesley Bloom transferred to Murray Brothers	Marquette Irma	Dec. 24, 1895
	George Logan	Marquette	Dec. 31, 1900 and Jan. 20 1902
KA	George Logan bought from Loyal Manning	Marquette	April 19, 1892
Z	George Logan	Marquette	Aug. 2 1897
	Frank Lundie	Marquette	Aug. 3, 1891
	Count Paul Breteche	Corbett	Oct. 3, 1884
	Count Paul Breteche transferred to Florence Breteche	Corbett	Jan. 15, 1892 Mar. 2, 1894
a/c	Charles A. Marston	Corbett	May 5, 1886
	Charles A. Marston	Corbett	Dec. 3, 1892
BN	Charles A. Marston	Marquette	Aug. 2 1897
	Flora E. Newton and Frank A Ingraham	Marquette	1882
2-K	Nuchols Brothers	Corbett	Aug. 19, 1890
WL	Albert L. Caillet bought brand from George Wise	Corbett	Nov. 15, 1886 May 16, 1891
ALC	Albert L. Caillet	Corbett	June 2, 1890
	Thomas Trimmer	Marquette	
	Dolly Martin Trimmer	Marquette	
	Frederick Morris	Marquette	c. 1904
	Andrew Martin	Marquette	
	Lee Upton	Northfork	c. 1902
	John Yeates	Northfork	1904
-B	Henry K. Barbee	Marquette	

	Name	Post Office	Date
KE	R.G. Miller	North Fork	1910
	N.P. deMauriac	North Fork	1916
T	Dwight Hollister		
3-	Jack Graves		
FV	Ben Simpers		
	Henry and Bertha Dahlem		mule shoe
K	J.F. Kelly		
3B- NP	Norman Price aka Jimmy Tuff		
	Jack Spicer later Lonnie Royal		lazy heart J
NF	C. H. Stonebridge		
	North Fork CAttle Co. (Stonebridge)		
S	Frank Slack		
4T	Art Reese		
Y	George Cles		flying y
W	Floyd and Lloyd Coleman		flying w
	Anna Moon Hall and Elmon Hall		mooncrest
YX	Jim Legg		
P-P	Nordquist Brothers, Lawrnce and Pete		
	Place eventually bought by Olive Fell who took the brand		four bear "four bar"
	C. J. Rhoads & Willard Rhoads		
	James Montgomery		
F	W. Hardy Shull		
	Claud Shull		
GE	Carl Johansson		
ON	William T. Borron		bar-on
	Ned Frost		
3C	Frost and Richard Ranch		

Kristina Murray with Johansson branding irons.

Below: Branding at Whit Creek. Ben Simpers with iron and Morris Simpers holding. Photo courtesy of Mark Simpers.

ↃXC Bronson C. Rumsey
Blackwater Camp, later at June Creek

Elephant Head Lodge

J Josephine (Mrs. Harry) Thurston

LV- Absaroka Lodge
John Goff's brand

Pahaska Tepee

Lazy Bar H. Ranch at Nameit Creek
Leonard Morris

The Circle H. Ranch
Chella and Bud Hall

Crossed Sabres – Holm Lodge

Some of these brands came to be associated as logos for North Fork lodges and dude ranches.

INDEX

A

B

C

D

E

F

G

H

J

K

L

M

N

O

P

R

S

T

U

V

W

Y

Map of Still Locations on North Fork

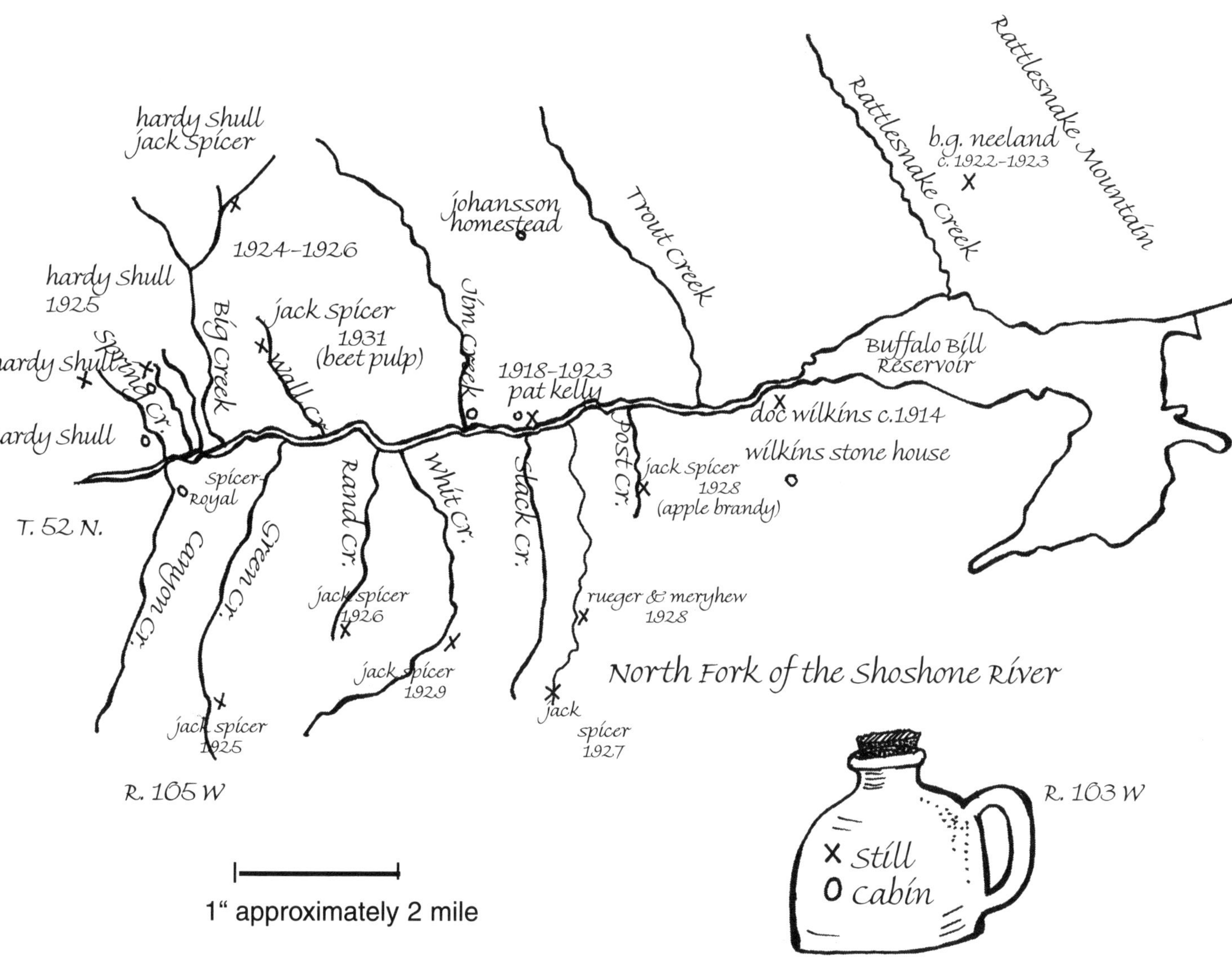